ADVENTURES OF A LANGUAGE TRAVELLER

By the same author

Babel in Spain
Getting On In English
Babel in London
George and Elvira
Choosing Your English
Action
Introduction To English Language Teaching
Think, Then Speak
Italian Labyrinth
In Search Of The French Revolution

ADVENTURES OF A LANGUAGE TRAVELLER

An autobiography

JOHN HAYCRAFT

Edited by Michael Woosnam-Mills

Constable · London

First published in Great Britain 1998
by Constable and Company Limited
3 The Lanchesters, 162 Fulham Palace Road
London W6 9ER
Copyright © Brita Haycraft 1998
ISBN 0 09 479000 0
Set in Linotron Sabon 11pt by
SetSystems Ltd, Saffron Walden, Essex
Printed in Great Britain by
St Edmundsbury Press,
Bury St Edmunds, Suffolk

A CIP catalogue record for this book
is available from the British Library

To Brita, with all my love and thanks.

'Wisdom is a butterfly – not a gloomy bird.'
W.B. Yeats

Contents

Contents

Acknowledgements

Thanks to the following for their helpful comments on parts, or the whole, of my manuscript: Katinka Ardagh, Tony Duff, Francis King, Nicky Lund, Pamela Nicholas, Heidi O'Shea, Paul Roberts, Colin Rogers, Elizabeth Rosenberg, Philippa Saunders, Thérèse Tobin.

John Haycraft, January 1996

Further thanks are now due: To Michael Woosnam-Mills for his skilful and appreciative editing, and to Nick Dobree for finding him, to Carol O'Brien for such positive response and support. I also want to thank Richard, Katinka and Jimmy Haycraft for their comments and all the IH directors who voted for the title of the book. As always, IH London has given instant assistance, Tony Duff especially. Matt Barnard, Maggie Javavas, and many others. Last but not least my thanks go to Maurice Cassidy for all his computer help.

Brita Haycraft, June 1998

Introduction

This book tells a story with zest and candour, which is fascinating in itself: of an Englishman with an original mind and an entrepreneurial spirit, who found himself almost by accident setting up language schools around the world, and creating a quite new attitude and system for teaching colloquial English to foreigners.

But the story of John Haycraft has a wider historical and social interest; for his remarkable career provides unusual insights into the crucial post-imperial decades when Britain had to adjust itself from being a dominant world power to being a more modest European nation, competing with others in the world market-place. John himself, as the son of an Indian army officer and husband of an adventurous Swedish language teacher, could see the transition in very personal terms, from different viewpoints. On one side he had a conventional British upbringing, at Wellington, in the army and at Oxford; like many others of his generation he saw at first hand the British empire dissolving, whether in India, in Palestine or in London. But he was one of the first people to realise that while England had lost an empire of territory, it was extending its empire of language; and he had a flair and endless curiosity which equipped him marvellously to turn language teaching into something much more creative and significant. And on his other side, through his wife Brita and his network of friends and associates across the world, he became a natural internationalist: not as a self-conscious or didactic missionary, but as someone who was constantly working alongside different nationalities and assumptions. The combination was evident in his own style: with his upright bearing and confident clipped speech he could look like a senior English army officer; but once speaking Spanish or French with suitable gesticulation he would be transformed into a Mediterranean enthusiast.

There was another duality in his character which he refers to in his book as 'my dual elements of monk and actor'. He always had a scholarly side, and wanted to be a writer: 'writing was perhaps my substitute for religion', he writes. 'In the nineteenth century, the romantic movement had replaced the priest with the muse . . .' But the key to his skills as a teacher, and as a teacher of teachers, was his love of acting and his ability to dramatise ordinary events, which led him to devise techniques and scenes which brought words and phrases to life for tongue-tied and bewildered students – the technique which the French called *linguidrame*. I will always remember watching students perform a short sketch at International House which made play with difficult constructions like 'I should have', with the man lamenting that he should have taken the girl out, with a humour which ensured that they would never forget it. It made me realise how crucially language was linked to drama, and how John had harnessed his own histrionic talents to his serious scholarship, to make teaching both more fun, and more memorable. And John's mixture of monk and actor combined naturally with his mixture of England and the Mediterranean, to allow him to break away from conventional English constraints.

In the 1960s, as a new British generation was kicking away their parents' imperial baggage and mocking the disciplines and follies of two world wars, John Haycraft's burgeoning academy of intrepid teachers and administrators seemed to me to represent a model of internationalism for the British, bringing out the best of their enterprise and dedication, and putting them alongside other nationalities in creative partnership, without any attempt to dominate. Whether in London, Paris or Beirut I would find English people working in the affiliated schools who gave me, as a journalist, new insights into other populations, with none of the aloofness of diplomats or (too often) the British Council. By the 1980s the climate had become more difficult, whether with the new insularity and xenophobia among British politicians, or with the turbulence in the third world which affected many of the language schools. But the links which the schools provided, and the cosmopolitan spirit which still emanated from International House, became all the more important, to provide a continuous connection between the island, the mainland and the continents beyond. And John Haycraft had ensured, through his own modesty and delegation, that International House would remain as a creative and self-generating institution long after he had left it.

From his other remarkable characteristic which shines through from his book was his lack of interest in personal gain. His own background, with his military father and his judicial grandfather, had given him the feeling that, as he writes, 'almost anything can be done without money'. It was not simply a negative fact, of not being very interested in business; it was a very positive sense of a mission to improve the world and enrich people's cultural lives, in which money was only a necessary means, never the chief aim. And this enabled John to inspire and motivate his staff with much deeper loyalties and satisfactions than the ordinary commercial language-schools. Today, in a much more commercialised environment, the lack of interest in profit is often despised as a left-over from earlier British attitudes, the belief in the primacy of empire and the contempt for trade, and as the cause of the collapse of many British institutions and companies. But John's dedication to his schools showed the most positive aspect of the long British tradition of public purpose; and his preoccupation with wider interests than money was really the key to the special character of International House. He was, to me, the ideal of post-imperial man, or woman, who rejected the old British habits of arrogance and domination but retained the public spirit, and added an intense curiosity and adventurousness among other peoples.

But the basic lesson behind this exhilarating and life-enhancing story is not ultimately a geo-political one; it is a more simple one, of how to humanise and vitalise an educational process. John's own life, as this book makes clear, mixed his private and professional life with no fixed boundaries. His achievement and public career were inseparable from his happy marriage, his family and friendships.

Introduction

Successful language teaching has always depended on motivating students with a love of words and of the culture and people which lie behind them. John's first breakthrough, as he relates, came when he began teaching English to Spanish waiters in London who desperately needed English to use when they returned home to cater for the wave of tourists hitting Spain. But the secret of their motivation was not only their self-advancement, but their fascination with their teacher Brita Haycraft, the Swedish blonde to whom they passed billets doux – including one from a Colombian: 'always i you luv!'

ANTHONY SAMPSON

Prologue: Under the Adam Ceiling

We threw three parties to celebrate my departure from International House.

The first was ten days before I left. About two hundred foreign students of English, aged between sixteen and eighty, from fifty different countries, clustered under the Adam ceiling in the large room overlooking Green Park.

Our name, International House, was not a particularly commercial choice for a centre that taught English and trained teachers. Perhaps a brothel staffed by different nationalities? International House is the name of an American pancake chain, and of a worldwide Methodist student accommodation service – there is a photograph of me in front of a highrise building in Nairobi, with 'International House' in large letters above my head. The name comes from when my wife Brita and I, on honeymoon in southern Spain in 1953, decided to stay and start a language school in Cordoba. We called it 'Casa Internacional', *casa* implying warmth and welcome.

At this first party there were about eighty British, American, Irish and Commonwealth trainee teachers. When we started in Spain no one, including ourselves, had thought it necessary to learn how to teach English. It was not taken seriously, for one thing, even by us. We intended to return to Britain and get 'proper' jobs. It was only because Cordoba was so entrancing and our new school flourished that we stayed for six years.

God was still an Englishman then, or had perhaps just become American. The important thing was to be a native English-speaker.

You were not expected to know about teaching or the intricacies of English grammar and word use. Language would somehow flow from teacher to student in the same way as life did through the divine finger on the Sistine Chapel ceiling.

But after six years in Cordoba, we knew how tricky it really was. Even in London, it was difficult to find teachers able to teach students of eight different nationalities all together in one class, necessarily using only English, with dramatic expression, pictures and objects brought into the classroom. So in 1962 we devised a short, intensive training course with daily observation and classroom practice. Its most novel feature was putting theory into immediate practice, Tuesday's instruction becoming Wednesday's teaching practice, with real students. Demand for the teachers' course was phenomenal. In 1978 it became certificated by the Royal Society of Arts. By 1990, 27,000 people had attended.

Under the Adam ceiling, trainees were talking and drinking with foreign students. It was a magic circle: our students practised their English with trainee teachers, who were eager to get to know them as they were the kind of student they would teach.

The speeches began: Carmelita Caruana, the new director of the London school; Ian Bell, one of our trustees; Tony Duff, who was my successor as director-general. They paid moving tribute.

In my reply, I emphasised that we had tried to create a new profession with its own standards and qualifications. We had also tried to help enemies get to know each other – Israelis and Arabs, Greeks and Turks, Germans and Poles, British and Argentinians, Christian Lebanese and Palestinians. On the neutral ground of English language learning, most had made friends.

To me, it didn't really matter whether they liked each others' countries, or Britain for that matter. What was important was that they learned about the world through the different nationalities they met. I thanked the students for standing behind us in times of crisis, such as the wars in Argentina and Lebanon, the tensions in Tripoli and Algeria. It was they whose enthusiasm had made classes such fun, and given International House its exuberant atmosphere.

Then I joined the students. A little group of Argentinians came up.

'I don't understand,' said a girl with glasses.

'What?'

'Why you are leaving. This is your school which you founded.'

'Well, it's an educational trust . . .'

'But you decide to leave?'

'Perhaps I've been doing the same thing for too long.'

'But travelling everywhere. Meeting so many different people. New teaching ideas.'

'I suppose I'm tired of being a kind of tent-pole supporting a bigger and bigger tent.'

They looked at me in dismay. Even after so many years I had allowed my feelings to overcome my teacher's caution in choosing language.

Why was I leaving, I wondered? I was in good health. True, International House was a young people's organisation. Although I didn't feel it yet, there could be problems with the 'age barrier' – though this is a peculiarly English concern: other cultures are more family-minded, live closer together, and tend to love their elders.

But I would have to leave International House sooner or later. So why not now, when everything was going well, rather than wait until I was doddering?

Certainly, the job itself could not be bettered. My wife Brita and I had never really earned much, but book royalties had helped. The work was a mixture of politics and education, commerce and diplomacy, pioneering, and meeting people all over the world.

And it allowed me time for writing. I started International House because Spaniards came to class in the evening, leaving my mornings free. I had kept the same timetable ever since, writing novels, history and travel books, textbooks and articles in the morning, while Brita delved into English pronunciation studies between family duties. The rest of the day we spent working at or for our schools. The introvert activity of writing contrasted with the theatrical world of International House. Thus both the monk and the actor were satisfied.

I had recently written two books requiring research: *Italian Labyrinth*, a study of contemporary Italy published by Penguin, and *In Search of the French Revolution*, which joined the plethora of books for the 1989 bicentenary. Neither had interfered with my International House work. Both had broadened my horizons.

Why was I leaving, then? I hadn't taught for two years. If you didn't teach, the real value of what you were doing didn't hit you. It could all so easily become petty battles of wills and money.

I suddenly felt sad. But Brita, my co-founder, was staying on. There would be nothing to prevent me teaching, or coming to parties, even though as guest rather than host. This week, my last, we had had our annual directors' conference – ninety people, representing ninety-two affiliated schools across the world.

We had a catalogue of schools in Italy: Turin and Campo Basso, La Spezia, Livorno, Perugia and Messina, Palermo and Arezzo, Napoli, Salerno, and four in Rome.

In Spain, from our beginnings in Cordoba, twenty-three schools had sprung up, from Huelva in the south to Santander and San Sebastian in the north. In Latin America we had three in Rio, two in Porto Allegre and Goiania and two in Buenos Aires.

There were two in Cairo.

The first east European school had started in still-communist Hungary in 1982. Now there were two in Poland, one in Tibilisi in Georgia, and other possibles coming up in Moscow and Yaroslavl.

There were surprisingly few in France, largely because the massive 43% employment tax made teachers, and therefore classes, expensive: two in Paris, one each in Lyons, Toulouse, Angers and Grenoble, and a new one in Nice. Like the schools in Hamburg, Freiburg and Munich, many were business English schools.

Once there had been Beirut, opening and closing with the vagaries of the civil war, until the director of studies, Philip Padfield, was kidnapped and killed as 'punishment' for Britain's helping the

Americans bomb Libya. Once there had been Algiers, Oran, Tripoli. But bureaucracy suffocated Algeria after an eight-year saga, and Gaddafi did for the Libyan schools after twenty years.

In Japan we had schools in Tokyo, Osaka, Kobe and Nagoya. But after eighteen years they were sold to a Japanese company. Bangkok, the only International House with a palm tree in its garden, had closed at the end of the Vietnam war when interest in English, anyway among companies, our principal customers, had waned.

Six schools in Turkey had also come to grief. We had disaffiliated them twice, partly because of Turkey's economic difficulties but also for the mismanagement which made it difficult to send them teachers.

International House still bestrode the English-teaching world. It taught the Portuguese navy and the Spanish army, and ran courses for the World Bank in Indonesia. It had given French teachers' courses in Brussels for the EEC. I had taught the late president Kekkonen of Finland in preparation for a state visit to Britain. We had sent a teacher to Jordan to teach English to King Hussein's children.

You could hardly go anywhere without meeting someone who had learned English with us or done our teachers' course. We had taught at least one-and-a-half million adults over the years, including Québecois, Outer Mongolians and Liechtensteinians, and a group of Chinese who arrived a week late because they missed the Trans-Siberian express!

Abroad, most directors were British. The Singapore school was directed by a Chinese, Michael Liew. We had three American directors: at one of the Paris schools, in New York, and in Aveiro in Portugal.

To begin with we owned schools. But the system of affiliation gradually spread and, when we became an educational trust in 1974, we made it a general rule, charging a small non-profit fee. In return we sent schools trained teachers, inspected them annually and arranged conferences in different parts of the world. On the whole it worked well; and the more trained teachers we sent out, the more standards improved.

Everything led, that hot, sunny week, to my final day of farewell and the last two parties arranged for it: one at midday for publishers, examination boards, the British Council, writers like Beryl Bainbridge, Francis King and Bernice Rubens who had helped with our writers' club, and a few people who had done us some signal service, such as Peter Banks of Strutt and Parker who had helped me negotiate the lease of this splendid building.

But it was the evening party that really launched me out of the International House orbit. Brita and I stood at the door greeting a procession of people from the past. We had tried to invite anyone who had ever worked for us.

Four hundred old friends swarmed in.

Yunus came, a wonderfully generous Malay who now had a school of his own in London. He gave Malay lessons on our first teachers' courses, to show trainees that an unfamiliar language can be taught without translation.

Silvana Orlando from Italy was there, my first secretary. I called her the 'conservative communist' because she was politically left-wing but very conservative in everyday life. Jean Peto, her incredibly efficient successor, was there. So was Edward Woods who had been on our first teacher training course in Rome; he had taught for us in Italy, Morocco, Japan, Indonesia and eventually London.

Opposite the grand staircase, the ceiling was festooned with multi-coloured helium balloons, set close together like huge shiny eggs.

It was time for speeches.

There were kind words from Eulogio Cremades. Ben Warren told the story of how he had been taken to hospital because I dropped a chair down the stairwell onto his head when clearing up after a party at his new school in Egypt. He handed me a cheque, a gift, which I passed on to Brita. Tony Duff indicated an enormous hamper crammed with bright parcels, gifts from our affiliated schools around the world.

Then came a poem in French, written by Anne Kempf, each letter of the alphabet prompting a comment about me. Then the school directors suddenly burst into something they had composed in a pub the previous evening, to the tune of the Seven Dwarfs' song:

> We teach, we teach,
> we never will get rich;
> we do it all for love of John,
> IH, IH, IH, IH . . .

By this time everyone was repeating choruses, laughing and making loud asides, and my farewell speech only added to it all. But when I said what a splendid opportunity it was for me to thank all those – teachers, directors, administrators, trustees – who had made this collective achievement possible, everyone suddenly looked solemn under the balloons. I remembered Brita asking please not to say anything tear-jerking. So I didn't. I just said how grateful I was and how lucky we all were to be able to earn a living teaching English anywhere in the world.

I raised my glass, to so many people I was fond of, and under the balloons we danced to a band which played so loudly it was impossible to communicate except through movement. So I escaped upstairs and helped dispose of the food and drink.

I talked to Charlotte Oakshotte about a house her family were buying in Lorraine, to Ann Samson, our 'queen bee' administrator who had started in reception in 1964, to Tom and Philippe who ran our canteen and had prepared all the food.

I thought back to when I had first seen this building at 106 Piccadilly. I loved it from the start, the Adam ceiling, the marble fireplaces, the sweep of the staircase.

But that, of course, was not how it had started.

PART 1

Hatching in the Sun

1 · Murder of a Major

My father wrote a regimental history of the 93rd Burma Infantry 1914–20, a record of gallant futility.

In 1915 he was in the trenches in France with his wretched Indian troops. One can imagine their brown faces peeping over sandbags, their turbans replaced by steel helmets, vainly longing for warmth and sunlight. Instead, it rained so hard that the water in the trenches came up to their waists. In their dugouts officers pored over maps, the water above their knees. In the end, the feet of many of the Indian troops swelled to the size of coconuts and they had to be evacuated.

The regiment was transferred to Mesopotomia, which is now part of Iraq but then belonged to the Turkish empire, with which Britain was at war. An army under General Townsend had advanced up the Tigris to within twenty-five miles of Baghdad. Repulsed, it had retreated downstream to a town called Kut, where it was besieged.

My father, a young lieutenant of twenty-four, was part of a relief force whose objective was to fight through to Kut and free the 9,000 troops there. On New Year's Day 1916, the ship bearing my father's regiment approached the Shatt-al-Arab, the waterway which today divides Iraq and Iran.

'Land was sighted,' wrote my father, 'whose memory must ever be a nightmare to those who survived. Of the eleven British officers, only five were alive four months later, while in the same period the battalion strength was reduced from 735 to 96.'

There was fierce fighting on both banks of the Tigris. To the left, the Turks had a strong position between the river and a lake. To the right stretched a flat plain about twenty miles long and ten broad, with undergrowth no taller than a few feet. Everything was visible for miles; attacking troops were 'mown down much as corn is mown down by a scythe'.

Equipment was deficient. 'Tents, except for those near General Headquarters, were unknown. One's normal habitation was a scrape in the ground covered with a waterproof sheet. Food was brought by mule and the wounded were carried twenty miles to the nearest dressing station in carts . . . piled in two layers and in this condition they jolted through ten weary and painful hours.'

Rainfall broke all records, 'covering the ground with sheets of water and at best leaving a slippery sea of almost impassable mud'. Lice flourished, 'and as everyone slept on the ground and considered themselves lucky with one bath a month, there was no difficulty in collecting them'. In the summer heat of 1920, flies replaced the lice and thrived on corpses: 'The fly one had just swallowed had probably lately arisen from the remains of the obese Turk just over the way.' There were also vicious sand-flies which nothing could keep out, and no fresh fruit and vegetables. Even potatoes rotted on the journey up, and there was widespread jaundice and the gum disease, pyorrhea.

Among the murderous battles was the climax of a night march over the flat plain – 20,000 men, accompanied by guns and transport: '. . . the rumble of the wheels, the shuffle of many thousands of feet, and the occasional neigh of a frightened animal made the column think the noise could be heard for miles . . . the sound resembled waves breaking on a far-off coast'. Through the haze of dawn loomed the Dujailah Redoubt, a large, oval mound some twenty feet high, such as commonly covered the remains of ancient cities in Mesopotamia.

'Had we gone straight for it,' adds my father, 'we could probably have occupied the redoubt without firing a shot, but the guns were called up to register and so advertise our presence, then the 28th Brigade, which was behind, marched through while the 9th halted.' The attack was three hours behind schedule. The result was a massacre. 'By the time 2,000 yards had been covered the ground behind was a forest of rifles stuck in the ground, bayonets first, beside casualties.' The colonel was killed, nine bullets in his body.

Many of the battles fought during these twelve months were equally futile, incompetently organised and wasteful of lives. Survivors sometimes had to put together a jigsaw of legs, arms and heads before burying their dead comrades. Fear must have been overwhelming. My father describes breakfast before an attack. 'Looking round a circle of friends and knowing that some are spending their last half hour on earth, one wonders if one is among the latter. Faces look pinched and strained, there is an unnatural glitter in eyes, the conversation is forced, and the slightest humour evokes an exaggerated laugh.' He describes feelings when 'a machine gun is firing onto the point where an attack is to take place, and the mental query about whether there is enough space between the bullets for a body to pass through'.

After four months, Kut surrendered. But the campaign continued. A new commander, General Maude, was appointed. He realised that success would come only after proper preparation and with adequate arms and equipment. In February 1917 the Tigris was bridged and the Turks retreated in panic. My father described Baghdad as 'decimated so many times by siege, sickness and massacre that its shrinkages and expansions are marked by a fringe of ruins which get more and more decrepit as they go eastwards until they merge with the desert itself'.

He went on up the Tigris to Damascus and took part in the final campaign in Palestine under Allenby. Amazingly, in three years of savage fighting, my father was only lightly wounded, although he won the MC and bar. The only damage was from a shell that passed too close to his ear and left him slighly deaf.

Remarkably, his book shows no animosity towards either the Germans in France or the Turks in Mesopotamia, as though it were all some macabre sport. He criticises bad leadership and administrative incompetence, but he also has the patience and modesty of the professional soldier. He reveals his ideal, common in those distant days, in his description of Major Simpson, killed in action: '. . . a perfect type of that perfect man, an English gentleman'.

He seems to have been a blend of two of his uncles. The more artistic writer's character came from his mother, the sister of the Edwardian novelist H de Vere Stacpoole, author of *The Blue Lagoon*, a love story on a desert island which became a best-seller and was twice made into a film.

His more stereotyped side may have come from a paternal uncle, Sir Thomas Haycraft, Lord Chief Justice in Palestine at the difficult period of the British protectorate, when any judgement, however impartial, seemed biased in favour of either Jews or Arabs.

After the war, my father took the boat back to India to rejoin his regiment, and met my mother who was part of what was unkindly known as the 'fishing fleet' – girls who flocked out to India hoping to hook a husband, white women of marriageable age being scarce. Pretty, lively, and twenty, my mother was swept off her feet before she even got to India; my father kissed her in the moonlight in the Red Sea. She once told me she had never realised such kisses existed. By the time they reached Bombay they were engaged, and were married ten months later in Allahabad.

I have my parents' love letters, passionate but humorous, full of exuberance and quaint pencil drawings, mainly of animals, by my father. None of the letters reproves or nags in any way. 'How I would love to have you in my arms this moment and smother your sweet mouth with kisses,' my father wrote three years after their wedding.

But Olive, my mother, was impatient with being a 'memsahib'. She was well-educated, played the piano, and spoke French, Italian and German. She could recite reams of poetry. I still have letters, all in verse, which she wrote to my uncle in a German prison camp during the first war, when she was fifteen. Olive was not good at managing servants, although she had been brought up with them. A memsahib was the matriarch of a large family. But Olive's great concern was to be with her husband, to read and talk and play the piano, without the intrusion of silent-footed minions. Her great passion, which she could indulge every day, was tennis. Officers' peace-time duties were usually light: a parade before breakfast, a few hours in the office, or firing practice before the heat of the day;

then 'tiffin' (lunch), followed by a siesta; tennis, a 'chota peg' (a tot of whisky); evenings were for dinners, dances, mess nights. Thursdays were usually kept free.

Often, though, my father and mother were separated. In the hot spring and summer, wives went to the hills while husbands remained with their regiments in the plains. My father would go on courses, or on active service. The longest spells were for six months, mostly on the north-west frontier. Olive would return to England. Once she went to Switzerland to play in tennis tournaments. They went to Europe together on leave, once meeting in Venice for a week at the luxurious Danielli Hotel; the pound was indeed strong then.

They bought a car, a Standard with a dicky-seat in the boot, for £600, which slashed their savings. My father earned the equivalent of £700 a year, reasonable in those days. He went to the Indian equivalent of Sandhurst at Quetta, where I was born, becoming friends with William and Una Slim. Bill passed out first in the final exam, my father fifth. Slim's report called him conceited and argumentative. In spite of this or perhaps because of it, he became a field-marshal long after my father's death, and commanded the Fourteenth Army in Burma.

After Staff College, my father was promoted to major, second-in-command of his regiment. My brother Colin was born. But when my mother was twenty-eight and my father thirty-seven, this happiness was shattered.

There was a new colonel of the regiment and when asked by a Sikh bugler for promotion to lance-corporal, he consulted my father, who knew the Sikh and said, in the man's hearing, that the bugler was not yet ready.

Later my father was watching firing practice. The Sikh approached with his section and, from five yards away, shot my father who slumped forward with a bullet in his heart.

The Sikh then tried to shoot himself, the bullet passing between the legs of an Indian warrant officer who had tackled him. The Sikh was described as mad, perhaps because promotion to the lowest rank in the Indian army seemed a trivial reason to kill someone; but obsession with rank is part of the human condition.

The murderer was hanged. Maybe, somewhere in the Punjab, they still tell of the brave sepoy who patriotically killed an imperialist oppressor. Certainly in Britain, at the height of post-colonial guilt in the sixties and seventies, I got little sympathy on the few occasions I told the story. 'What was he doing in someone else's country anyway?' was a common question. People couldn't believe promotion was the only motive; hadn't my father seduced the bugler's wife, or some such thing? Or perhaps the bugler shot the wrong man?

Two officers' wives were sent to the Murree hills, where my mother had just arrived with me, aged two, and three-month-old Colin. The ladies arrived in the early evening. One of them said later that my mother seemed to know why they had come before they opened their mouths. At first she broke down. Then, as the colonel's letter to my Uncle John puts it, 'she composed herself in an astonishing manner'.

Down in the plains at Nowshera, my father was being buried. The funeral was conducted with great pageant, and the affair took on considerable importance. Not that it made any difference to the poor, dead centre of it all, prone in his wooden box, or to his widow, whom the two officers' wives were reaching at about the same time.

Amazing what can happen in a day. Waterloo is fought and Napoleon flees, a king of England is executed in Whitehall, a Tsar of Russia is shot with his family against a wall. More humbly, an officer is killed in India for revenge, marking his family for the remainder of their lives.

Up in the Murree hills, my baby brother and I both got dysentery. My mother thought we would die and leave her quite alone. She would watch to see if there were any signs of digestion in the milk which went right through our little bodies. Finally, when we were very weak, there were the first signs of brown patches, and we got better. Olive put it down to the sudden change to Allenbury's baby food!

We went to stay with Uncle Arthur and Aunt Faith, who in 1990 celebrated her hundredth birthday. Their son, the novelist Francis

King, then about six, remembered my mother not wanting to do anything except play tennis, as though to drug herself by getting as tired as possible. The family were shocked, as she left us entirely to the Indian nurse. The pain must have been unbearable, particularly as the day before his murder my father had taken her up to Murree himself, and they had said goodbye for the last time.

The pain, though, was driven below instead of being expiated in mourning. Years later I read Geoffrey Gorer's *The English Way of Death* about how the enormous First World War casualties caused the disappearance of community mourning in Britain. Gorer says those who disperse the pain of mourning in other ways often break down later. This happened to my mother. Her menstruation stopped when my father was killed and she developed ovarian cysts. She got blood poisoning three years later and became disturbed and incoherent. Only an operation in Switzerland restored her.

Of course I remember nothing of my father. I thought I recalled him bending over me in a tent, but discovered this was a photograph. I suppose what I know of him best is from his book and other photographs. He had smiling eyes, regular features and a high forehead. Partly because of him, no doubt, unlike many of my contemporaries I have never been ashamed of the British role in empire. And I had direct knowledge of it as a young officer after the Second World War in India, Egypt and Palestine.

After my father's death, we stayed on in India for some months, until financial arrangements had been made. My mother's pension was £400 a year with £80 for each of us until we were twenty-one. She also had about £150 a year of her own. So, although not rich, she had enough. The strong pound made it cheaper to live abroad. My mother's passion, tennis, needed the sun. So after a long journey to Bombay, we sailed to Marseilles. For seven years, we lived in France, Switzerland, and Italy as a one-parent family. We became aware of different languages, and of the charm of being nomads.

2 · A Touch of German

My mother's family had a secret. Her mother, my grandmother, by blood half Bavarian and half Italian, was German. This would hardly call for concern today. Nor did it at the end of the last century when my grandparents were married. Britain admired Germany then. Wasn't the royal family German? Didn't Queen Victoria and the Prince of Wales have guttural accents? Wasn't Germany leading the way, with its welfare state, the first unemployment benefits and old age pensions? Hadn't it produced the internal combustion engine? Wasn't its educational system unsurpassed, with the new 'kindergartens' and all those eminent philosophers, historians and musicians? The English admired the Germans for their diligence, energy and sense of order. They were almost blood-brothers, certainly closer than the Latins or the Slavs. In the 1880s it was common for an English gentleman to follow royal example and find a bride in Germany.

My grandfather, Lucas King, came from an Anglo-Irish family which had settled in County Clare. His grandfather was a bookshop owner in Dublin, his father headmaster of a respected Irish public school. After Trinity College, Dublin, Lucas became a lawyer in India and then a judge. But when he was thirty, his bank crashed with all his savings. So he postponed marriage until he retired from India at the age of forty-five, with a replenished fortune. He knew a wealthy Bavarian family with several eligible daughters, and visited them soon after his return. The youngest, Philomene, a sturdy blonde lass who rowed across the lake every morning, was only seventeen with round, rosy cheeks. He was grizzled and almost thirty years older. But he proposed and was accepted.

Her father was a cavalry officer, Major von Fischer, who had entered Paris with the victorious Germans in 1870. His family owned half Augsburg. Liszt gave piano lessons to Philomene. Her great-grandfather had been finance minister to King Ludwig of Bavaria, which must have been a difficult job: Ludwig had a flamboyant Irish mistress called Lola Montez, whose extravagances fanned revolution. In 1848 Ludwig lost both his throne and her.

Lucas and Philomene married in 1887 and rapidly had many children of whom eight survived. The growing family wandered about Europe, renting houses in places from Dresden to Bromley as they saw no need to buy property. On the way they picked up nursemaids and all the trappings of Edwardian England from pony carts to second gardeners. In 1905, Lucas got blood poisoning from a nail in his boot when mountain climbing near Strasbourg. There was no penicillin then; he died at the age of sixty-three. My mother was five at the time and remembered little about him. The only memory my Aunt Lucille had of him was of going into the drawing-room and seeing an old man reading a newspaper, which he lowered to reveal a wrinkled face, half hidden by a grey beard. He looked at her for a moment through thick-lensed glasses without a word, then raised his paper once more.

Widowed, Philomene continued as before, renting a large house in Malvern and often visiting her sisters in Germany. With growing tension between the two countries, she said that if war broke out she would hang the German and British flags side by side above her door. She had a benevolent naivety which I have since met in other aristocratic German ladies. From 1939 to 1942 she stayed with us, by then old and bent, but still with unlined, chubby, rosy cheeks like a white-haired cherub. She dressed in black with a black velvet choker, and smelled of moth balls. Plumes of smoke emerged from the kitchen when she tried to be domestic. Her sense of charity meant there were queues of the unemployed at the front door wanting 'the lady who gives out money'. She was terrified of the telephone, and thought the radio could be heard both ways, so she told us to hush when Hitler was making a speech. Colin and I thought she looked like Dopey of the Seven Dwarfs, and I recently came across an old china toothbrush holder representing Dopey with 'Granny' scrawled underneath in childish hand.

On 28 July 1914, three days before Germany declared war on

Russia, Philomene set out with five of her children to visit her sisters in Germany. Despite Sarajevo and the threats and rumblings, she left England with a complete lack of concern. When Britain entered the war a week later, she and her daughters were interned. Her son Cyril went to the Ruhleben POW camp for the duration. The rest of the family was confined to a hotel in Baden Baden, a tranquil Black Forest spa. The owner was Jewish and understood Philomene's dilemma. The town had been one of the fashionable resorts of the international beau monde. It would be fascinating to know who the family met there.

They were allowed one day a month to travel to a neutral country. But Philomene was always unwell on that day, clinging perhaps to the nation which had reared her and where her sisters lived. But one November she was well enough, and they travelled to Vevey on Lake Geneva. The German residents studiously avoided them because they were English, and the British would have nothing to do with them because of Philomene's German accent. They took a villa, and later recalled that the bald man living next door was called Lenin, forever being visited by crowds of noisy Russians.

The girls went to school and attended the English church. One Sunday the vicar shouted in his sermon, 'If I could get hold of a German, I would strangle him with my bare hands!' The family was shocked. There had been anti-German feeling in England before they left, with the stoning of dachshunds and shops with German names. But they had never known such outspoken virulence, and in a church!

The story impressed me at an early age. It was perhaps the source of my hatred of judgements against individuals simply because they belong to a country or class or sect that is disapproved of. I imagine Philomene crouching in her pew in that Swiss church, trying to make herself invisible, turning timidly to see if anyone was looking at her and perhaps weeping at the way the world had changed.

In 1916 came the terrible news that Philomene's second son Willy was missing at the Somme. His identity disc was recovered, but not his body. He had gone to Argentina before the war to learn to train race-horses, then moved to Canada and enlisted in the cavalry, from where he was posted to France with the Leicestershire regiment. He was one of the brightest of a bright family.

Partly because they had lived most of their lives in England and gone to school there, the four girls wrote intensely patriotic poems. In 1916 Lucille and May were old enough to return and volunteer for war work. They were treated with suspicion passing through France, and when they got to England. Why had their mother gone to Germany just before the war? Were they spies? How did they feel about being half German? They were allowed, reluctantly, to work on the land. A family story had it that on this journey my aunts were stripped during an interrogation, and writing was discovered on their buttocks, taken to be a secret message – confirmed when, using a mirror, the writing was seen to be about the war. Only then did the girls remember using newspaper to protect themselves from unhygienic lavatory seats on their travels.

When the war ended, everyone was reunited in England at a house in Eastbourne. Cyril read classics at Cambridge and became deputy headmaster at Bedales. Lucille joined the Howard League for Prison Reform and later the pacifist Peace Pledge Union. May did social work, and Eveleen went to China, pining for a friend who had killed herself by jumping off a Channel steamer. She came back and died of a broken heart in a hospital in Earl's Court. Arthur, with whom we had stayed in India after my father's death, died of TB in 1936.

I always found my aunts pessimistic and diffident. Much of it came from the war. Philomene, the innocent cause of all the disruption and persecution, died in London in 1944. She was taken to the morgue at New End Hospital in Hampstead, where her heavy German rings were stolen, leaving her chubby fingers forlorn and bare.

3 · 'Zuppa Inglese' and 'Marmellata'

Living as we did in Switzerland, Italy and France for seven years, with local friends, learning to speak French and Italian as part of the environment, I think I only became aware of being foreign when I went to a French school at the age of seven. Differences suddenly stood out and were commented on. We were at the age to feel that what we had, or belonged to, was best – no matter why. So Britain, that distant, unknown island, became a glorious source of pride, just as it had for Lucille, May, Eveleen, and my mother during the war.

When we arrived from India, we stayed in Nice at the Tsarevitch Hotel which was full of White Russians. A girl called Tanya dominated us and a small English boy with a phobia about rubber: we only had to show him our inflatable cat and he would rush away screaming.

Tanya once led us to a hill, beside which stood a house, half concealed among the trees with smoke drifting from the chimney.

'That's where the giant lives,' she whispered, as we crouched and wondered if the smoke meant the giant was cooking captured children for his supper. When the wind swayed the branches, Tanya warned us that the giant had come out and was hiding by the trees at the top of the hill, blowing down on us. He would suddenly leap up, charge down and capture us for his next meal. In delirious panic, only half believing but savouring the excitement, we fled, looking back anxiously over our shoulders.

There was a Russian count in the hotel who would tell stories, one about a nobleman who finds a dead cockroach in his pudding. 'Oh no, sir, that's a currant!' insists the cook, who pops it into his mouth and swallows it, smacking his lips. We loved it.

At one stage we had a Russian governess, who used to take us to church with her. It was a pageant of candles, gold leaf, and little old women crossing themselves frenziedly. A priest in gold vestments would appear and chant 'Bogi! Bogi! Bogi!' in a deeply melodious voice. The governess said 'Bogi' meant God, but we were more inclined to associate the word with things found in our noses – an early example of difficulties with translation. Language acquisition indeed holds many mysteries.

From Russia-in-France we went to Lausanne in Switzerland, when I was four or five. I remember my mother leaning against a rock in a garden and saying she had to go into hospital. I was concerned because I loved her, and sad that we would not see her for a while. But we were used to her going away for tennis tournaments, and I certainly did not feel insecure or abandoned. Anyway, I had no idea what a hospital was.

Once home again, Olive was intent on winning tennis tournaments. Without my father, tennis was her life, a social activity without commitment. For she was reluctant to get married again: it would have meant losing both pension and independence. Although she had loved my father, I think she resented the subservience of marriage. Tennis could satisfy ambition, and could bring equality. She took a game off the famous French champion Suzanne Lenglen, who got quite angry as she normally beat everyone 6–0, 6–0. Tennis kept Olive healthy and pleasantly exhausted, which helped cure her restlessness.

So we followed the sun. We lived in hotels which were not luxurious but comfortable and homely, where Olive could get good discounts for a lengthy stay. People have often said how unsettling it must have been not to have a home of our own – but these are people who had a childhood home and cannot imagine being deprived of it; they just see us living in foreign countries whose languages they probably don't know.

But we had never known anything else, like circus children. Changing hotels and switching countries, our single parent often away and a governess to look after us, was routine. We knew we were loved. Our mother was beautiful, loving and humorous. I can't speak for my brother, whom I tended to shove out of the nest with the jealousy of a cuckoo; but I loved my mother dearly and my love was reciprocated. I remember sitting by her, watching her play the piano, her fingers moving over the keys in the lamplight. In a first intimation of death, I realised that one day those fingers would be lifeless and still. I clasped them and would not let go, to the jarring of notes.

Philomene used to visit and tell us German fairy stories. Colin said, 'Granny has her head full of stories and Mummy has her heart full of songs.' We were lucky.

Behind the Hotel Salisbury in Alassio were broad, empty fields, today no doubt covered in modern villas. We spent much of our time in them, or swimming or, copying Olive, on the tennis court. We joined a gang of ragged Italian boys and had friendly fights with staves on the roofs of ruined cottages. When Olive sent a photo-graph of this to Uncle John in Cardiff, she received a worried letter expressing doubt about the way we were being brought up.

In the fields, we charged the nettles with swords made of cactus spikes. We built extensive palaces of intertwined palm leaves, where we lay back in the shade and devoured clusters of wild grapes. Looking back, I realise we were experimenting with adult role play. Our palace made us builders, then house-owners. We set up a shop where we sold plants and fruit to each other. There was a goldfish tank to one side of the hotel, where we became fishermen, trying in vain for a catch, with a piece of bread on a window hook tied to a piece of string. In the end, impatiently, we took the plug out of the tank and the gardener had to hose down the gaping, squirming fish. I often wonder whether a lot of adults are not pursuing careers which they once enjoyed playing at as children.

What was so wonderful about being in Italy so young was the Italian love of children. The Arighettis, who owned the hotel, never tried to hush our noise, never reproved us for thundering down the stairs – not even for stealing window hooks to catch the fish in their tank. Signor Arighetti was a big man with the frown which many Italian men seem to have when in thought, and often belies their gentleness. He had fought in the same regiment as Mussolini, whom he described as *un uomo rude*, a rough man. Signora Arighetti was an ephemeral lady with a delicately boned face, alabaster skin, wispy dark hair and small freckles on a beautiful nose. They had no children and vented their gentle feelings on us, running their hands through our hair and saying 'Belli bambini!' just as people would to our own children in Rome thirty years later.

Colin had an accident of considerable excitement. While the grown-ups were having dinner downstairs, Colin sat on a chamber pot which broke, making a great gash in one of his buttocks. I supplied my pot and he sat there, howling and gushing blood while I fetched mother. The Arighettis arrived with two maids and the hall porter, crying, 'Povero! Povero!' Colin's tears were wiped away. Signora Arighetti tried to embrace him, almost pulling him off his pot. A weeping maid was sent to summon the doctor, who stitched Colin up to further agonised yelps. For some time, under 'distinguishing marks' in his passport, Colin had 'scar on left buttock'.

The kitchen staff became warm friends. We would take eggs to the kitchen and be rewarded with marmellata omelettes. We sometimes helped the maids clean up or peeled potatoes, not because we were particularly industrious but because we liked their company.

Olive was tentatively attending church, something she had not done since girlhood. Although a small seaside town, like this whole Mediterranean coast Alassio had a large British colony. The 'squire', one Hanbury-Williams, had started the tennis club and built the Anglican Church. But Olive was too Voltairean. The sermons filled her with wicked mirth. She was too much of an impulsive will-o'-the-wisp to fit into a congregation of stuffy, elderly British expatriates.

Miss Owen, our English governess, returned to Britain. Her replacement, for the short time before we moved to France where I would start school, was an Italian peasant called Maria whom we and the hotel staff disliked heartily. She had rough skin, coarse hair, and a raucous laugh like a tricoteuse watching the heads fall. We prissily thought her vulgar. She slept in the same room as us, farted frequently and peed noisily in her chamber pot in the small hours. She called jam caca, which put us both off jam for a long time. The staff detested Maria because they felt she was no better than they, yet put on airs and ordered them about. At bedtime we would hide from her in the kitchen. When her footsteps clattered on the stone stairs, we were shoved into a cupboard.

'Have you seen the English children?' asked Maria, loftily. 'For some reason they spend a lot of time down here.'

'No, no,' one of the maids would say casually, while in our dark hiding place which smelled of tomatoes and melons and mice, we trembled with anticipation. As the footsteps disappeared upstairs, the kitchen staff would pull us out of the cupboard to smother us with kisses and fill us with custard, which we then knew as *zuppa inglese*.

Things were happening in the world. Olive won the women's singles at a tennis tournament in Turin. In Marseilles the king of Yugoslavia was assassinated with the French foreign minister by a Macedonian. Alassio was visited by Crown Prince Umberto who, after the war, would become the last king of Italy. There were processions and bands played the fascist marching song *Giovanezza*. Vivid in my memory is a *carabiniere* in a three-cornered hat and splendid dress uniform, striding proudly under a fig tree and a plump fig falling and bursting on his chest, smearing his medals.

We were rowed out to visit three Italian cruisers. We climbed onto a seaplane and across steel decks, and were hoisted up by laughing sailors to sit astride the guns. Years later, in 1942, the cruiser we boarded was sunk by the British at the battle of Matapan.

These Italian years were my Garden of Eden, with sunlight, warm sea, freedom to do what we liked, and people everywhere who were exuberant and kind. I have never felt more healthy, brown, or windswept, swimming like a porpoise, playing tennis in the soft evenings, playing about with the *ragazzi* in the fields behind the hotel.

I look back on this time with naive mystification, as even now I don't really understand why people can't be healthy, loving and exuberant most of the time. Perhaps it is all a question of luck and the right environment.

4 · 'I Bit My Brother'

The last afternoon in Alassio our cat, which we were leaving behind, crawled under a bush and died. The gardener had miscalculated and poisoned it too soon. We left in tears because we were also leaving Alassio, and drove sadly in a hired car the thirty-odd miles to the French frontier at Ventimiglia, and then to Menton, about fifteen miles from Nice. Sturdy umbrella pines grew round the bay and, lower down, palm trees and tropical vegetation stood out against the blue sea.

We settled into a pleasant seafront hotel with an Italian name, the Stella Bella, small and cosy. Olive arranged for tennis and enrolled me at the Collège, the enormous local school. A new governess looked after Colin during the day, and both of us when I was not at school. Eugénie Lang from Strasbourg was young, dark and pretty. We called her Nini.

At the Collège, tall buildings grouped round a huge quadrangle, I had three problems: I had never been to school before; I couldn't write, only print; I could speak Italian and English, but not French. I gradually adapted, copying sentences, joining up different letters between tubular lines in my exercise book. I don't know how I learned French. I was seven, the language was around me all day at school. Nini spoke no English, so it was French in the hotel too. Gradually French words became associated with real things. Even today, *une plume* is something different from a pen – a long, smooth, wooden instrument, dark blue, red, or brown, culminating in a beautiful bronze-coloured nib with a small heart-shaped hole in the middle. *Encre*, ink, is a marshy liquid with bits of blotting paper, hair, and the dry encrustations of previous evaporations, as the white china inkpots set into our desks had no lids. The *cahier* is the most beautiful of all: the shiny blue, red or yellow cover with the Gallic cockerel, his crest as luxuriant as a lion's mane, the paper smooth as cream, a surface so pure I was reluctant to besmirch it.

Mademoiselle Macon wore a wide-brimmed hat in class, her long face heavily powdered. She had beautiful violet eyes, and was middle-aged and *sérieuse*, wielding authority with the confident precision so characteristic of France, certain things accepted and others not, and that's all there is to it. She called me *mon p'tit Anglais*, and helped me where she could, leaning over my desk and revealing the top of large white breasts that curved away into darkness and mystery.

My class had about a dozen local boys from different backgrounds: Jean-Claude, the doctor's son, squinting and vociferous; Pierre was unctuous, with neat clothes and watered-down hair, probably the son of a lawyer or businessman; Nicolas was fair, an expression of quizzical insolence on his long face, which I have associated ever since with the word *gamin*. With the adaptability of a child of seven, I gradually became one of them. But because I was identified the whole time as 'anglais' I became aware of my different nationality. I grew curious about where I came from. We had gone to England occasionally for a month or two, to Eastbourne or to Cardiff to visit Uncle Johnny, but had never lived there.

To me, accustomed to moving around, there seemed nothing special about being English. It may seem extraordinary now, but Britain really was the most powerful country in the world then, with the largest empire, the strongest navy; its shipping and commerce filtered everywhere. It manifested itself to us in the band of the Scots Guards on a courtesy visit to Menton, and our hearts swelled with pride at the busbies, the splendid uniforms and the music, familiar from Olive's piano playing.

When Mademoiselle Macon had the temerity to tell the class that the French empire was the biggest in the world, I pointed out fiercely that there was more red than blue on the map. In the end, she agreed that her *p'tit Anglais* was right, and obviously approved of my patriotism.

King George V's jubilee took place. We saw the royal family in the newspaper in all their finery. Distant, small subjects as we were, we imitated the king's apparel, making cardboard medals and epaulettes, broad ribbons, and a Star of the Garter. Nini had a lean and sallow communist friend, Adèle, who would remove *O, for the Wings of a*

Dove or Kreisler's *Liebesfreud* from our gramophone and put on the *Internationale* instead. She slipped a hammer and sickle under our 'medals', which in our innocence we welcomed as yet another decoration, doubly welcome because not made of cardboard.

One day there was an anti-foreigner movement at the Collège. I found myself fighting against hordes of excited French boys, back-to-back with a White Russian boy, the only other foreigner. I felt a great bond with my ally. We stood together at an angle of the wire on one side of the playground, each facing his attackers singly, like Horatius on the bridge. We punched and ducked indignantly, until the bell sounded and we returned to class. Everything became normal again, as we absorbed ourselves in the history of *nos ancêtres les Gaulois*, 'our ancestors the Gauls'.

From my homework at this time, the educational standards at the Collège were high. I still have neatly corrected assignments on history, geography and maths, including equations and fractions. But there was no play element, no music, no social activities even at Christmas, no organised sport. Everything was very serious – but effective. Perhaps because of Mademoiselle Macon, I found learning pleasant. For the annual prize-giving, a platform draped in red, white and blue was set up in the quadrangle, with seats for dignitaries and parents, pots of flowers and tricolour flags. Between events, a band played patriotic music and ballads such as *En Passant par la Lorraine* and *Sur le Pont d'Avignon*. We wore little grey shorts with dazzling white shirts, our hair plastered down with water. Monsieur le Directeur addressed the mass of boys and fashionably-dressed parents, talking of *le destin, le travail, la patrie* and even *la gloire* – as only a Frenchman can. Each boy went up to receive his *Cours d'Honneur*, a certificate showing school progress. I still have mine, written with a dip pen and many flourishes. The ceremony ended with the *Marseillaise* and everyone trooped off, beaming.

Back at the Stella Bella, Nini was proving affectionate but severe, bringing French order into our lives. There was school only in the morning; in the afternoon, she introduced us to the siesta. We lay looking at the chinks of sunlight between the slats of the closed shutters. If only we could steal out, a kind of never-never-world would surely be revealed, with brighter sunlight and happier people. They stayed with me, those siestas: later, in Franco's Spain or communist eastern Europe, while saddened by the closed shutters and darkened rooms of dictatorship, I was often surprised at how idyllically their people imagined we lived, in lands where you went where you wanted.

I quarrelled a lot with Colin, basically I suppose because there were two of us and only one mother. We jostled for the sunlight; as the oldest, I usually won. Colin compensated by playing the violin better than me. We learned with Madame Gherardi, a plump, theatrical Italian whose technique combined exuberant praise with twisting your arm into positions that immobilised you. We played in a little concert which she organised for her pupils. I played atrociously, nervous at all these people, and forgot the music. Colin, on the other hand, a dapper child of five, played superbly, and was the centre of an admiring crowd afterwards.

Our quarrels became worse. In one frenzied fight, I bit him. Nini was horrified. Biting was an animal act – and to bite one's brother! Not even Cain had done that! Nini prepared a placard which I had to wear next day at lunch in the crowded hotel dining room. It read: '*J'ai mordu mon frère*', which means 'I bit my brother'. The placard was attached and, like a criminal on his way to execution, I was propelled into the dining room, tears in my eyes. There was a hush as I sat down. Some people looked at me with disapproval, others whispered to their companions to ask what the placard said. One man got up, went round behind me and returned to his seat: '*Il a mordu son frère*!!' he reported audibly in shocked tones. I hardly ate anything. I can't remember my mother's attitude, or even if she was there. She seldom interfered with our governess's decisions, but comforted us afterwards.

Nini also used emotional blackmail. For one punishment, I was forbidden to give her a Christmas present. I ended up begging her to let me spend some of my diminutive pocket money on her, like a desperate, thwarted lover. But I had my revenge on Nini.

When there was no school, she would take us to the pebble beach below the promenade. She would change into her swimsuit behind the large rocks and we, and probably passers-by, would often catch a glimpse of white breast or buttock gleaming in the sunlight. She would then meet her *camarades*, sun-burned youths who teased and bantered with her as they sat on the pebbles. We sat further down the beach, or among the rocks. As we played, alone, we were aware of mysterious tensions, with Nini at their centre. There might be raised voices, and Nini would come and sit with us, muttering about how *bête* some people were. The climax came on the way back to the hotel one evening. I noticed a placard on Nini's back and pointed it out gleefully. She was dreadfully embarrassed. It said: A LOUER (to let). This meant nothing to us. My revenge was in her having a placard on her back!

Meanwhile, I had fallen in love with a little English girl called Honour, although with my deficient English spelling I wrote it 'Onna'. She was slim and fair with the whitest of skins, and lived with her family in a small house near our hotel. I became obsessed with her. Even at eight, I went through all the romantic love symptoms: dreams of our being together for ever, misery when I was not with her, bad temper if she seemed indifferent, sensitivity when Philomene, who had come to visit us, teased me archly about her. From Olive, I wheedled eighteen francs to buy her a little pink handbag with sequins, and cut out cardboard chairs for her doll's house. She of course was very matter-of-fact, as if small boys fell in love with her every day.

The outside world impinged. We were asked to play with a little boy called Marcel Ophuls whose family had just fled from Germany. He turned into the director of such films as *Le Chagrin et la Pitié,* about people in France who sympathised with Germany in the war. He was a skinny little boy and we were reluctant to play with him because he looked like a child star called Freddie Bartholomew whom we had seen and despised in *Little Lord Fauntleroy.*

In class, Jean-Claude told us a bomb had gone off at his father's house because he belonged to the Croix de Feu, a prominent fascist organisation. In England George V died. Philomene bought a long black veil and insisted we wear black arm bands. When the Collège learned I was in mourning for a king, they were terribly impressed. Mademoiselle Macon gave a talk, holding up her *p'tit Anglais* as an example of what children should feel for their *patrie* and those who ruled it.

I have often wondered what happened to Mademoiselle Macon and all the others in 1940, four years after we left. I can imagine her in tears in that sunny classroom, telling her class that France had fallen. But it must have been a source of pride that Menton was the scene of the one French victory. The Italians, perhaps including men we knew from Alassio, were pushed back to Ventimiglia.

Things started changing. A small, crinkly-haired waiter called Albert was found in bed with Nini, who was dismissed. Suddenly, there was no Nini. Our departure for England was approaching. I would be nine in December, and Olive thought I should start climbing the ladder of preparatory and public school, particularly as it was only going to cost our widowed mother £10 a year. Colin was still too young, but we would all go to England, and find him another school for a year or so. I found the idea exciting, and felt more grown up. I would be going 'back' to my country which I so admired. I was already reading British boys' magazines from Britain. I began imagining what school would be like with 'rotters' and 'decent chaps' in striped ties and blazers, punctuating everything with 'I say, old chap'.

We left Menton in the evening, to catch a train to Genoa where we would board the *Oldenbarndeveldt*, a Dutch ship, which would stop at Tunis then continue to Southampton. There was a stiff breeze. I looked through the car windows at the swaying umbrella pines and the waves like insolent white tongues on the dark sea, and thought agonizingly of Onna, of her indifference at our parting, and of how, whether she liked it or not, I would find her and marry her when I was nineteen.

PART 2

Play Up and Play the Game

5 · Dictatorship of Fear

We went down to Wellington where I sat a scholarship exam on which would depend my education for the next nine years. Olive could not have sent me to a boarding school without it being subsidised. The exam was not very difficult. Mademoiselle Macon had not let me down.

Summer at Folkestone was much like Menton, with tennis and swimming. I planned to build an aeroplane and amaze Folkestone by sweeping over the rooftops. I hoped my wood-and-newspaper contraption was to be driven by an enormous rubber band. I don't know how I believed it would actually fly. Was it the feeling I still have, that projects are worth undertaking simply to see if they will work?

Colin visited our great-aunts in Germany. An outspoken child, he shocked them by saying he thought Hitler was an idiot. The aunts were terrified it would get around and implored him to be discreet.

September: time for me to go to school.

Olive took me to Waterloo, where there were other boys in grey short trousers and jackets and a cap with a large B. Parents clucked as their sons looked aggressively at each other like dogs on leads. I realised this was not a mere lark. I was going away, to an unknown place with all these unpleasant little boys. As the train drew out I waved tearfully to my mother, feeling I would never see her again. I turned to a compartment of sullen boys, one of whom said a 'chap' doesn't 'blub' when saying goodbye to his 'mater'.

Next morning I awoke miserably in a room with seven other boys. I realised with horror that I didn't know how to tie my tie. I couldn't go down to my first breakfast in an open shirt with all these superior little boys and doubtless supercilious masters, simply because my mother had never taught me something so elementary. Another new boy called Wemyss tied it for me, and later taught me how to do it.

The Menton Collège had occupied us only in the mornings. I began to realise that this school claimed us all day and evening. Compared to my carefree life in Alassio and Menton, it was like a prison. There was an exact time for waking up and breakfast, followed by half an hour at the outside loo, sitting over a bucket with the wind whistling between your legs. Then prayers in the gym, followed by morning lessons. After lunch there was football (in any weather) or cricket, depending on the season, and more classes till supper, then homework, called 'prep'.

There were morning classes on Saturday, then sport or compulsory cheering at home matches. Then, at last, there was time for hobbies: marbles, stamp-collecting, squabbling, reading. Or in the evening, a film with Margaret Lockwood, Dame May Whitty, Naunton Wayne or Basil Rathbone.

Sunday meant a morning walk, the whole school winding in a crocodile of blue raincoats down damp lanes, followed by letter-writing to parents, letters handed in by lunchtime and doubtless read by the authorities to check on 'unreasonable' complaints. We actually had the afternoons and evenings to ourselves. But we were so conditioned to doing things compulsorily all the time that I didn't stop equating Sunday afternoons with boredom until I was adult.

One of the worst things about this regimentation was how disagreeable everyone was. Coming from a naturally exuberant existence, I couldn't understand why. It was like living in a cave with a lot of bad-tempered dwarfs I couldn't get away from. Why couldn't they just be spontaneous and affectionate without all this offensive jeering? What I didn't realise was that they were just as frightened as I was. All of us lived a lonely life, with no one to go to for comfort. One way out was to join an élite. You did this by following the strongest or most popular. Outsiders were called 'swank', 'sneak', 'yellow', or 'swot', even 'girlish'. Rules would emerge suddenly. Parting your hair on the right was suddenly 'girlish', or your tie had to be knotted in a particular way.

Another mystery was popularity. One morning, everyone suddenly disliked you; next day, they were friendly again. You never knew why. Everyone was so touchy and competitive that being outstanding in any way didn't help, unless of course you were brilliant at games. Then you could behave like an oriental prince. The secret was to be dull yet at ease, not obtrusive or pushy, but calmly wise, blinking gravely from your corner like an owl. This was impossible for me as I tended to be spontaneous, and even here expressed my feelings freely. Such behaviour was deemed 'silly'. It was dangerous to express anything you felt because small boys have the unerring knack of using anything you really care about to torment you. Mothers fell right into this category. On Speech Day, it was important that your mother look dull and respectable. Otherwise, you would be assailed because she had too much lipstick or a hat like a cream bun. If you were clever, you could keep precious feelings hidden for a time, like being in love with pretty Miss Godley, the matron, or being depressed enough to go weeping to Miss Miller, who taught drawing; or hero-worshipping a boy called Chapman who was so muscular that when the gong was struck by the strong-man at the start of J Arthur Rank films, the whole school would shout 'Chapman'! We learned to adopt a stiff upper lip if, for instance, a close relative died. No wonder that, until recently, Englishmen had a reputation for reserve, coldness and hypocrisy. It came from the days when only those who had been to boarding school could afford to travel. The mask became a permanent fixture.

Just as I was unused to the barbarity of aggressive small boys cooped up like too many rats in a cage, so I had no experience of those sacred pastimes, cricket and football. I won a swimming cup. But there was no kudos in that, or in tennis, doubtless because neither was a team game. To add to the unpleasantness created by insecure little boys, terror was made manifest by corporal punishment, regularly administered by the headmaster on bare bottoms.

He had glasses, wore grey suits, drove a second-hand Rolls-Royce, smoked a pipe, and was a snob. He often had talcum powder on his cheeks, which made them look like unbaked loaves. He had written a play, *The Cannon in Residence*, which he inflicted on parents and boys every five years when there was no one left who had seen it before.

If the school existed today, parents would be suspicious of an unmarried, middle-aged headmaster who always attended bath-nights and watched his naked pupils drying themselves, and who spanked the bare bottoms of at least five small boys every week. He did not teach and rarely met us, so probably knew us better without our clothes on. I never knew of him 'interfering' with anyone, although he openly took individual boys on 'treats' during the holidays, presumably with the parents' permission. In his study, he had a range of instruments in order of pain: the simple strap, the razor strop, and the 'little swish', a short ivory cane, all used with the culprit lying bare-bottomed across the man's knees. More out-rageous offences, such as stealing apples from the orchard at night, or trying to go home in the boot of your parents' car, were punished with the dreaded 'big swish', the birch, a longer cane which he used standing up to get the necessary leverage. The number of strokes depended on the severity of the offence: two with the strap for leaving a towel in the swimming-pool, up to twelve with the big swish for exceptional offences.

Every Monday, which we called Black Monday, punishment was ritualised especially grimly. Those who had worked poorly the previous week were dealt with during Monday evening prep. Tension mounted as evening came, particularly for people who felt their week's work had not gone well, everyone listening intently. First came the footsteps. A classroom door opened, a voice was heard. The door closed, and two pairs of footsteps disappeared down the corridor to the headmaster's study. The dragon had carried off its first victim. Within minutes the footsteps came again – the wretched boy summoning the next miscreant. Sometimes several went from one class. Other rooms would be missed out altogether, and through them a great surge of relief would roll.

Young though we were, some boys were made prefects, responsible for dormitories being quiet after lights-out and for boys not breaking the rules. We were thus trained at an early age to assume authority impartially and with dignity. Meanwhile, games taught us the importance of blending impulses and personal ambition in the bid for team victory.

The masters who taught us were an undistinguished lot. I don't think any of them had university degrees, but it probably did not matter as we left at thirteen. Mr Marshall was a young master whom Olive found handsome. Sarcastic and scornful, he eventually succeeded the headmaster. Mr Quinn, who taught mathematics, left precipitately after being caught getting into little boys' beds – including mine, but I was too immature and petrified to be abused.

Mr Kingdon was in his forties and had clear grey eyes. He had fought with the Sherwood Foresters in the war and regaled us at lunch with stories about the trenches. He taught us Latin with a bundle of ancient sticks brown with age, like long cigars. He handed them out, and if you answered a question correctly you gave one back. Dunces were thus left with most of their sticks at the end, their ignorance displayed to all. There was also Mr B, the headmaster's younger brother, a quiet black-haired man with glasses and a strange way of emphasising the ends of words. The brightest and most unfortunate was Mr Gilbert, a young master with an exuberant smile. He took singing classes, which must have been torture for him as they were always chaotic.

Educational standards were nevertheless high, and I learned a lot. Strangely, it was a good school, well-run, with excellent facilities and spacious grounds. But efficiency and quality are not enough: little boys also need warmth and encouragement.

Towards the end of my first term we all assembled to hear Edward VIII's abdication speech on the wireless, everyone breathlessly aware of the uniqueness of the occasion. In London, Olive told me later, they were singing in the streets:

> Hark the herald angels sing,
> Mrs Simpson's pinched our King!

In the holidays we lived in hotels, in those days very cheap. I remember the Loftus Hotel in Gloucester Road costing Olive £2 a week each for board and lodging. She played a lot of tennis on the covered courts at Queens Club and got into Wimbledon, but lost to a seeded player in the second round. In summer 1938 we went to La Baule in Britanny, where Olive won a tennis tournament which Colin umpired although he was only nine. I fell in love with a little Dutch girl who dangled her legs on the gate of the hotel – my last passion before adolescent shyness and school's monastic atmosphere overwhelmed me.

Looking back, I wonder how Olive managed so well on her small income: tennis, travel, living in hotels, eating out, with no feeling of deprivation in everyday living. I suppose with such low school fees, no house, no car, no smoking, no alcohol, no inflation, she had significant expenses only when we were with her.

In Paris for Christmas 1938, we bought our first wireless, which was just becoming popular. Television was almost unheard of, although I remember seeing, in 1936, a scratchy programme with actors speaking affected English in a shop window in Shaftesbury Avenue. None of us was at all mechanical, and we assumed the wireless plugged into the light socket. There was a great flash as we fused the whole floor of our hotel.

It was a grim, dramatic time – the Munich crisis just over, the Spanish civil war about to reach its climax, the annexations of Czechoslovakia and Albania looming. Once we got the wireless working, it heightened everything. Through whistling noises we heard disembodied voices in different languages, from mysterious stations like Luxemburg and Hilversum. They presaged war and disaster. Frenchmen we talked to were fiercely pessimistic. We thought nothing was more gloomy than a pessimistic Frenchman, the language and gesticulation threats in themselves.

It was now that Olive sowed my interest in the French revolution by taking us to Versailles and the Musée Carnavalet. Versailles then had hardly any of the furnishings it has today. In winter it was a gaunt, empty hulk, unheated and dimly lit. Paint flaked off, the decorated ceilings were blotched and dim. In many ways, it was more evocative than with today's bright restoration and crowding tourists. I merged the horrors of the wild revolutionary mobs with the menace from Hitler over the Rhine, and from Stalin beyond Poland. The world we lived in was doubly threatened, with the probable renewal of the bloody quagmire which had ended only twenty years before, this time with the additional prospect of aerial bombing. Olive was especially apprehensive of communism, having read how well-to-do ladies had been made to sweep the streets in Russia. As we entered the fatal year of 1939 in our Paris hotel, one of my most troubling experiences was the film of HG Wells' *The War of the Worlds*, with its prophecy of war breaking out in 1940, mass bombings, and final, fruitless stalemate.

Sex raised its blissful head. We saw a French film starring Yvonne Printemps. A tennis friend of Olive's, Mademoiselle Belliard, came with us. It was a light romantic comedy. When, with a schoolboy's bristling scorn, I said it was 'soppy', she responded archly, 'You will like that sort of thing, *mon petit!*' I didn't understand. I was soon enlightened. Back at school, my Uncle Cyril came to visit me, a charming, gentle man who ended up as second headmaster of Bedales. Tufts of hair stuck out of his ears and nostrils. The other boys of course said he looked like the wild man of Borneo. We went for a walk in the woods. As we trod on the wet leaves, Uncle Cyril tried to tell me about sex. As I had no father, he obviously felt it was up to him.

'The man passes the woman a sort of jelly,' he said awkwardly, as if it were done with a spoon. 'This gives him pleasure.' He didn't say if it gave the woman pleasure. But I could guess a certain amount and had heard rumours.

A boy called Croucher became interested in a Spanish stamp I had, showing 'La Maja Desnuda', a Goya painting of a naked woman lying on a couch with her arms above her head. Croucher used to borrow this stamp in the evening and return it in the morning. I didn't understand then, but realise now that things must have been pretty desperate if he had to use a postage stamp and a torch under the bedclothes.

My true awakening came when I fell in love with the mother of a boy called Clark, at the edge of a playing field one Speech Day. I was bewitched by the black eyes under delicate, curving eyebrows, the soft brown skin, the short, curly hair. She began to appear, naked, in blissful wet dreams, and I would wake up, desolate that she wasn't there. I was much nicer to her son than before. I felt scruples about lusting after his mum, although my dreams were hardly my fault, and it all seemed so blissfully pure. But the sense of purity soon left me when I started imagining other women naked: Margaret Lockwood and other actresses, even the lady who held up the torch at the beginning of Columbia movies. As my obsession grew, the solitude and the unreality of it began to oppress me. I felt I was the only person, apart from Croucher, who did this. If I was discovered, everyone would point at me in disgust. I would be expelled. Wellington would hear about it and I would lose my scholarship. I would become a pariah, hounded, notorious!

Thinking back I find it strange, in this post-Freudian age when sex runs out of our eyeballs and is constantly in print and on celluloid, to recall this tremendously guilty start to my sex life. Sex seemed part of a criminal temperament, not an essential part of life which everyone shared. When sin was mentioned in chapel I equated it with sex, with the accompanying fire and brimstone.

Drugs were unheard of at school, and as far as I know there was no smoking or alcohol. But we found escape by making each other faint. You clasped someone tightly round the chest while he held his breath. He would go limp, and lie prostrate for a few seconds. I enjoyed it because I had vivid dreams of palm trees and blue oceans. As I awoke, the dreary schoolroom seemed itself the disagreeable figment of a previous dream; my reality was still the palm trees and the blue ocean. I would hover between the two, uncertain which was real and which was not. As the classroom finally established itself, the dream faded.

Was there another world where everything was equally real? In this probably dangerous experiment, I had touched on something that was to develop within me all my life: the belief that there are multiple realities, that something illogical on one plane can be logical on another. This applied particularly to religion, with which in those days even children were more concerned. Thus you could dismiss miracles or immortality on rational grounds, but find there might be a different world with a different logic that made them acceptable. If you tried to explain how an engine worked to a child, he would obviously understand in a child's way, with conclusions different from an adult's. So, perhaps, it was with religion or god or the universe, with us drawing valid conclusions that on another plane might seem irrational. The important thing was not to be literal or over-definite, to think your own reasoning was necessarily right. The real fools were the fanatics who made little patches of truth their own and dogmatically insisted there was nothing else. Significant, too, was my dream of blue oceans and palm trees, juxtaposing my earlier Mediterranean existence with now, trapped at this school.

Another escape I enjoyed was writing adventure stories. I devoured boys' weeklies like *Champion* and *Wizard*, frowned on by the headmaster, and the Henty and Ballantyne books in the school library. I began writing a story about a cabin boy at the time of the Armada. I wrote in little notebooks, and hired them out for one used stamp. I seem to remember completing six notebooks and collecting a large number of stamps, which I gave to the People's Dispensary for Sick Animals. All this gave me great pleasure. I escaped into the adventures I was creating, writing page after page on Sunday evenings, wishing I could spend all day doing this, feeling exuberant as I went upstairs to bed.

I started a different book each winter. I still have one about a youth captured by a press gang in 1809 and whisked off to become a lieutenant in the Peninsular War against Napoleon. I wasn't sure what to call him, and Croucher repaid me ill for the loan of my Spanish stamp by mischievously suggesting David Fulham, the hero of Stevenson's *Kidnapped*, which I had not read. Miss Miller, the drawing teacher, as ignorant of *Kidnapped* as I, inscribed 'The Adventures of David Fulham' in splendid gothic letters on the cover. It was only much later that I became aware of my unwitting plagiarism. By page 117 I was tired of David Fulham. So I ended the narrative, neatly and omnisciently, saying David Fulham died of pneumonia on his journey home.

I became the tribal story teller in my dormitory, improvising stories on any subject they chose. Someone would say, 'Tell us a story about a cabbage leaf', and I would create an exciting story – they always had to be exciting – about a caterpillar that gets turned into a Crusader by a magician and goes to Palestine with Richard the Lionheart. One day, just as he is about to be squashed by the ferocious if chivalrous Saladin, he turns into a butterfly on a cabbage leaf.

Colin joined the school in 1938. Like a mother hen, I worried in case he put a foot wrong. But he shrugged me off. Brilliant at both games and work, and less spoiled than me, he could go his own way. He was more determined to plough his own furrow, not be buffeted by every wave as I was.

In summer 1939 we moved from London to a rented house in Torquay. Unlike her mother in 1914, Olive foresaw the war and, presumably for all our sakes, took us out of London to a relatively safe place which also had covered tennis courts. The house was a small, undistinguished, pebbledash semi-detached. But it meant enough cash to continue our basic existence of tennis, restaurants, and all the sweets, chocolates, ice-cream and toys or books we wanted, compensation for having to leave home for nine months every year. There was general acceptance that war would shortly break out. In class, Mr Marshall weighed up the forces on each side and concluded that both had a good chance. None of us really believed him, or was even greatly concerned. Busy with our own pursuits, we did not understand what defeat might bring. We took it for granted we would win, whatever the odds.

On September 3rd, Olive and I went for a walk on a deserted Torquay beach. We had just heard war being declared by Neville Chamberlain on the wireless. Of course nothing looked different. The sea broke with little, gentle waves, the sky was still grey and cloudy, the seagulls still shrieked. As I recall, we were dazed, anticipating immediate air raids. But the only news was that a lone

German plane had bombed Clacton. Some afternoons later, we had tea at the house of a boy called Seymour. The battleship *Royal Oak* had been sunk by a U-boat in Scapa Flow. The wireless broadcast the survivors in the water, singing *Roll Out the Barrel*. Their cheerful singing somehow compensated for that first disaster of the war.

6 · Wellington

We put up black curtains, which let out chinks of light and provoked the wrath of the air-raid wardens. Under the stairs, we accumulated a mass of tinned food and felt more secure. A neighbour reported that lights had been seen flashing from the cliffs above Anstey's Cove, and that there was a German spy in our midst. We felt furtive in case it got out that Philomene, who had taken refuge with us, was of German origin – although it was hard to imagine a white-haired old lady scrambling about on the cliffs to flash at U-boats. Philomene took badly to yet another war. Again she had relatives on both sides, and was torn between them. When people asked her nationality, she lied and said she was Swiss.

Back at school, the blackout had been put up with the usual impeccable efficiency. They gave us wool and knitting-needles to make warm clothing for our troops in France. I knitted a long beige scarf. I had two terms left before going to Wellington. I was now older, less subject to harassment. But I felt I hadn't done very well, not considered for promotion to prefect or put in for a scholarship which, if I had got it, would have meant Olive paying no fees at all at Wellington. Olive got the date wrong and I arrived at Wellington a day early. I stood in the sunlight on the white gravel of the broad drive, massive rhododendrons on either side, the impressive façade of the school before me.

Wellingon College was majestic, built in memory of the Iron Duke and vaguely like Versailles. The top two floors around several large courtyards contained the dormitories, named after Wellington's generals: Hardinge, Combermere, Murray, Hill, and Lynedoch, which was mine. Each dormitory was a discrete administrative unit with housemaster and prefects, and housed about forty boys aged from thirteen to eighteen. Each had a small partitioned-off room. A long central corridor served as social and assembly centre. There were gaunt stone stairs with iron railings, and a gas-ring for heating sardines, baked beans and other snacks. The school grounds were magnificent, the long drive stretching between woods on one side and playing-fields on the other. There was a lake and a swimming-pool, more playing-fields and other houses in clearings in the woods.

In peacetime, Wellington had apparently been a tough, brutal place, taking principally boys who planned to follow their fathers into the army. Beating for trivial offences and bullying had been common. The war changed all that. It was even possible not to belong to the military training corps and do landwork instead. There was a young new headmaster called Longden, a humane, modern man who was far more relaxed than his predecessors. Many teachers were also new. All this made Wellington educationally excellent, with an almost university-like informality for older boys.

No sooner had term begun than the Germans invaded Belgium, Holland and France, the sunny days dramatised by their advance. Arras fell, then Amiens. With Dunkirk, the newsreaders tried not to sound too desperate. We could hardly believe it. German troops marched under the Arc de Triomphe and an armistice was signed in the same railway-carriage at Compiègne in which the Germans had surrendered in 1918. There was a new, sad song: *The Last Time I Saw Paris*. We were disturbed but not worried. With the collective confidence of past British victories, this seemed just a temporary setback. As we said, the English always win the last battle! On the last day of term we had the usual fags' party with chocolates and sweets, then still unrationed. There were too many Smarties, and we threw handfuls at each other over the partitions after lights out, little realising we would regret this waste in the ten years of rationing ahead.

During the holidays, the Battle of Britain was remote from Devon.

British defiance strengthened confidence. In September I wished the Germans would invade so I wouldn't have to go back to school. I was sure they would disrupt the railways sufficiently, and then of course be thrown back into the sea. I once told this to some Americans in New Orleans. They were shocked, as if I had somehow put my childish desires before the interests of the entire British people. But along with a lot of other people in Britain, I took it for granted that the Germans could not win. I have sometimes wondered how typical was my blindness to the possibility of defeat, and whether it was not this exaggerated confidence which helped Britain stand alone for so long. The German invasion was postponed. Daytime bombing virtually ceased, but now sirens sounded all night long. As we went down to the concrete shelters in the woods, the German bombers buzzed like malevolent hornets looking for somewhere to sting. As far as we were concerned, they found it.

I had flu and was in the sanatorium when the siren wailed one evening. We went down to the lower floor which had new wooden beams supporting the ceiling. Suddenly there was the most terrible series of crashes, like a volcano erupting next to us. We were terrified, but the ceiling didn't crack and the vertical beams continued to support the floors above. The all-clear sounded and someone went to find out what had happened. The headmaster's house, next to the sanatorium, had been hit. Longden was just coming out when a cluster of bombs fell directly on him. He was killed. No one else was harmed because they were in the shelters. Another bomb eliminated Grubbies, our tuck-shop, about two hundred yards from the school. Wellington being near Sandhurst, and both having lakes which reflected the moonlight, the Germans confused them. Ours were drained, and no bombs fell on us for the rest of the war.

Because we were only thirty-two miles from London, the sky was often blood-red, sleep continually interrupted by sirens. At all hours, sometimes several times a night, we had to trek through the woods to the shelters, bare concrete with wooden bunks and lilos. The new acting headmaster decided it was better if we slept there as a matter of course, so we tramped down in the dark with blankets around our shoulders, re-emerging next morning. We did this until early 1942, when the raids tailed off.

I felt more at ease at Wellington than at my awful preparatory school. I was of course older and more used to the tribulations of boarding, and participated more. I still remember the exact moment I decided I would put everything into sport and work: it was just as I was crouching over the starting-line for a hundred-yard race, which I won. I had absorbed one of the most important principles of the psychological training we were undergoing: it was not enough to be what Italians and Spanish call *simpático*, for which English has no exact translation. Popularity was temporary. More lasting was respect for achievement. While fame may have been the spur, public opinion was a whore. This did not mean I had changed within myself. I was like a hermit crab which had found another shell. I went through the ranks: prefect, head of dormitory, school prefect, and finally head of school. I was also head of athletics and 'master of the hunt', the Wellington name for long-distance running. But I did not feel, as the French say, comfortable in my skin. Ambition meant tension. I shall never forget the agony before 'Bigside', the annual five-mile race, or a boxing match.

These years at school marked me. For good or bad, I had a worriedly conscientious attitude to everything I undertook, which also marred my early approach to women. I thought the way to succeed was to impress with achievement, rather than simply being relaxed. The school hierarchy had its rituals. Every boy was a fag for his first few terms, polishing a prefect's shoes, tidying his room. If a message needed taking, the broad dormitory corridor resounded to the cry 'Fag!', and the last boy to arrive would take it. Fagging probably did more harm to the prefect than to the fag, because it meant he was pampered and waited on. Fags were treated loftily by those they served and rarely got to know their masters well. One of my prefects was named Whittal, a bulky, tempestuous boy, an excellent rugby player, loud and abusive, with a broad red face and a mass of black hair. I later met him at the Oxford Union, now a Catholic priest, subdued and reasonable. But I was still in awe and, in a typically English way, never asked how he had come to be a priest.

Belonging to the 'Upper Ten' was particularly ritualistic. This near-priestly title was the privilege of the top few school prefects. All it meant was you walked into chapel in front of the entire school, in a white surplice. At a certain point in the service, you rose from your special seat and read the lesson at the lectern, with its great bronze eagle. At the end, you walked out of the chapel before all six hundred boys. A prefect applied the instructions of the masters and was responsible for order, a kind of sergeant-major for everyday administration. He did this all for glory, and to serve the community. The role continued if he joined the foreign or colonial services, the armed forces, or any manifestation of the Establishment, though there was a discouraging feeling of starting at the bottom all over again and struggling up the same kind of ladder. This did not apply if you went into 'trade', but at Wellington there was a strong anti-trade bias – although many fees could only have been paid because the parents were in trade. A boy called Miller unluckily mentioned what his father manufactured, and was known ever after as 'Shirty' Miller.

I was reasonably happy among my friends as we were less insecure and therefore less aggressive. We went through adolescence in our various ways. One boy looked like a coot, with a coif of black hair sticking up at the back and a turned-up nose. Hopeless at everything, he did little but design and build roads and canals by the lakes. He became a fabulously wealthy engineer. One large bullock of a boy convinced himself he was homosexual because he had a crush on a younger boy. He asked to consult a London psychiatrist, who assured him it was a normal phase and that he seemed healthily heterosexual. Then there was the kleptomaniac who stole bicycle parts and stashed them under his bed.

Once, a pile of excrement started appearing each night in the same place in a quadrangle. The prefects patrolled, eerily expecting a shadowy figure to emerge from between pillars and squat down in the darkness. But no one appeared. We couldn't stay up too late, and in the morning the usual pile was there. The perpetrator became known as the Crapper, and at breakfast word went round: 'The Crapper strikes again!' A prank? A lunatic? Could it be a member of the staff? A sleepwalker? The affair became as intriguing as a murder mystery. The nightly deposits ceased. What had happened? Had the Crapper overslept, tired from missing so much sleep? We would never discover his identity.

Then came the breakthrough. One of the cleaners complained she had to empty an exceedingly dirty chamber-pot morning after morning. She revealed whose it was, and said she wasn't cleaning it any more. A watch was kept on the boy it belonged to. That night the prefect on watch heard scuffling and clanking from the boy's room. He went in and found him sleepwalking with the window open, the pot in his hand. The prefect put the pot down and gently led the boy back to bed. The boy was as surprised as anyone to discover he was the notorious Crapper.

Teaching at Wellington was flexible, with streams adapted to different talents. Thus, in 1940, we had many of the advantages of a comprehensive school. You could be in the best class for French and the lowest for mathematics. If you were near the top of your general class, you often skipped the next when promoted, thus taking the General Certificate, the equivalent of 'O' levels, as early as fourteen, as Colin did. Your general education then stopped, and you specialised in classics or history or languages, science, or a category known simply as 'army', a general course for an armed forces career. I had thought of doing modern languages, but fortunately was persuaded to take history instead. I have never regretted it, as I have found it more sensible to learn languages in their own countries. The wonderful advantage of history is that it helps you understand both your own and other countries, making for greater tolerance.

At the top of the dormitory staircase there was an iron bar connecting the banisters to the ceiling above. For extra security, another bar crossed to the wall opposite, above a shaft plunging eighty feet to the concrete floor below. At the end of this bar was a small window. Rashly, two other boys and I swung across, Tarzan-like, and wrote our names on the wall below the window. The dormitory master noticed them and, feeling I was the ringleader, told me to go across again and rub the names out. It was one thing doing it spontaneously, quite another being compelled to. My hands were slippery with fear. With trepidation, I swung over again and scrubbed at the names. But I had left smears.

'Haycraft!' yelled the master. 'You haven't done it properly! Go over again and erase them properly!'

I was terrified. I leaned a ladder between the staircase and the wall, which would have made no difference had I fallen, but at least gave me the illusion there was not sheer emptiness below. With sweaty hands, I swung across again, removed all traces, and swung back. I climbed down to the stairs almost singing with relief. The result was I lost my confidence with heights, and respect for the dormitory master. We had defaced the wall, and there was a certain justice in one of us putting it right. But had I fallen he would have lost his job and been hounded by the press, haunted for life by the memory of his rashness.

At home and at school, the war continued to impinge. Boys who seemed to have only just left were reported killed. One was the brother of a contemporary, who wept uncontrollably in his room on hearing the news. Another won a posthumous Victoria Cross for charging a Japanese machine-gun post.

Torquay was strafed by what were called 'tip-and-run' raiders. It happened while we were, as usual, on the tennis courts. I remember sheltering behind a large plane-tree as a Focke-Wulf 190 roared down with machine-guns like incandescent devil's eyes in its wings. As it swooped and climbed, it was hit by an army cook who rushed out of his kitchen, grabbed a machine-gun, and fired. He was court-martialled for acting outside his sphere of duty, and acquitted. The Focke-Wulf rose, its tail in flames, then faltered and nose-dived onto the beach in a bonfire exploding with bullets and cannon shells.

Olive had a narrow escape one Sunday morning. Our rented house was by a church, and a Focke-Wulf raider dropped a bomb during Sunday school, killing nineteen children. Olive had gone under the stairs when the siren wailed. But the house shook and the windows facing the church were blown in.

Gradually, the time was approaching when I would leave school and join the army. In autumn 1944 I went to Oxford for a scholarship exam. I found those few days intoxicating: freedom, a sense of the threshold of adult life, the beauty and peace without the traffic that plagues it today. I deplored the imminence of my military service and was delighted to get an exhibition scholarship at Jesus College, although I felt I had waffled during the exam and displayed only the pretentiousness which I imagined was a sign of intelligence. I later discovered I had been awarded the exhibition only because I was head boy at Wellington and interviewed well. 'They wanted someone who would make a good president of the junior common room,' said Major House, the headmaster. Little did they know that I had finished with this period of conventional ambition, of striving for status. Henceforth, I would be more like Colin: he had never been a prefect, and had dropped his rifle in the lake during a field day and been 'court-martialled' for it. On the whole I had enjoyed Wellington. I had shaken off the submissiveness and traumas of my prep school. I had adapted to British ways without losing my Italian and French memories. Any religious sense had been expunged by chapel every morning and twice on Sundays – although it did teach me most of the Bible. My spontaneous passions with girls had been replaced, ever since the little Dutch girl who swung her legs in La Baule, by agonisingly shy and ineffective worship from afar.

The term ended with thunder-flashes and smoke-bombs. This last Christmas of the war, our exuberance was even greater than usual. The Duke of Wellington's nose, protruding from his bust on the library roof, had been painted red so often that by now it was almost black. Not a light showed amid these revels; it was as though, tired of keeping up their imitation of Versailles, the shadowy buildings were waging war against the occupants.

7 · 'Brighten Up, Haycraft!'

I got an official message amid the Christmas mail, saying I had been conscripted into the Coldstream Guards and was to present myself at Caterham Barracks on January 4th. At Caterham we were processed rapidly, receiving uniforms and kit in an enormous warehouse. Then we went to our barrack room where blankets were neatly rolled at the foot of low beds. We got a short-back-and-sides in a long, low room echoing to the snap of scissors, a carpet of multi-coloured hair underfoot.

We lunched in a large dining-room on mashed potatoes and sausages, served from vast cauldrons.

That evening we were addresssed by the trained soldier in charge, Hardy. He was twenty-four and had fought in Normandy, where he had been shot in the head. He spoke in strident, menacing tones, and called us a lot of civvy street milksops. But now we belonged to the finest unit in the British army, whose standards it was up to us to maintain. We looked a right 'shower', he went on: that would have to change. From now on, we would learn to be good soldiers and smarten up. For the next six weeks we would not be allowed out of camp, even at weekends. Instead we would polish our brass and boots, and blanco our equipment. We broke up in depressed silence. In a few hours, life was transformed. Yesterday we had been free men. Now we were on a treadmill.

Next morning, a bugle woke us at six-thirty. 'Rise and shine!' yelled Hardy. 'Show a leg!' We stampeded here and there, scrambling to be smart, in line, on time. Meals, inspection, neatness, blanco, spit-and-polish, square-bashing, dismantling and assembling bren guns, crawling in snow-covered fields, yelling as we bayonetted straw sacks. The object of it all was to ensure we were good at killing, and to avoid being killed ourselves. The worst thing was not knowing how long this prison sentence would last. The war seemed to be ending, but the Germans didn't know when they were beaten. They launched a surprise offensive in the Ardennes, looking at one point like repeating their 1940 drive to the Channel. The offensive collapsed, but now the Germans were defending their homeland and would not surrender easily. Then there were the Japanese, unlikely to give up without being invaded across thousands of miles of sea. And then there would be the extra time it took to be demobilised. Hardy added to our sense of uncertainty with his whims. One moment he was telling us the details of the first night of his honeymoon, the next he was punishing us because someone had used the urinal bucket after 9:45 when it was forbidden. In a fury, he poured the contents into the stove. It gave off a green, ammonia-smelling mist which shrouded us as we slept that night. Some said it was all because of being shot in the head. It was certainly difficult to get on with him. I once accused him of treating us like serfs. For answer, he came at me with fists raised.

'I'll show you!' he said.

'Fine.'

'Come outside.'

I did, and we stood prancing absurdly in the snow. 'Come on,' he said.

'You were going to show me something,' I reminded him. We continued the dance, as he tried to make me hit him so he could get me charged for striking a superior and I repeated that I thought he wanted to show me something. It ended when the duty sergeant appeared and we scuttled back to the barrack like scared rabbits. A sergeant said he was going to show us the best way to polish a chin-strap, dangling one before our eyes like a long French bean.

'First you put brahn polish on, but not too much or too little. Then you hold the strap in front of the stove, but not for too long. Then you spit on it, but not too much. Then you rub it with this clorf, but not too much so you rub all the polish orf. This you do again and again, until you can see yourself in the leather. In the end, you might 'ave something to attract the girls with,' he leered, 'long, polished and glistening.'

*

A few days later I discovered there was a squad of officers in training at Pirbright, nearby, conscripts like us, who had been marked out for commissions. Why shouldn't I be on a course like that? I had been a sergeant-major in the military corps at Wellington. So I asked the platoon officer, a young Grenadier, who advised me to get my mother to write to the colonel and apply. I was interviewed by a white-haired lieutenant-colonel. The prospect of transfer gave me hope. At least this toil would lead to something tangible – unless of course I was hopeless, which did seem a possibility. To my amazement, I was told my application had succeeded and I would shortly move to Pirbright.

But when I did, I saw I had exchanged a cheerful, varied band of 'rookies' for a reserved and superior group of public schoolboys. At Caterham there had been Baxter, the butcher's assistant, who never stopped talking about his febrile sex-life. Or Sparks, who had strong religious beliefs which made him get down on his knees every evening before lights-out. Most were colourful and earthy. Apart from Hardy, I had met no one truculent or aggressive. When they heard I was going, they seemed to accept it, without envy. They wished me luck, assuming my 'toff' accent had wafted me to more refined spheres.

The platoon at Pirbright was indeed a refined group. Most were ex-Etonians whose inherent sense of social superiority seemed to inhibit self-expression and stifle displays of emotion. Two had impossibly complicated double-barrelled names. Many ignored me because I was unfamiliar. But I still made some good friends, in particular Alan Cooke. We coincided later at Oxford, where he became president of the university dramatic society and then went into television. Like me, Alan was one of the few who was not an Etonian. He detested the bullying of the NCOs who, if they had a down on you, would chivvy you mercilessly: 'That useless man, Haycraft, in the back rank! Pick your fucking feet up!' At Caterham, the most common words were four-letter ones. But among these more refined officer recruits they were less usual, the domain largely of sergeants and corporals who used them to abuse us. Otherwise, the rhythm was just as frenetic. Just before 6:30 the bugler's tread outside the window would wake me from my warm cocoon, realising that in seconds Reveille would sound, lights slam on, corporals roar, the barrack room resound to imprecations and scurrying feet. All my resentment boiled up in that moment. The hateful thing was being completely in the NCOs' power. At Caterham sloppiness was punished and forgotten. But here we were under continual review for our commissions, with the fear of being rejected and returned to the ranks of the underprivileged. Gradually, though, things improved. We got to know each other better. Spring replaced winter. We went off on specialised courses: Wrotham, full of blue-bells; Swanage, by the sea with Corfe Castle nearby.

News came that Mussolini had been strung up in Milan with his mistress Clara Petacci. Hitler committed suicide. Montgomery signed the surrender document on Lüneburg Heath. There was, incredibly, peace! We were allowed up to London for VE day. Some of us went to Buckingham Palace and cheered the royal family. We danced in the streets. I picked up two happy girls in Leicester Square, and at Lyon's Corner House we queued endlessly for whale steak. We spent the night kissing and caressing in St James' Park, with myriads of others all doing the same thing. At last Pirbright came to an end. The platoon sergeant actually shook everyone's hand in farewell. When he came to me he just said, 'Brighten up, Haycraft!'

We were now on our last stage, at Mons, the wartime equivalent of Sandhurst, under a new platoon officer, Captain Lloyd, a wealthy landowner in the Coldstreams. He was one of the first people I knew who had a car, a Hillman Minx which used to wait for him beside the parade ground like an obedient horse. He gave us a lot of variety, including long route-marches with full pack, and assault courses under fire. He reinforced assessment by getting us to write what we thought of each other, and asked us to give short talks on anything we liked; I chose telepathy. We also had grenade practice. The officer in charge once fumbled a grenade, dropped it after he had pulled the pin and screamed at us to scatter and lie down. One cadet threw himself onto the grenade. It turned out to be a hoax, devised to scare us. This puzzled me. If the brave cadet thought the grenade was live, his act was surely heroic. Yet nothing much was said in his praise. Of course he might have been part of the hoax, in which case it wasn't heroic at all. I realised that as far as acclaim is concerned, the situation is just as important as courage or motivation.

As officer-cadets we wore white ribbons in our caps, and even sergeant-majors called us 'sir'. But the abuse did not diminish. You would find yourself being asked, 'And what the fucking hell do you think you're bloody well doing, *sir*?' or, 'Look at your fucking brasses, *sir*! As filthy as a whore's fucking undersheet, *sir*!' Freedom to abuse certainly stimulated the NCOs' creativity. I felt they competed in producing images of startling obscenity, often without making sense. One cadet was told he 'looked like Venus on a fucking rock-cake!' At Mons, we had the sergeant-major of all sergeant-majors, Regimental Sergeant-Major Britten, known to thousands of officers and the popular press. RSM Britten was enormous. Everyone was terrified of him, including some senior officers. He had an extraordinary voice and way of delivering orders. He stood at the edge of the parade ground, a frown on his walrus face, swagger-stick under his arm. To give an order, he began by drawing in his breath, his Sam Browne belt loosening as his vast paunch shrank in towards his backbone. Then, increasingly loud, came the word 'Squa-a-a-d!', rising in an extended falsetto, the single syllable wafting up and up. As he reached top note, he drew in his breath again and suddenly unleashed the whiplash, '*Halt!*', his vast stomach hurled back against his Sam Browne as if trying to split it. Woe betide any poor bugger caught stamping his foot down a second late.

For some time now we had been allowed to go out on Saturdays and Sundays, sometimes getting a pass for the whole weekend. We were near London but as far as I know none of us had a girl-friend; we were no doubt all white-skinned virgins.

The majority of 'other ranks', as privates were called, talked about little except sex. But they had been at mixed day schools and were in constant touch with girls. When we officer-cadets talked about sex, we did so with boastful, unconvincing flippancy. We budding officers just had our fantasies. Perhaps the paralysis of most young public schoolboys confronted with girls was another aspect of empire training. Sex was an entanglement which would interfere with the self-sufficiency needed for living in Africa or India. Occasionally I would go to a dance and pick up a 'wallflower'. But the object was not specifically to go to bed. That was something one might fantasize about afterwards. But shyness made it well-nigh impossible to buy condoms, and one might catch VD or father a baby. What would I do, anyway, if by some miracle I succeeded? My sex education had barely begun. I knew a lot about my own body, but nothing about a girl's, outside complicated charts in manuals. So I trod on my partner's toes and made glazed conversation – almost certainly the last thing she wanted.

Gradually the time approached for our lot as potential officers to be decided. We went on manoeuvres to north Wales in August, hearing in the train about the atom bomb and, later, that the Japanese had asked for an armistice. Whatever happened now, we were basically awaiting demobilisation. Oxford and freedom seemed closer. Little did I know they were more than two years away.

Captain Lloyd began a series of personal interviews about our 'future'. I had just scraped through. Lloyd told me a Guards officer needed a personal income of at least £100 a year – a quarter of Olive's income – if he was to be 'comfortable' in the mess. I was shattered. I explained I had nothing except my pay which, as a second lieutenant, would be three pounds ten shillings a week – and I needed to save as much as possible for Oxford. Perhaps, suggested Lloyd, it would be better to put myself down for one of the 'line mob', as the Guards so loftily called other infantry regiments.

So I joined the Queen's Royal Regiment, its insignia a pascal lamb, formed by Colonel Kirk in Tangiers in 1685 and still known as Kirk's Lambs. I was being commissioned at only eighteen, faster than if I had gone through more standard procedures. With my army allowance, I bought a uniform at Hawkes in Savile Row. I was absurdly proud of my glistening Sam Browne and the single golden pip on each shoulder. Colin came down for the passing-out parade on a windy September day, which ended with Handel's slow march, *See the Conquering Hero Comes*. We saw *Giselle* at Covent Garden, smoked Balkan Sobranie cigarettes at dinner, and felt we were really adult.

I realise now I could have spared a thought for my father on such a day. He would have been proud, particularly as I was to go to India, after a short period at regimental headquarters in Maidstone. I know now from his letters, which my mother kept, how much he cared for me during those two years before he was killed. But I had never known him. I felt exuberant, and the sixteen years since that murder seemed an age, my whole infancy and childhood.

I had leave until just after Christmas and worked on a tortured novel which aimed to discover the philospher's stone and to express my doubts about myself and life around me, as movingly and self-pityingly as possible. Much of my spare time was spent with Olive who lived alone in a house she had actually bought. So we were possessors of a semi-detached 1930s dwelling which looked small from outside, but was really quite large, with garage, small back garden, breakfast-room, two reception rooms and four bedrooms, plus a couple of attics, one of which I made my writing room.

Olive was happy alone. The real problem about solitude is boredom, something she never experienced. The wireless, after that memorable start in Paris, was now her main source of entertainment. In the style of earlier centuries, her bedroom was her living-room. She would often lie down in a dressing-gown after breakfast and spend the morning listening to the radio, reading, or cutting up the newspaper to fill her innumerable scrapbooks. Her conversation was replete with jokes she had read, or heard on the air. Some became family jokes and many were to do with language, like the lover who says '*Je t'adore!*', only to be told, 'Shut it yourself!', or the English priest who takes a service for French soldiers and ends with the benediction '*Que Dieu vous blesse!*' She loved ridiculous verses:

> There was a man, and he was mad,
> who thought he'd died before he had.
> This one idea his whole life saddened,
> and when he died, he thought he hadn't.

Like Philomene, Olive belonged to an age when young, wealthier ladies knew nothing of cooking. Nevertheless, she managed with tins, boiled potatoes, and ice-cream or cake. She combined cooking with her musical sense, discovering that potatoes would boil by the time she had played a Beethoven sonata.

Altogether, Olive was a wonderful parent, never snubbing or inhibiting, amazingly tolerant, even of the obscene limericks we brought back from school. The only thing she objected to was bad temper. If Colin or I was grumpy, she expressed her dislike of this as if we were grown-ups. But I never remember her punishing us, which must mean we didn't take advantage of her. Somehow we respected her as a woman, and were grateful for her easy-going, vibrant liberalism. Above all she was not possessive, as widowed mothers can be. For this reason, I have a phobia of possessiveness in all its forms. People might assume it is because I had possessive parents. But it is precisely the opposite that makes me realise what an outrageous vice possessiveness is.

Olive and I had a tacit pact, meaning I did not tell her about my disasters and agonies so they wouldn't depress her. She, I presumed, did the same. This gave us a sunny, humorous, affectionate relation-ship, which some might think was shallow or avoided unpleasant or hurtful 'reality'. Despite foreign influences, our relationship was probably very English: calm, cheerful, superficially unemotional, based on the assumption that one's difficulties should not burden others. The one great difference was the demonstrable, almost Latin affection. I was as concerned as anyone about her loneliness, wondering whether she wasn't putting on a brave front. This question became crucial for me: the less self-sufficient she was, the more bound I was. I could never have lived and worked so much abroad, if I hadn't been sure she was contented alone at home. One advantage of a boarding school had been to allow each of us to get used to living independently, making it easier to leave the nest. Certainly, I never saw any sign of sorrow on her part when I left home. The one exception was the time when I left for India.

The train left in the early morning. We went down to Torre station together. Tears came to her eyes. Was it association with India and my father, and the time she had last said goodbye to him seventeen years previously? I had never seen her cry before, and didn't know what to do. As the train came in I kissed her warmly, climbed aboard, and in that dim December dawn waved frantically to conceal my feelings, the station lights still shining.

It was the last time I would see her for eighteen months.

8 · In the Last Year of the Raj

We embarked at Southampton on the 20,000-ton *SS Strathnaven*, once a liner, now a troopship. It took seventeen days to sail to Bombay. On board were veterans who had fought in Burma. They resented being shipped out again for only three months before demobilisation. There were a few women sailing out to rejoin husbands, and a ballet company due to tour Bombay, Delhi and Calcutta. Junior officers and newly commissioned subalterns, like me, were going out to join the Indian army. A new friend on board was Peter Atkins, a sculptor and painter. We spent a lot of time discussing books and paintings, and what it was like to be an author or an artist. Far left politically, he later became a communist. We discussed the strangeness of going to India as part of a colonial army when we had been taught how wrong the Germans were when they occupied other people's countries. We met the troops at boat drill, and were each given a platoon. The men were older than us nervous teenagers. It was a gruelling experience, brown faces leering at us, whispering insults and obscenities, giving us cat-calls when they were in an anonymous mass.

With a winter sea in the Bay of Biscay, we went through the agony of seasickness. Then the straits of Gibraltar and my first view of foreign land since France, seven years previously. On the left, the dry, bare mountains near Gibraltar were my first view of Spain, that country I was to know more intimately than any other. As we sailed further into the Mediterranean, I grew more exuberant, remembering Menton, Nini, Mademoiselle Macon, and my *camarades* at school in Menton. Further down the coast, there were memories of the Hotel Salisbury, the Arighettis, the nests full of eggs.

I was attracted to one of the ballet dancers, and looked at her as she passed. But when she met my eyes I dropped my gaze. I plucked up the courage to ask her to dance, but was so paralysed I could scarcely open my mouth, and my voice trembled as I asked her where the ballet company was going in India.

It got hotter as we neared Egypt. Crowded into stuffy wardrooms in the lower part of the ship, the soldiers petitioned to sleep on deck. The request was rejected. So they mutinied. On New Year's Eve we had a dance in the first-class staterooms. Here we were, young adolescent officers with our newly polished pips, prancing under the mistletoe with the only pretty women on board. The troops charged en masse up the staircase, banging on the windows and hurling insults through the open doors.

'Get your knees brahn!'

'Wipe yer mother's milk off yer lips!'

The band stopped, and the girls clustered timorously behind us as if the Indian mutiny had broken out. The commanding officer calmly lured the turbulent soldiery away to the main deck to discuss their grievances, finally allowing them to sleep in the open. The rest of the journey passed peacefully.

At Port Said, kite-hawks circled and the sea was dotted with boats, rowed by wheedling men in dirty robes and embroidered caps. They sold everything from cheap watches to Spanish fly, and small boys dived through the scummy water for coins. We passed through the Suez Canal at night with a half-moon over the desert, then into the glare of the Red Sea where my father had first kissed my mother. A few days later we were gliding over the Indian Ocean, with flying fish flopping onto the decks. Through my porthole one dawn I saw Bombay a few miles away, under the first sunlight.

Born in India, and recalling what Olive had told me, I felt excited at what was in store. The experience would be heightened by the fact that this was 1946, the last year of the British Raj.

We were lodged at a seashore camp near Bombay with a long hill above it, shaped like a sleeping giant. The place swarmed with boys selling bananas, something we hadn't tasted since the end of the 'phony war', and devoured eagerly. Peter and I put ourselves down for the First Punjabis, which I thought had been my father's regiment. Awaiting confirmation, we went into Bombay. We visited the hanging gardens and the Parsee 'towers of silence', where corpses of the newly dead are exposed to vultures. For the first time, we were confronted by real poverty. Gaunt women proffered wasted babies and demanded 'baksheesh'. Legless boys slid along the pavements, waving sticks and asking for money. Even the cows were bony, wandering amid the rickshaws and horsedrawn tongas, people crossing gingerly between them with loads of planks or bales of cloth.

We visited a temple with silver Buddhas with diamond eyes, and a market with monkeys, a peacock for fifty rupees, exotic parrots, dogs I wanted to take home. The colourful chaos delighted us, but the poverty made us feel guilty. It was not *our* doing, perhaps, but we both 'belonged' to those responsible. It also made us wary, expecting that people so much poorer would cheat us. Even the meekest Indian suddenly seemed threatening. We took a taxi, beat the driver down, and gave him no tip. He was a shrunken, whiny man with shabby clothes, the whites of his eyes brown and veiny. We felt it our priggish duty not to be bamboozled, although we couldn't tell if he was overcharging. It would only encourage him, we thought sentenciously, to try it out on others. For the same reason, some years later, I fled from a friendly whore in Rome, and didn't keep a rendezvous with an enthusiastic coloured man in a taverna in Tarragona – for fear of not being able to extricate myself from a situation for which I did not feel equipped.

Before travelling nine hundred miles to Jhelum, our regimental depot in the Punjab, Peter and I acquired a 'bearer'. The camp swarmed with men from all over India. Bombay was an entrepot where 'sahibs' returning to Britain left their bearers to be taken on by new arrivals, like us. A bearer's job was to look after your clothes, pack and unpack, run errands, bring early morning tea, clean your room, bring hot water for the tin bath, and do your every bidding. Ours was called Yussuf. Worried-looking and about our age, he came from Bihar.

We boarded the evening express to Lahore. Officers always travelled first-class. Yussuf was automatically allocated a wooden seat in third, near our carriage. It amazes me, now, how we took the master-servant relationship for granted, including the low wages. It seemed 'normal', like the sun rising each morning, with nothing to be done about it. To pay more would have been naive, as the bearer would have been disappointed with his next employer. I once offered a bearer an orange. 'Oh no, sahib,' he said. 'Thank you but I might like it too much and I couldn't afford it.'

Train journeys in India were slow. First class was comfortable: black leather sofa-beds and bunks that folded down, suspended on strong black leather cords. Stations could sometimes suddenly look like Wolverhampton or Torquay, with the same iron bridges and roofs, the notices for 'Gentlemen' and 'Station-Master', the buffet menus offering Horlicks, Ovaltine and welsh rarebit. Our train had no restaurant car but stopped for an hour for lunch and for supper at station restaurants where the air was cooled by a *punkah wallah*, a boy who pulled a rope moving a large wickerwork mat suspended from the ceiling. Eager youths tried to sell us anything and everything. I was offered two black piglets for five rupees.

We saw a forest fire our first night, with flames shooting up from

a vast jungle. Three weeks earlier, we had been in crowded, dom-
esticated Britain. Now we were in a fierce wilderness which writhed
and burned only fifty yards from our train. Dark plumes of smoke
rose into the night, like jinns released from their bottles with loud
hissing noises. The fire seemed a suitable introduction to the vast
chaos of this empire. Although it was red on the map, the Union
Jack flying from every flagpole, a mere 100,000 Britons ruled a
population then numbering 300 million. I heard tell of Indian
villagers who did not know the British were in charge, after almost
a hundred-and-fifty years.

A member of this tiny ruling minority joined us. He was a district
commissioner in his late twenties bound for Bihar, where he would
be responsible for thousands of square miles. He seemed adaptable,
enthusiastic and intelligent. It was his first DC job. He would
supervise the welfare of close to a million people: education, roads,
hospitals, police, justice, settling disputes, suppressing riots – all
came within his jurisdiction. He of course had the local civil service
to help. But the ultimate decisions were his. What had appealed to
him, in his previous post as assistant DC, was riding in the dawn
from village to village, staying a day in each to deal with problems,
learning and practising the language, trying to understand this
different mentality, making new friends. Peter felt it was all patriar-
chal and condescending, that the job could as well be done by an
Indian. But I was enchanted, envious at doing everything possible to
contribute to order and prosperity. It was like being a prince, able
to decide, to be creative, yet under distant supervision, encouraged
if you did well, your power curtailed if you abused it. It seemed
somewhat to balance the hungry eyes of the mutilated beggars in
Bombay.

Jhelum was a cantonment town with streets of small bungalows,
church, cinema and officers' mess, all set in hygienic isolation.
Beyond lay the real town, with its open scum-filled gutters, bullock
carts swaying past tiny shops where owners sat cross-legged in what
seemed open French windows, their wares stacked around them. We

soon discovered there was very little to do in this regimental depot. There was a parade or exercise every day. I spent the rest of the time discussing art with Peter, learning Urdu which carried a hundred-rupee reward if you passed the exam, writing my diary, and reading.

Mess night was once a week, the history of the regiment reflected in the battle flags hanging from the walls. Regimental silver glittered on the tables: vast fruit salvers, tankards, plaques, even an embossed ram's horn containing snuff. At certain points, Sikh pipers with kilts below and beards above marched round the table playing Scottish tunes. The food was delicious, served by bearers with elaborate turbans and red cummerbunds. But I found the conversation listless. I was not interested in 'shop' and was diffident about asking questions. I regret it now: the most fascinating stories about a closing epoch must have lain in the memories of those around that table. Who knows? They would probably have liked to be drawn out.

One evening Peter and I explored a village and talked to some children playing in the street. They all spoke remarkably good English. To their great amusement, I rode one of their donkeys. They seemed surprised to learn we were British officers. We were joined by their families, who asked us endless questions. They were particularly curious to know if we had been to church the previous Sunday, exchanging glances when we said we hadn't. I realised Hindus felt they were superior in faith and spiritual observance, despite our superficial technical and administrative skills.

In March I was told I had been posted to the northwest frontier, on the Afghan border at a place called Razmak, where my father too had been posted. I felt uncertain about it. What were we doing, thousands of miles from home, slaughtering and being slaughtered? But without us, the Afghans would have swept down through the Punjab, devastating everything, as they had done before.

I said good-bye to Peter Atkins, whom I was not to see until twenty years later when he got off a train at Blackheath. Another subaltern, Hywel Hughes, and I set off for a town called Bannu, a staging post for the fortified towns in the mountains. We travelled through desert. The white sand, the absence of humans or animals, the mountains showing dimly through the haze – as if on a different, mysterious planet. The sun came out as we approached the Indus. Broad and muddy, the river flowed against the base of massive peaks above a town of square buildings, heroically resisting the river's fierce sweep. Beyond, the desert gradually gave way to more fertile land. Little round bushes stuck out of the sand, like the tails of up-ended rabbits. The mountains began to recede, and fields of corn to encroach on the scrub.

Twenty-four hours after leaving Jhelum we reached Bannu, a town of around 20,000 inhabitants, mostly Pathans. They had rough clothes, blue eyes set in brown faces, and shapeless turbans. Bannu made me think of imperial Russia. There was a surly feudal air about the crowded streets and markets, a sense of underlying violence and resentment in the faces that looked at us impassively. We were just the conquerors of yesterday. The convoy up to Razmak made me realise how effortlessly the British got what they wanted: through delegation. The trucks in which we left that morning were not owned by the army, but hired from an Indian contractor. As we drove up through the Waziri mountins, the isolated forts looking down on us were manned by *hasridans*, British-paid Pathans to help us if necessary. There were more in one of the trucks, their job to ensure we were not attacked. Pathan vendettas are fierce and long-lasting. A raider would think twice before adding to old scores by killing a Pathan when attacking a British convoy.

The Himalayas made the journey up to Razmak. The ground was flat for the first few miles. We passed camel caravans loaded with the belongings of nomadic families, from mats and saucepans to small children. Then armoured cars joined us and we climbed steeply into scrub-covered mountains. Below were the tall, grey towers of villages, looking from a distance like termites' nests, with loopholes instead of windows. Pathan families lived at the foot of the towers. When the men went to work in the fields, they were covered by snipers up on the flat roofs or peering through the loopholes. At times the drop was so sheer that it seemed we were flying. Mottled valleys cut into the rock thousands of feet below, with the snowy Himalayas as background. After three hours of swerving and climbing to six thousand feet, we drove into a long, broad valley with snow-covered mountains on both sides. At the foot of one, on a slope in the distance, lay Razmak, surrounded by walls in which gates were pierced, like a mediæval township.

You could only enter or leave Razmak in a military convoy. Anyone caught on his own would either be shot or, if he had the sacred red hair of the Prophet, be taken away to breed children in the neighbouring villages. It was an entirely male community, really just the garrison and a few shopkeepers, and we were more cooped together than at Jhelum. Half the mess were Indian, the commanding officer a Hindu, the second-in-command a Muslim, and number three a Sikh. The most senior British officer was the adjutant, Captain Bell.

To us subalterns, it made little difference whether officers were Indian or British. A major was a major, and as a lieutenant you saluted him and called him 'sir'. With fellow subalterns we were all on an equal footing. We British may have had more confidence, but the Indians brought in a pleasantly frank element of bawdy talk. It was they who had to adapt more, forgetting their traditional enmities. Hindus had to suspend their caste system and eat with 'untouchables', which both we and the Muslims were.

The sepoys had great character and charm, quite able to separate military discipline and the personal approach, even on parade. They would tell you with great smiles if your tie was crooked, but this did not prevent them obeying orders promptly. They were traditional in their tastes. I remember not wanting a tablecloth on my table, but my batman said, 'All sahibs have tablecloths, sahib.' I got my way, though, and I feel he never really regarded me as a sahib as a result.

The sepoys were simple, cheerful, never admitted being tired, and greatly respected physical strength as well as learning. Unlike British soldiers, they showed little envy or resentment, seeming to accept their status more readily. I loved their slapstick humour, but got a bit tired of the endless giggles about my Urdu. They once tried to teach me to smoke a hookah. I inserted the mouthpiece, and was told I must inhale strongly. The smoke came surging into my lungs, producing immediate coughing which had me writhing on the ground. I was assailed by the hysterical laughter of the entire platoon, ecstatic that their trick had worked.

I never had the kind of discipline problems as on the boat with British troops. In Britain we tend to protest as a matter of course, and I remember an experienced officer telling me that if the troops weren't grumbling then something was really wrong. In India, protest had never got anyone anywhere. The close-knit family, with its parental discipline, has produced cohesive communities that follow age-old rules, against which it would be futile to protest.

Certainly in my only real crisis, which I brought upon myself, the sepoys followed me faithfully. Every few weeks, one of the garrison battalions was sent to the hills at the head of the valley to protect a new convoy coming through, spending a night under canvas in the process. I was ordered to take out a patrol of a dozen men in pitch darkness. We came to a slope covered with large stones, and started a tumultuous avalanche. Invisible animals moved in the bushes and bullets began to whistle overhead from a little way up the hill. I felt we should turn back, but had only a vague idea which way to go. Haphazardly, I chose what I guessed was the right direction, praying it wouldn't lead into an ambush. By a miracle, twenty minutes later we found ourselves in camp. I have often wondered what would have happened if we had started wandering through the trees and bushes in ever-larger circles.

It surprises me that I was given so much responsibility at barely nineteen. Yet I had been trained for it since my early teens. Perhaps it is old men's self-interest that tells us responsibility should not be assumed early. Revolutions have often given amazing power to men in their twenties, while in recent wars many majors or lieutenant-colonels were striplings. In the eighteenth century, East India Company employees like Clive came out from England at thirteen. But responsibility only came to me in surges. Most of the time, we were at leisure within the walls of Razmak. I was devouring all the books I had heard of but never read, by Huxley, Lawrence, Greene,

Waugh, Maugham, and others now hardly remembered such as LS Myers, Rex Warner, Charles Morgan. I read the classics too: Flaubert and Fielding, Gautier and Dostoievsky, books on Hinduism, *What Is Art?* by IA Richards, and works by Herbert Read. I wrote industrious summaries of each, noting my reactions. I think I read more widely during my two-and-a-half years' commissioned life in the army than in three whole years at Oxford.

As far as my writing went, I wasted a lot of time through lack of confidence. I felt nothing I wrote was any good, constantly tinkering to get that mysterious 'alpha quality' which had cursed us at Wellington. I was highly sensitive to other people's criticism. It did not occur to me that while some people might dislike what I wrote, others might like it, and that the real value of criticism for the writer is that it may reveal things he had not suspected. Writing was perhaps my substitute for religion. It was similarly intangible. In the nineteenth century, the romantic movement had replaced the priest with the muse, the creative writer becoming oracle and sage. The advantage of wanting to write was the way it encouraged me to record experiences of possible value, making people interesting *per se* because they might become or contribute to characters. The negative side was that it made me more detached, more analytically cerebral – fine for a journalist, less so for a novelist, which was what I aspired to be.

I filled my days in Razmak with reading, and writing my diary and short stories. I kept one notebook of quotations and a second for my dreams, which I wrote up immediately I got out of bed.

After a couple of months of this, I was posted for a fortnight to a small hill fortress called Alex, reputedly the highest fort in the British empire. The garrison consisted of Captain Malik, me, about twenty sepoys, and a number of goats, chickens and rabbits, our food during our stint there.

Round the top of the fortifications was a crenellated parapet with a machine-gun at each corner. The views from 8,000 feet up to the valleys below and the Himalayas above were extraordinary. Clouds changed continually, at eye-level, blotting out the sky, misting the tops of hills, filling the valleys with diaphanous, shimmering, wispy drapes. They would be pierced by hot, sharp sunlight, the great circle of the Himalayas above emerging, like the vast, snowy crater of a volcano or a fluted white seashell. From vegetation nearby came the cries of animals and birds, and the gurgle of a brook full of melting snow. As at Razmak, it was dangerous to step outside the fort. Malik told me not to go onto the battlements: there was supposed to be a group of 'rebels' with a machine-gun about. This emphasized our isolation, like being on a raft, surrounded by hostile sea creatures. Once in the moonlight, I saw a lantern moving below the fort, lighting the branches on either side of a narrow mountain path. I felt like a Roman soldier, peering at a solitary traveller from Hadrian's wall.

When I returned to Razmak, we were told volunteers were needed for the ordnance corps in southern India. The commanding officer made his usual boring joke about volunteers, and the northerners told long stories about the south, which everyone laughed at but no one understood. I had little idea what the ordnance corps did, but the opportunity to go south seemed too good to miss. Transfer involved a preliminary course in Madras, which meant crossing India from north to south with perhaps a brief visit to Delhi and Agra on the way. The south with its heat and black-skinned Dravidian people, its seas and jungles and fantastic Hindu temples, attracted me. There I, too, could carry a lantern and explore. The alternative was to stay in this majestic but confined environment, most things only glimpsed at a distance. I said goodbye to the sepoys in my company, the Jats, the Sikhs and the Muslims, to my bearer who still hadn't succeeded in getting me to buy a tablecloth, and to the officers in the mess. The third-in-command got quite sentimental, like an elderly aunt with false teeth saying farewell to a favourite nephew:

'I am sorry you decide to go. But remember we do not separate. We are all together in human race.' He patted me on the shoulder.

[71]

It hailed, the morning I left. But as the convoy started, the carpet of ice was beginning to melt, sending mist up into the rays of the sun which had broken through, giving a sense of exotic purging and peace.

9 · Going South

This was the first of many times that I experienced the delight of setting out into the unknown alone. There is initial nervousness, worry about coping, anticipation of loneliness. But with the first welcoming face, stimulating conversation or intriguing event, you take off with the freedom of a bird. So it was going from Bannu to Madras, with many changes on crowded stations, white-turbaned coolies shouldering the luggage. The cold of the north gave way to the temperateness of the Punjab, the heat of Delhi and the blistering air further south.

Until Lahore, I shared a compartment with a Muslim captain who was respectful about the British as successful military colleagues, but fiery about the Hindus, despising them as clerks and shopkeepers. The Rajputs apart, he said, they were not a military race. In his colloquial 'classy' English, he termed them 'filthy fellows', with their phalluses and temple prostitutes and obscene gods and goddesses – and daring to call Muslims, Christians and anyone else 'untouchable'. If the British left India, he said, the Muslims would create their own separate state, and would fight for it if necessary. He echoed the historical awareness that, until the British arrived, Muslims had ruled India for over four hundred years. I had little sympathy. To me, Hinduism was more fascinating than Islam, more vividly mystical, less militant, with the interesting underlying idea that as god was in everything, everything should be worshipped. The one element that jarred was the caste system.

In those days, the transport of individual army personnel was casual, India being so vast. You were given vouchers and made your own arrangements. If you took a few days off in the middle of a journey, nobody knew or cared, provided you didn't turn up weeks late. So I spent a couple of days in Delhi. Railway stations in India were like oases. Within the labyrinth of corridors, shower rooms, offices and store rooms, restaurants and waiting-rooms, you could usually find a cheap room for the night.

I was fascinated by the traces of the great 1857 mutiny. After their initial uprising in Meerut, the mutineers had marched to Delhi to rally round the last Moghul emperor, Bahadur Shah II, then in his eighties. Styled the king of Delhi with an allowance of £120,000 a year from the British, he was a powerless figurehead. The Moghul empire had declined after the death in 1707 of Aurangzeb, the fanatical Muslim emperor who sliced off the heads of carved stone elephants as the Prophet forbade representation of animal or human forms. Aurangzeb's rule covered all of India, oppressing the great majority of his subjects. It was inevitable the Hindus would rebel on his death to form their own kingdoms, as did Aurangzeb's former viceroys.

In the eighteenth and early nineteenth centuries, the British gradually extended their rule as an alternative to chaos, using the Moghul emperor as a pawn. When the mutiny broke out, Bahadur Shah declared for it, as did his sons. The pipul tree under which fifty Europeans were slaughtered still stands in the courtyard of the Red Fort.

When the British retook Delhi four months later, the reprisals were terrible. Anyone captured during or in any way connected with the mutiny was strung up. Two of Bahadur's sons and his grandson were shot without trial. British soldiers whose relatives had been massacred went on an unchecked rampage.

These events of such savage cruelty made me question the relationship between the British and the Indians. I had taken the Indians very much for granted. I mixed with them when I could, more than with my compatriots. They stimulated my curiosity because I did not know them. It was extraordinary. Here we were, ninety years after the mutiny, and although there were rumours that the Labour government would grant India independence, we were still ruling autocratically. The war had left me sensitive to comparisons between us and the Germans. The difference, I concluded, was that the Nazis had been inspired by a cold, vicious philosophy which led to the holocaust, while British troops after the mutiny had been intoxicated by revenge. Neither was acceptable; but 'our' doings had the excuse of being hot-blooded. Thoughtfully, I took the train for the long journey down to Madras, to find various British government ministers, including Lord Pethwick Lawrence, there for discussions on independence. Most young British officers, and of course the Hindus, were in favour. But some older officers felt India would never be able to govern itself. Anglo-Indians were worried because, while their European blood gave them an advantage with the British, they would be rejected by the Hindus who considered them 'untouchables'. The Muslim officers were indignant that the idea of a separate Muslim state had been rejected.

In contrast to the eccentric tranquility of Razmak, there was tension in Madras. In the officers' mess, a wag changed the name of the newspaper from *The Dawn of India* to *The Eclipse of India*. In the heat, we started our course on ordnance procedures, with, I learned, responsibilities for supplying army equipment, particularly guns and ammunition. We supervised the filling in of forms and invoices, stocktaking, and dispatch, working only in the morning, so we were not exactly hard-pressed. But the work had nothing to do with people. I realised it had to be done by somebody, but felt it was unworthy of human creativity and imagination, and should be done by robots instead. No wonder the ordnance corps was so short of staff it had to call for volunteers.

Only one of the other subaltern volunteers had known what he was in for. 'Scottie' wanted to be a businessman and felt the ordnance corps would be a better preparation than the infantry. We often went to the bazaars to look for carpets he could take back to Britain and sell at a profit. He didn't know what business he would go into so long as it was lucrative.

At weekends, we explored Madras and the coastal villages, where we tried to fish. Once out in a small boat with some fishermen, we playfully rocked the boat, until the terror on their faces made us realise the sea was infested with sharks. Another time we found an immense jellyfish trapped between two boats, at least twelve feet long, the head two feet across. It lay pumping away like a great disembodied glans, trying to escape from between the boats. We tried to extricate it, but only broke off threads of gelatinous string. Finally a fisherman leaned down, grasped it firmly by the head, and dragged it onto the quay where it lay helpless, like a monstrous white intestine. I passed an inquisitive finger along a thread and the sting remained with me for days.

Scottie and I got five days' leave, and went up the coast to what was then the tiny French colony of Pondicherry. All the signs, advertisements and street names were suddenly in French, the police in French uniforms. People gestured in a Gallic way. The churches had a look of Normandy. It was a striking example of colonialism: the people were Indians, just like those a few miles away over the border. They were Hindus and their native language was Tamil. This was France with a brown face.

We passed the British consulate and went in. The consul was a cheery old man who complained about wearing a cocked hat with ostrich feathers so often, the French loving processions. 'I loathe ostrich feathers!' he exclaimed, 'They make me sneeze!' He told us Pondicherry had been captured five times by the British, whenever the two countries had been at war, mainly in the eighteenth century. At the end of hostilities it would be handed back.

We found a shabby hotel, owned by the French widow of a Hindu businessman. We flirted intensely and clumsily with her daughter, Mademoiselle Magry, who was like a provocative firefly, incandescent and shimmering at a touch of the hand, or when clasping one's arm in discussion. She was attractive in a rough, sensual way, with her jet-black shining hair, thick red lips and well-formed body. She played us along until we became impatient at the other's presence. On our last evening in Pondicherry, we decided that one of us would feign illness, so the other could be alone with her in the little salon beside her bedroom, and see how things developed. We tossed a coin and Scottie won. I retired to bed, he to the salon with its dark sofa and easy chairs, tulip lampshades, and the plaster statue of Ganesha the elephant god in the corner.

I was woken by a depressed-looking Scottie. 'Nothing,' he said sourly. 'She kept asking about you, your background, what you were going to do after the army, and kept on talking about marriage. I didn't even get a kiss!'

I got out of bed and, still half-asleep, opened the door of our room and closed it quietly behind me. Suddenly I was in absolute darkness, with not a glimmer from a window or from under a door. Moving slowly, hands outstretched, I touched an armchair, which told me nothing. Suddenly, I could distinctly hear breathing. Listening carefully, I decided where it came from. Eagerly, I moved a little faster, stumbled suddenly, and fell onto what felt like a flimsy bed. A warm body beneath me let out a cry as it tried to wriggle free.

'Mademoiselle . . .' I whispered tenderly. The body writhed free and sat up.

A light snapped on and I found myself on a camp bed facing Madame Magry *mère*, hideous and wizened, with curlers in her greying hair and blotches of cream on her cheeks.

'*Je m'excuse, madame*,' I burbled, 'I stumbled in the dark . . .'

'*Mais monsieur*, where on earth are you going?' Her bed, I saw, lay across a closed door, which I guessed was her daughter's.

'*La toilette* . . .' I mumbled, bowing absurdly and repeating '*Bonne nuit, madame*,' as I went.

Next morning, as we paid our bill, we saw nothing of Madame, but Mademoiselle was as smilingly provocative as ever. 'I hope you slept well!' she said pertly.

'I hope you did,' retorted Scottie.

'Oh, I was disturbed in the middle of the night. Such a noise,' she said, looking at me, 'but it did not matter. *C'était amusant.*'

10 · Falling by Moonlight

I shall always remember Secunderabad, partly because I kept a detailed diary. I also started an immature novel, set in the ordnance depot, about how spontaneity, sexuality and enthusiasm are dulled by working with things rather than humans in vast offices and warehouses. The depot was a collection of huge sheds, some used for storage, others for offices where Indian clerks sat in front of piles of forms which were continually replaced, like some relentless Greek legend. I imagined this work continuing all night, the moonlight shining through the broad windows, the ghosts of dead clerks shifting forms from tray to tray, condemned for all eternity to the routine which had sucked their lives.

The land around was flat, broken by patches of jungle and palm trees, mounds of jagged rock protruding from the plain. Little domed shrines stood beside the dusty roads from one shabby village to another. Eight miles away the great grey fortress of Golcunda covered an entire hill with its crenellated walls, terraced palace and ruined buildings, while flocks of emaciated goats scampered along the winding paths.

One evening, I glimpsed the full moon shining over the great pile of rocks behind the depot. I decided to climb up. The rocks looked silvered at the top, with shadowy gaps between, where the rain had eroded the earth. The effect was like the columns of a ruined temple. I thought I spied an eagle sitting motionless in the moonlight. But, as I came closer, I saw it was just a strangely shaped boulder.

As I moved up among the rocks, a furry animal bolted into the bushes from under my feet. I thought of rock pythons. A snake charmer had shown me how to clasp one below the head and under the tail, and I had held it around my neck as instructed. I reassured myself that even if there were pythons among these rocks, they would be more frightened of me than I of them. Anyway they were

[77]

harmless unless they found a grip for leverage, and the rocks seemed too bulky. Climbing was easy. Now it was the countryside below that was silvered, the town twinkling in the distance. The stars stood out brightly. Here I was, actually in India, poised over this countryside under this splendid sky; only two years ago I had been at school. I wanted to climb higher, out of the shadow into the moonlight to the jagged summits. Ahead, a stretch of rock sloped gently upwards, higher than where I was standing. I would have to jump a narrow gap and then lever myself up with my elbows.

I jumped. But my elbows were not properly on the rock, and I had no foothold. I glanced round to see if I could get back. No: to turn round, I would have to relinquish my handhold. I struggled forward a few inches, but slipped back.

I was frightened. I couldn't see how deep the shaft was, but on the way up I had seen some thirty or forty feet deep. Falling would probably mean a slow, broken death, predators sniffing eagerly around. Perhaps my body would never be found. Presumed kidnapped by freedom fighters, I would appear on that sinister list, 'Missing'. Desperately I struggled up, but only bruised my elbows. I began to slip and stayed very still, like a large lizard in the moonlight. Never have I savoured such a terrible feeling of helplessness, of being doomed to fall whatever I did. I slipped again. Then suddenly, with a cry, I fell.

Black shapes whisked before my eyes. I hit the earth. The shaft was only six feet deep and I had only hurt my foot. For a moment I lay breathing heavily with relief. Then, feeling idiotic, I scrambled painfully down through the shadows. A rabbit scampered out, his white tail a patch of silver. I limped slowly back to the cantonment.

What amazes me still was my foolhardy confidence, in such contrast to my diffidence with people. The fifty-foot drop over the staircase at Wellington came back to me. Perhaps it was the very essence of empire training which prompted me, with hardly a thought, to climb those unknown rocks in snake-infested India at night.

*

We British officers felt we had the right to ask for anything. Once a couple of us went to the Nizam's armoury and asked to borrow a shotgun to shoot leopard. We were courteously refused. We may have not approved of the Raj, but we were British officers and very much part of it.

One afternoon I went out to visit the residency, an enormous house built in 1802 for the British East India representative. The dining-room was a quarter of a mile from the bedrooms. A deputy commissioner told me most of the building had been shut down as, despite the masses of servants it was still possible to recruit, it was too draughty and inconvenient. We talked about tiger hunts and he told me how he had recently seen a tiger playing in a river, splashing the water and pouncing on the ripples like a kitten, until suddenly he had sensed humans watching. He growled and bared his teeth, then jumped out of the river and loped off through the trees, sunlight on his fur and his tail swishing crossly from side to side.

One day I explored a leopard's cave with some Anglo-Indian friends. Although he used the cave to sleep during the day, they said it was all right provided we didn't corner him with his back to the wall, because then he would attack. Gingerly we advanced, treading on bones, some recently chewed, overwhelmed by a nauseating smell of cat urine. In the semi-darkness, with only the light from the entrance behind us, we stopped at a curve in the rock leading into impenetrable blackness. We never knew if the leopard was there. The thought of him leaping out of that darkness with outstretched claws was too much for us. We retreated.

My most extraordinary contact with an animal in India had nothing to do with hunting. In Bangalore, I bought a slow loris from a snake charmer. The slow loris, of the sloth family, is furry with great gooseberry eyes like car headlights, and the size of a small monkey with long limbs for climbing.

I returned from Bangalore to Secunderabad by night sleeper. Bandits had been getting onto trains and robbing passengers, so compartments were shared by both sexes on the assumption that the men would protect the women. I had my slow loris with me in a small net bag, concealed from the other passengers. The idea of a small wild animal in the compartment might add to the worries of the two women, already upset by thoughts of bandits and sharing sleeping quarters with two unknown men.

I slept well, but was suddenly woken in the darkness by female protests from the bunk below.

'What is it?' I asked sleepily.

'You touched me!' accused the distraught voice.

I reached for the net bag. It was empty. The loris was somewhere in the compartment, long legs and arms pulling it slowly along. Soon there would be protests from other bunks, the light would go on, and there would be pandemonium, the loris probably getting thrown out of the window in disgust. If I reached down in search of it, the woman below would probably grab my hand as proof of interference, and scream. The one small comfort was that there was nothing to connect the animal with me.

Suddenly I heard a gentle scrabbling. Against the window, which was lighter than the rest of the compartment, I could see the silhouette of a small mannikin, its small hands scratching at the glass. I sat up, swept my arm down, caught the loris round the waist, and hoisted him back into the net bag, tying it firmly.

Next morning the ladies said nothing, though the one in the bunk below gave me a curious look as we said goodbye.

In my room at Secunderabad, I installed a large branch in the corner, and the loris climbed onto it. He moved very deliberately, ate mashed bananas, and slept during the day in a furry ball. I could leave him safely in my room with the door open while I was at work. At night, he roamed as he had in the train, climbing up the mosquito net or the shutters.

I called him Boris and became very fond of him, though he was hardly demonstrative or affectionate. He couldn't bite as the snake charmer had flattened his teeth. After work I would rush home to see how he was. I began to feel sorry he was in captivity, and one evening let him out for the night. His slow movements wouldn't get him very far, and I would easily find him in the morning.

But I spent all next morning looking for him, assisted by a crowd of excited bearers and fellow-officers. As we combed the bushes in vain, I began to feel glad he was free, no longer confined by his daytime torpor to the branch in my room, nor limited to clambering monotonously over the same mosquito net at night. I looked up at the trees and imagined him in a furry ball under the leaves, to emerge at night with his slow, awkward gait, staring into the darkness with his globular green eyes in search of grubs and insects.

Suddenly one of the bearers cried, 'Sahib! Look! There he is!' From the top of an electricity pole hung a motionless, furry shape – Boris, dangling from long arms, one hooked round the wire, the other hugging the pole, electrocuted while exploring yet another of man's impositions on the wilderness, his staring eyes now lifeless.

11 · Temples and Tombs

The one certainty to emerge from the independence negotiations was that the British were determined to leave. The question was, when?

In January 1947, we were among the first troops to be shipped from Bombay. I was going to Egypt and was glad: it was nearer home. Soon, perhaps, I would be released and go to Oxford. I did not realise how lucky I had been to travel all over India at the end of the Raj, learning Urdu and with time to write short stories and read more than I ever had before. I was given a week's leave, for me a climactic farewell to India.

On my way to Bombay, I visited Agra where my parents had been on honeymoon, remarkable for both the Taj Mahal and the neighbouring palace town of Fatehpur Sikri. The Taj took me by surprise. I was talking to an Indian cadet when it appeared suddenly between the trees. I had of course heard much about this memorial to Mumtaz Mahal, favourite wife of the penultimate Moghul emperor,

Shah Jehan. In his last years, he could admire his supreme creation only through a window in the palace where he had been imprisoned by his ruthless son Aurangzeb. He had planned a replica in black marble for himself on the opposite bank of the river Jumna.

Perhaps it was the sudden vision that moved me so. The translucent marble surface, lightened by arches and fretwork, is simple, majestic without being fussy, flanked on four sides by slender minarets. A long pool in front mirrors the dome. We examined it all – the white walls inlaid with precious stones, the marble tombs of the emperor and his wife. We climbed up a minaret to small arches opening onto circular platforms only a foot wide, a seventy-foot drop below.

I left reluctantly, aware I might never come here again, and walked over to Akbar's fort, a blend of Hindu and Muslim styles. Akbar did more than anyone else to bring together the separate threads of Hindu and Muslim culture.

We took a train to Fatehpur Sikri, also built by Akbar, a palace so large as to be almost a town, today no doubt overrun with tourists. Then, this extraordinary group of buildings, some in ruins, walled on three sides within a seven-mile perimeter, had no people. Instead, monkeys gambolled towards us, scurrying over battlements and parapets with their long tails as if the place had been built just for them.

Mostly of red sandstone, as easy to sculpt as wood, the buildings were sited here on the advice of a holy man whose vision had not included the need for water. Akbar's court only stayed a brief while before the lack of it forced them to leave. Fatehpur Sikri was built for airiness and lightness, against the hot sun. A white marble mosque houses the mother-of-pearl tomb of the holy man responsible for the fiasco. Criminals were tried in the council chamber, the emperor seated atop a pillar. Two hundred yards away is a stone ring where a rogue elephant was tethered. After a death sentence, the victim was dragged across the courtyard to be trampled. Perhaps the most beautiful building is the 'palace of winds', an ethereal structure of five open terraces, one above the other, affording shade for the court ladies. One is decorated in Hindu style with bells, animals, and women's nipples like black buttons, many later defaced by the incurable Aurangzeb.

Outside the walls, we watched boys diving eighty feet into a slime-covered pool, then climbed the 170-foot 'victory gate', barbed wire round its minarets to foil the monkeys. From a rope-ladder dangled an incongruous bed, a cradle for the workmen getting rid of the bees' nests in every crevice in the walls. We looked out over the modern town, a maze of brick walls, thatched roofs, winding rocky paths. Its clamour rose: children's cries, old women hawking their wares, quarrelsome screeches, cocks crowing – the noises of eternal India, its poverty sprawling beside crumbling palaces. I felt that in contrast to this chaotic liveliness, we British, with our cantonments and stations, statues of Queen Victoria and cemeteries full of tombs, were leaving behind little worth looking at.

From Agra, I took a series of devious trains to Aurangabad, east of Bombay, travelling with a Muslim captain named Mir, who thought the Hindus' religion primitive and barbaric. Aurangzeb only got a plain marble slab, almost hidden by tall buildings, without roof or dome, a modest final resting place for the great fanatic, the last Moghul emperor. Perhaps there was such chaos when he died, in 1707, that there was no time to erect anything spendid; or perhaps no one cared enough.

From Aurangbad to Daulatabad, an extraordinary fortress covering a hill rising 600 feet above the plain, a paranoiac's dream: three walls and moats, the gates garnished with spikes to stop elephants being used as battering-rams. Whoever penetrated those defences then faced stairs tunnelled through the rock, cauldrons of boiling oil placed in cavities on each side. Escape-holes plunged seventy feet into the moat. Anyone who got to the top of the stairs found an iron sheet made red-hot by a blazing fire on the other side. We learned the fortress was captured only once, and then by treachery not assault.

A crowded, dust-filled bus took us to Ellora, to see temples not built so much as carved into a cliff, one as big as the Parthenon. The earliest courtyards, shrines and temples, dating from 200 BC, are decorated with representations of the Buddha, staring out with upturned palms along halls ribbed like the inside of a whale. The most recent ones, from 700 AD, are dedicated to Hindu gods. Ravanna, the demon king, holds up the Himalayas on which sit Vishnu and Lakshmi. The natural alternates with the horrific. The goddess Parvathi plays a game with Shiva of the many arms, a belt of skulls around his waist. She wins and refuses to throw again, infuriating him. Then she reappears as Kali, a skeletal figure holding a bowl to catch the blood of a demon who has just been killed.

At the heart of every shrine is the phallus, representing Shiva who is, among other things, the god of creativity. It is set in the vagina of Parvathi, Shiva's wife.

'You see what I mean!' said Mir triumphantly. 'It's disgusting! Amid all these idols! You see how depraved these Hindus are!'

We left Ellora by bus for Ajanta which had a 'dak' bungalow, special government housing for visitors, small and modern, the whitewashed walls usually contrasting with the crumbling chaos of the village. We ate omelettes, hot and greasy, in chapattis. Children played at our door; a dog watched hungrily. There was a full moon. Waking in the small hours, I looked out at the countryside, rectangular hills rising from the plain like dice thrown in the gods' careless game. Next morning there were three bullock-carts at the door, competing for our custom like an auction in reverse. We trundled uncomfortably off to the Ajanta caves a few miles away. From a little glade, we walked up a path to a ravine formed by the river Waurga. In the low cliffs were pillared verandahs and the black mouths of about thirty caves, as old as what we had seen at Ellora. It looked idyllic. From their doorways, the monks saw trees and soft grass on the opposite bank, the river gurgling between. The caves were not discovered until 1817. The remarkably well-preserved frescoes on the walls and ceilings predate Giotto's discovery of perspective by nearly a thousand years. There are exquisitely done court and love scenes, pictures of bees buzzing among flowers, warriors, elephants, and events from the life of the Buddha. Someone brought up in the Christian tradition may be perplexed by such distractions in monks' meeting halls and stone dormitories. But they are something quite different from any Christan monument. Nirvana is reached through a merging of Atman, the soul, with Brahma, the 'real' world outside. The Buddha at the end of the hall represents Atman; Brahma is symbolised by the worldly frescoes. Christians may find this contradictory because they tend to separate god from the observable world.

The bullock cart trundled us back in the evening. The hills and the soft grass were golden. A bus careered past and drove us into the ditch. The bullocks gave a mighty heave and pulled us out. I was lulled by the strangeness of it all. I felt even more alien after these final few days in India. An empire seemed little more than a dog cocking his leg against innumerable lamposts to mark his territory. Maps were coloured, flags flapped, bands played. But real life continued after the dog had gone, indeed while he was still around. It didn't matter, though, that I felt alien. I could still enjoy the extraordinary legacy of other civilisations, and learn to understand them better. The trouble was, it was all coming to an end. Tomorrow I would be in Bombay, to take ship and leave India, perhaps for ever.

We were back at the Kalyan camp near Bombay, the sleeping giant still stretched out along the top of his hill, as if he had been dreaming the last year away. Just outside my door stood a tripod, with chains and erratic scales, for weighing luggage. Our luggage was painted black and marked with our names and an 'O' denoting our ship. We were afraid it would go to the wrong one. Mustafa, our bearer, was so anxious to get everything done and be off that he rolled up my mosquito net while I was still asleep. We left Kalyan in disorganised confusion. At the window as the train moved out, one officer had his glasses whisked off; another got a mouthful of betel-juice full in the face.

We sailed on the *Britannic*, the tugs pulling to port, their sirens yapping like tough little terriers, churning the water frantically. At scarcely discernible speed, we crawled through the narrow channel between harbour and sea. Down on the dock, a khaki-clad man performed flying somersaults, his hair brushing the stone slabs each time. I felt taut as I watched him: one slight miscalculation would smash his head against the pavement. Stopping, he looked up expectantly and saluted. No coin descended; he stood like an unnoticed clown. He started saluting again and again, until four- and five-anna pieces began bouncing down like metal rain onto the sunny, dusty dock. Once through the channel, the ship accelerated. The figures on the dock became tiny, wispy specks. Soon Bombay was a line of buildings with, to our left, the blue hills above the bay. Then it dissolved into brown smudges, uncertain shadows in the distance. A curtain of rain suddenly blew across, as though the performance had ended.

When the shower had passed, all traces of India seemed to have been washed away. There remained nothing but a slender horizon and the choppy, foam-crested sea.

12 · Legionnaire in Palestine

Few people now experience the joys of sea travel. Going by air is like clicking television channels. Take off, doze, eat contents of plastic box, doze, land thousands of miles from where you took off, exchange New Bond Street for the open sewers of Calcutta.

For two centuries British soldiers, officials, merchants, and their families travelled to and from India by ship. Most of the time you read, chatted, played deck quoits, plunged into the canvas swimming-pool on the upper deck – leisures interrupted by vast meals where, beneath chandeliers, you chose from elaborate menus. The ship was a bustling, floating township – purser's office, multiple staircases, long corridors smelling of polish, shops, ormolu lamps, bars, restaurants.

In contrast to our journey out, this was cheerful, everyone glad to be westward-bound, no mutinous troops, less uncertainty about what we would find on arrival. In the sunny water the porpoises rose and fell. Flying fish, bigger and with darker wings this time, glided perilously close to the rail. I tried fishing for shark, begging hunks of raw meat from the ship's galley and attaching them to a hook suspended on a cable through my porthole, close to the waterline. But Buddha watched over his own. I peered into the swirling sea for the dark triangle of a shark's fin. But there was no snap of razor-sharp teeth, no wild thrashings below my porthole, no cruel glimmer of small, wicked eyes. The rushing water revealed meatless hooks, and my supplies gradually vanished.

In the Red Sea, small isolated islands appeared under the hot sun, scrub-covered hills sloping to empty sand beaches. To our left, the mountains of Africa were hazy beyond the brilliant, sunny sea. The ship was unloaded at Port Said by German prisoners-of-war in denims and Wehrmacht caps, wearing the passive expression of military slaves. On the platform where we took the train to Cairo, there was a turmoil of ragged boys: 'Peanuts!' 'Dirty pictures!' 'Spanish fly!' As in India, I wondered how many would ever climb above the poverty line. People the world over were poor and uneducated, except for the thin band of middle and upper classes to which I belonged. We may never have gone hungry, but most of us found our full stomachs balanced by a sense of guilt and unease.

On the train, I woke at 6:30 and went into the corridor for my first glimpse of Egyptian countryside. Flat, fertile fields stretched beneath ragged palm trees. White cranes hunched their heads between bony shoulders, staring moodily or hopping stiffly into a ditch as we passed. Early morning mist suddenly appeared in long banks, wisping aside to reveal glimpses of *fellahin* tramping to work along narrow paths between desolate hovels with crumbling walls, untidy heaps of firewood stacked on the roofs. The sun appeared, slicing through the haze, grew into a dome tapering at the ends, then rose as a flat gold coin, scattering the frost and warming the dark fields, the stacks of firewood, and the cranes' white feathers.

Cairo was the first cosmopolitan city I had seen for over a year. Although capital of a British protectorate, its spirit was French. The

Nile and the Suez canal its supply routes, it had sucked down Mediterranean people and others – Greeks, Armenians, Jews, Spaniards, Italians – who shunned local Muslim schools and found what they wanted in French-dominated classrooms. Shop assistants were reluctant to speak English, both because their French was better and because there was an underlying detestation of the British, far greater than in India, with a sense of that particular hatred which the French reserve for their old enemy. Naively, one might ask what crimes we British had committed. Hadn't we saved Egypt from Rommel and the Germans? Hadn't we given it some sort of independence, with its own king? But the point was, we were still the occupier. From the corner of our mouths we preached liberty, yet we bared bulldog teeth in the interests of an empire which, for the moment anyway, still existed – not even bothering with the American excuse of 'saving people from communism'.

Most British troops in Cairo were too busy being tourists to ponder such questions. We rode camels at the pyramids, visited Mehmet Ali's mosque, viewed the contents of Tutankhamen's tomb in the chaotic museum. Some soldiers hired the women being hawked by their brothers, perhaps even their sons: 'You want my sister? Very good, very sexy, very cheap.' A man with a fez asked me, 'You want jig-jig with green-eyed girl on top of pyramid?'. Everything was blatant and uninhibited under that cynical playboy, King Farouk, who once said that soon the only surviving kings would be those on playing cards.

We left for Palestine in a train with windows shuttered against stones and bottles. The whole territory up to Lebanon and Syria was then virtually under British rule. Transjordan had been detached from the Turkish Empire in 1919 and made a kingdom; a British officer, Glubb Pasha, commanding the most powerful unit in the Jordanian army. In Irak, also under British protection, TE Lawrence's friend and ally Faisal was king. Likewise the Gulf states were only nominally independent.

British rule was more direct in Palestine, under the 1920 League of Nations mandate entrustment. By 1947 it was prey to constant attacks and sabotage from Jewish terrorists determined to create a state of Israel where other Jews, many of them holocaust survivors, could find a home.

Arab communities reacted fiercely. Britain attempted a compromise, limiting the number of Jewish immigrants. It might have seemed a small-scale, local affair, but the focus was international: Palestinian Arabs had massive cultural and religious links throughout the Middle East; the Jews had strong financial and political ties with the western world, particularly the USA. At the storm's centre was the fall guy, Britain, battered and impoverished by the war it had helped win, sending in troops like me who, it hoped, would contain the two irreconcilables and thus fulfil its 'imperial responsibilities'.

Fifteen months later, in 1948, the British would withdraw. It was my fate to be among the last occupying legionnaires in both India and Palestine. My doubts contrasted with my father's belief, a generation earlier in the same two places, in the value of what he was doing. I had been in an extraordinary variety of regiments: the Coldstream Guards, the Queen's Royal, the First Punjabis, the Ordnance Corps, and now the East Surrey, a battalion of which occupied tents on the plain between Haifa and Acre which, with its castle and crusader memories, lay a little down the coast.

Here Richard Cœur-de-Lion had fought Saladin, who chivalrously sent him ice-cream made of snow when he was ill. Napoleon was checked here by a British fleet under Sir Sidney Smith. In 1918 my father had been part of Allenby's army which swept the Turks away. We settled down with tents, hurricane-lamps, camp beds and army-issue rugs.

My batman was a youth called Roberts from the East End, with hair-raising stories of life there before the war and during the 1940–41 bombings. Unwanted babies would be thrown from bridges to smash on passing barges. It wasn't enough to throw them into the river, Roberts explained, as they might be found and traced. He told these stories in gentle, wondering cockney tones, relating the most grisly details. I was particularly shocked, thinking naively that such things didn't happen in Britain. Poverty, yes. Crime, yes. But callous barbarism, no. Like many a teenager, much of my rebelliousness was based on unreal assumptions.

I found others who also felt we were in limbo, doing a job we did not believe in. Although the allies had won the war, our values and beliefs were distorted by parallels with the Nazis. One day a captain gave us a lecture on how to handle riots. 'Identify the ringleader,' he said, 'and order one of your soldiers to shoot him.' I imagined a small dark Jew in open shirt and baggy trousers, shouting venom. Then a shot, and he was writhing on the ground, killed by a soldier who was not really involved but just obeying orders – perhaps mine.

I realise now that this was a period of general malaise, particularly for people in what was really a war zone. The defeat of Germany and Japan had created further problems, Palestine among the most obvious. Churchill's speech at Fulton had warned of possible war with Russia. Nothing final had been achieved; the war was perhaps just a prelude.

Palestine was beautiful. The flatlands rose to gentle hills cradling ancient towns inhabited mainly by Arabs – Bethlehem, Nazareth, with narrow streets and rectangular houses of baked earth, glimpsed as our trucks passed. But we could not explore them. The fields were full of olive-trees, and oranges grew in vast groves close to the sea, golden fruit peeping from the leaves and reminding me of summer in Menton.

The Arabs we met looked like Jews, with dark faces and hooked noses, while many Jews seemed like Germans with the fair hair and skin of their east European origins. We often had to examine identity cards on buses. It seemed fairly pointless, as we were not looking for anyone in particular, and anyway the Jewish groups could forge anything they wanted. The photographs were usually out-of-date and hardly recognisable, mostly taken before the war, fresh young faces contrasting to the furrowed skin and greying hair before us.

We sometimes manned roadblocks, stopping and searching every vehicle without ever being told the reason. I once stopped a jeep with two captains in it, in a tearing rush. I was a lieutenant, so their commands to hurry amounted to an order. But feeling suspicious, I dawdled and took their papers into the guardroom, which made them even angrier. Probably absurdly, I thought they were terrorists in disguise. I let them go, but felt uneasy. In retrospect, it is interesting how concerned I was, caught up in this war willy-nilly.

One night I was leading a patrol over a field, when suddenly an oil tank exploded in distant Haifa, throwing great orange flames into the black sky. Years later at Yale, I got a lift down to New York with a friend who had an Israeli in the car. I mentioned I had been in the British army in Palestine. The Israeli lashed out, covering me and the British with abuse. But, I retorted, while perhaps what the Jews had wanted, the British departure had cost thousands of lives and unbalanced the region. Personally, I insisted, I had nothing to be ashamed of or conceal. He calmed down and we began to talk of our experiences. He had been in the Irgun Zvai Leumi, led by Menachem Begin. When I recalled the exploding oil tank, he said, 'I was in the group which laid the explosives. It was all fixed beforehand. We paid the man in charge fifty pounds to let us in!'

The only pleasant thing about patrols or road-blocks was staying up all night, owls hooting over the dark fields and Mount Carmel bright in the distance with Haifa's bright lights like necklaces. Out of the darkness would come a white flock of sheep, the patter of their feet soft and muffled. From midnight, cocks would crow like mediæval watchmen chanting 'All's well!' Sunrise could be splendid, a curtain lifting over a line of hills, a long slab of light growing brighter, occasionally dismissing the competing silver horn of the moon, as if nature had changed its mind.

Preventing immigrants from arriving by sea was less pleasant. Thousands of war survivors were cramming into leaky boats in south European ports. British policy being that Jewish immigration should not swamp the Arab population, ships were stopped and diverted to camps in Cyprus. The flashpoint came when the ships actually touched land. The filthy, miserable passengers, released for a moment from their floating prison, had to be pushed back from the shore and prevented from escaping inland. We knew perfectly well that these were the same people who had survived the concentration camps.

One morning, I went up to Divisional HQ on Mount Carmel. It reminded me of Cap Ferrat in southern France – umbrella pines and the deep blue sea below, the water almost transparent, a rowing boat seeming to glide on air.

Near a promontory lay an illegal immigrant ship, small, grey and listing, with thirteen hundred Jewish refugees crammed into holds. We could see little figures jumping into the sea and wading ashore. But soldiers lining the beach pushed them back to clamber hopelessly aboard again. One slipped through, but was caught. Two soldiers threw him into the water, like a sprat they had caught but did not want. The ship lurched off down the coast, searching for another spot. But two destroyers shadowed it, like cats after a mouse, and escorted it on its way to Cyprus.

Early one morning, we too were ordered to line a beach. There were people visible everywhere, crowded like flies on a floating carcass. They shook their fists and shouted abuse, close enough to see their strained faces and scruffy clothes, some of the women naked, to make it embarrassing for the soldiers to carry them. At least it showed British troops did not inspire fear of rape. Any moment the sea might become black with heads as these famished people struggled to reach the promised land to which they were so close. We would have to repel them, their desperate breath on our faces, hands clawing our uniforms. I believed in restraining Jewish immigration to maintain equilibrium with the Arabs. But these were human beings in a pathetic plight, not statistics. Fortunately for us, a destroyer escorted the boat off before the immigrants could reach us.

I managed to talk to individual Jews and Arabs. In a café in Haifa, out of uniform, I listened as Jews from Poland at the next table described the relatives they had lost at Auschwitz. One talked of his mother with tears in his eyes: 'Why did they do this to us? What had we done?'

An Arab lawyer sympathised with the Jewish dilemma but feared the British would yield and the Arabs be ejected from land and houses they had owned for centuries. 'After all, we have been here for almost fifteen hundred years and Zionism only dates from the beginning of this century. Why should it be us who pay for Hitler's sins, just because Moses led his people here three thousand years ago?'

I asked him about my great-uncle, Sir Thomas Haycraft, chief justice in Jaffa in the early 1920s. To my surprise, he had heard of him. 'Ah, yes,' he said, 'he was impartial, the first judge to give a verdict in favour of some Arabs whose property had been seized. May it continue – but I doubt it!'

There was talk of finding another area for the Jews to go to, in South America or Africa, but nothing came of it. Where could such a place be found? The territorial imperative would always be too strong, even if only for a patch of desert. Some of my fellow officers and I wondered urgently why the British had taken on the whole burden, with its attendant assassinations and bombings. This was something of an anti-empire feeling not felt before, similar to my attitude in India. For good or ill, my generation represented a mood which, in the next few years, was to change everything.

In April I was back in Cairo, on my way home, ecstatic at the prospect. Perhaps I would be demobilised this very summer and go up to Oxford in October. It seemed incredible. Although the year had been fascinating, I had jibbed at the restraint and discipline, the obligations, the way my time was not really my own.

The return home was of course the slowest possible: a ten-day journey in a 'victory ship', an old merchantman adapted for troop-carrying. The slow journey through the Mediterranean and the Bay of Biscay was my last experience of counting off the days, of waking and thinking, 'This time next week . . .'

The incredible day dawned. We disembarked at Liverpoool in the afternoon and I was soon travelling, as if in a dream, through the green fields of Wales – first-class, of course, even for lieutenants, to avoid being in the same compartment as privates or warrant officers: it might have been embarrassing, broken down that barrier of non-communication on which all class hierarchies depend.

'Very good country for defence!' remarked the fatuous captain opposite.

I changed at Bristol and then, beyond Exeter, began the familiar coastline along the Exe through Dawlish, brief tunnels penetrating dark cliffs, the sea sucking at sand and shingle. I had witnessed it all so many times before, with the same sense of joyful release. We puffed up the Teign valley: mud flats at low tide, circling birds, green slopes rising on the opposite bank. There are always landmarks to ecstasy. Modest Newton Abbot station, the bijou bungalows approaching Torquay, a brick chimneystack like a tall, grubby finger in the failing light as we slowed for Torre station, where my odyssey had started sixteen months earlier.

There were porters in those days. My luggage, painted black and marked 'O', had not gone astray. It was put on a trolley and taken to a taxi which drove up Teignmouth Road, past the Technical College.

'First house on the right, with a green roof!'

Olive had loaded the table with ersatz cream cakes of the type she had provided throughout the war, in shadowy memory of easier and more indulgent times.

13 · Onstage with German POWs

I spent my eight weeks' leave working at the novel started in Secunderabad, basically a jumble of personal incidents and emotions masquerading as fiction. It probably would have been better as short stories. Seriousness and lack of self-confidence produced a burdensome mixture.

At the end of my leave, I was instructed to attend an infantry training course at Warminster, which seemed a waste of time as demobilisation could not be far away. But it was interrupted by an absurd accident: opening a tin of beans, I severed the upper ligament of my right forefinger. I bandaged it and reported for duty, only to be sent to the military hospital in Shaftesbury for an amazing five weeks, surrounded by people who had mangled their bodies in various dramatic ways, most in bed with limbs suspended. I was derisively known throughout the hospital as 'Finger'.

An awkward brigadier came round once, with two standard questions: one, what was wrong? and two, how had it happened? I was last. Anticipation grew in the ward, the others grinning and waving their fingers at me when the brigadier's back was turned.

'Well, my man, what's wrong with you?' he asked the man next to me.

'Well, sir, I've fractured my leg.'

'Have you? Terrible.' The brigadier asked his second question. 'And how did you do it?'

'My motorcycle ran over a cliff, sir.'

'Terrible!' the brigadier repeated his favourite adjective. He turned to me as I stood by my bed.

'And you?' he asked, relief in his voice at reaching the end.

'Well, sir,' I began, 'I've cut my finger . . .'

There were snorts of suppressed laughter. A captain with a broken collarbone laughed so much it hurt, and he let out a sharp cry.

The brigadier looked perturbed. 'Terrible!' he said, uncertainly. Then, clutching at routine: 'How did it happen?'

'I cut it on a tin of beans, sir . . .'

The laughter became almost uncontrollable, and the brigadier looked even more embarrassed. 'It's small but important,' he said defensively. 'Small but important!'

'It's nothing,' I insisted.

'It's small but important,' repeated the brigadier, nodding to the ward and departing hurriedly.

In the end my finger never was cured, and to this day is still bent at the end, partly because I couldn't take it seriously and played tennis regardless when allowed home at weekends.

During my next leave at the end of the course, I hitchhiked to Castle Barnard to see my brother Colin, who was stationed there, and also to familiarise myself with a Britain I had been away from for so long. In those days hitch-hiking was an easy, safe way of getting to know a country, with drivers taking you because they wanted to talk. Politics, jobs, love lives were discussed without inhibition, because you would never meet again.

I received my last posting in October, to a prisoner-of-war camp at Colley Weston, near Stamford, a collection of Nissen huts among trees on a long, windy ridge. Six hundred and fifty German prisoners were working, in two shifts, at the brickworks near Kettering, one from ten at night, the other from eight in the morning. Their main task was moving bricks off the production lines, like swivelling robots, then wheeling them to the stacks. In my perhaps naive way I was appalled that, two-and-a-half years after the war ended, Germans should still be slaving for eighteen shillings a week. They were 'compensating for' houses destroyed in the blitz, and with so many troops still busy occupying Germany, it was difficult to find British workers.

I found them fascinating. Many had been in Rommel's Afrika Korps, whose adventures I had followed avidly in the school reading room. My driver, Neumeier, had actually driven Rommel! Most had been captured in Tunisia in 1943, and often did not know where their families were in the chaos of postwar Germany. Few got letters. Some seemed dulled by events. One, a poet, had hanged himself the previous summer, with a placard round his neck reading, 'Here, Engländer, you see a victim of your slow revenge.'

A few were heavy and tactless. The official interpreter, Krause, was particularly pushy, inflated by his position. He treated me with ill-concealed scorn as a mere youth, the only one in the camp who had never been under fire. He saluted me reluctantly, rarely called me 'sir', and made invidious comparisons between England and Germany. I decided to pay Krause in his own coin. I told him we all knew how efficiently the Germans ran prison camps, barked at him to stand up straight, to salute when we met, and to call me 'sir'. The effect was immediate. Krause treated me with exaggerated respect thereafter.

Neumeier was different, small and squinting, his eyes twinkling in different directions. He had a sense of humour, but his pride and joy was his car which I nicknamed his *Schatz* (treasure). I had learned to drive as an officer cadet, but had forgotten much. He gave me practice on empty roads and instructed me with the tenderness of someone revealing the charms of his beloved. But one afternoon I hit the accelerator instead of the brake as we turned into camp. The wooden barrier hit the canvas roof, twisting it to one side. Poor Neumeier was shattered. His sense of hierarchy prevented him from expressing himself, but he became sullen, as if in mourning, and gave me reproachful, doglike looks. He repaired the car himself, and it was days before his twinkle returned.

Neumeier was a continual source of information about what the prisoners felt. He said what they most resented was their defeat. It was only this which had weakened their Nazi beliefs. The British tried regularly to indoctrinate them. Batches were sent to a place called Wilton Park at weekends, for lectures on democracy. Most were unimpressed. Neumeier showed me a satirical drawing by one of them: a POW sitting on a box marked 'Liberty', scanning a newspaper called 'Freedom of the Press', a bubble coming out of his mouth saying 'Free Speech', thick rolls of barbed wire around him and notices saying 'You shall work for fourpence an hour!', 'Don't escape!' and, of all things, 'It is forbidden to climb trees!'

I mostly got on well with the prisoners, and enjoyed practising my German. Behind my back they called me *der Bube* (the boy). I never mentioned Philomene's origins because they might think I was more of an ally than I was. They were surprised when I hummed German folk tunes like *Freut euch des Lebens* or *Magdele ruck-ruck-ruck bei meine grüne Seite*, which I had heard my mother sing at the piano. Neumeier said it was extraordinary the English should teach schoolboys German songs and kill their soldiers.

They could be affectionate. I particularly liked Koch, the cook, and invited him into our mess for a sherry when I was alone. We talked about his war experiences, which riveted me. On my twenty-first birthday, about which I had said nothing, he led a delegation to present me with the most splendid cake, with cream and 'Happy Birthday' in dark chocolate letters, and little silver balls which Neumeier had bought in Stamford. The prisoners had found out when my birthday was and had each contributed a sliver of their rations. We put the cake on the table and I cut a slice. They watched as I bit into it. I don't know whether it was the rationing or the heavy German style of baking, but the cake was too stodgy. They asked if I liked it. My mouth like an earthmover clogged with clay, I could hardly answer. I waved another slice around and said I was quite overwhelmed. I cut enormous slices for everyone so there would be nothing left for me. They ate with relish. It was a positive exercise in international relations: however little I liked the cake, it was a symbol of friendship which I accepted; that was the important thing.

The camp was guarded by a sergeant and half a dozen pasty-faced tommies, obviously picked because they were hopeless. One was illiterate, which amazed the Germans. There were two officers, so I was second-in-command. A gloomy captain was CO. He had a gentle Alsatian called Dastur. We shared the 'mess', just another hut with a sitting-room and two small bedrooms. When I asked about the prisoner who had hanged himself the previous summer, he shrugged his shoulders and said, 'You can hardly blame him.' When I said many still seemed to have Nazi sympathies, he said, 'What can you expect? You can't de-nazify people by keeping them in prison. They'll get over it.'

One night the captain was out and I was minding Dastur. There came a timid touch at the door. Dastur barked. I sensed something malevolent lurking outside in the dark. I opened the door and thought I saw a shape standing about ten feet away, motionless.

'Hallo,' I said.

The shape moved. 'Please excuse . . .' said a nervous voice.

'What is it?'

A prisoner came into the light, a scarf over his face.

'What is it?' I repeated. Cold in the wintry air, I beckoned him in and gave him a chair. He sat, hesitantly.

'I sorry, sir . . .' he began. Removing his scarf he looked at me awkwardly from under bushy black eyebrows. I had not seen him before.

He suddenly started talking rapidly in English. His name was Gruber, and he had just been posted to this camp from one in the north. In the last camp he had informed on prisoners still with Nazi sympathies. He showed me a letter he had just received, the envelope marked with a cross.

'It is a sign!' he wailed. 'Now they know, they vill come to get me!'

'How do you know it isn't just some post office mark?'

'*Nein, nein, nein!*' he shouted. 'I vill that you put me into detention solitary, then I shall be safe!'

'But I can't arrest you for nothing. The other prisoners will wonder what is going on.'

'Otherwise, they kill me.' He put his hands over his face.

'How could they?'

'They vill. I have always been friend to England.'

'Look, the captain is out. Wait till he returns. Go back to your barrack for the moment.'

Gruber looked as if I had condemned him to death. 'Please, sir . . .'

'Come on.'

He stood up reluctantly and looked at me beseechingly, putting the scarf back over his face. He plunged into the darkness.

I gazed blankly at my unfinished story. Whether Gruber's interpretation of the cross was right or not, he seemed sufficiently hysterical to do anything. Neumeier had talked of Nazi groups. Perhaps I should have taken Gruber to the guardroom, at least for the night, and discussed everything with him in the morning before anyone discovered where he was. Perhaps he was already beaten up or dead in a corner of his barrack. By arguing bureaucratically about putting a prisoner into detention, I might look back in shame on this night for ever.

Dastur and I were both glad when the CO returned. But he was drunk, and could only burble about brandy and bodies.

'Shit!' I said. I went to the guardroom and asked the sergeant to follow me. As we walked, I told him what had happened.

I put on the light in Gruber's barrack. There was no one there as they all worked nights. Blankets were rolled neatly at the end of empty beds.

The sergeant pointed at a partition. I tried the door. It didn't give. 'It's locked,' I said.

'No, sir. None of the doors lock.'

We pushed. It gave with a crash. '*Töten Sie mich nicht . . .*' said a terrified voice from the shadows. I put on the light. Gruber had fallen on the floor. He recognised us and relief suffused his face. 'I thought they had come,' he moaned.

'Don't lay there like a bloody beetle!' barked the sergeant. 'Stand up when an officer comes into the room! Come on! Get up! Get up!'

Gruber scrambled to his feet and the sergeant marched him briskly out of the barrack into the darkness. 'Left! Right! Left! Right! Pick your fucking feet up! Left! Right! . . .'

At the guardroom, Gruber crouched and took my hand. 'Thank you,' he moaned, 'Thank you.'

'What d'you think you're fucking doing?' shouted the sergeant. 'Stand up straight! Quick march!'

And Wehrmacht-trained Gruber marched with swinging rigid arms into the safety of a British guardroom. Only in a madhouse would anyone be so grateful to be locked in solitary.

It was a miserable, wet autumn. The rain beat down on the corrugated roofs and the winds shook away the leaves, making the trees stark and creaky as they scratched at the dull, grey sky.

I took an acting course in Peterborough. The class put on a one-act play at a theatre festival, a disaster for me: I forgot my lines and wandered about the stage repeating the previous one, 'I must think of something!', while the prompter hissed, 'Medicine! Medicine!' from the wings. The class included an ex-serviceman called Tooley and his wife Adrienne. They both felt as I did about the prisoners still being here, and had already invited some home at weekends. We discussed the possibility of having them put on a show in village halls on Saturday evenings. It could be called *German Follies*. Tooley worked at the town hall and would contact local councils, while I would ask the CO. We hoped to get a group together, encourage them to write and rehearse sketches, and I would compère the shows.

'Do you think there'll be hostility?' I asked Tooley.

'I'm sure there won't, particularly if we give the proceeds to the Red Cross.'

My request for volunteers got an immediate response. Several prisoners had been musicians or actors. Many others were teachers, and we also discussed weekend German classes – conversation exchanges, with English and Germans 'paying' each other with their languages.

We got military permission for the show, subject to the captain's censoring eye. We used an empty barrack to devise sketches, sing songs and rehearse. Tailors made dresses for those playing female roles, painters produced scenery. The leading spirit was Zimmermann, who had been in theatre in Berlin before the war. Of course this was amateur dramatics – but there were sparks of genuine talent. Three weeks later, we peeped through the curtains and saw the village hall fill up until people were standing at the back.

'There is a lot of interest!' Zimmermann was surprised. They had feared no one would come, in protest. But a crowded hall might also mean hostility; it only needed one extremist to abuse 'those who had killed our boys', and it could all break up. In that pre-performance tension, we squatted nervously behind the curtain.

Groschen struck up his medley of German folk songs on the piano as a warm-up. Then I went on and said it was a pleasure etcetera, and that the first sketch was about a lady called Die Lorelei who sang bewitching songs from her rock on the Rhine, luring sailors to their deaths. The curtains opened on 'sailors' rowing a pasteboard boat, while Furlein sat, with a long blond wig, on a superbly painted 'rock'. A curious dialogue had Lorelei complaining that sailors no longer crashed into her rock; the sailors told her she was at least five hundred years old and needed a facelift and singing lessons.

The audience were a bit mystified but did their best to respond. Sketches followed about sausages, jerries in both senses, cricket, and a German trying to buy a bicycle in ambiguous English, interspersed with songs. My task was to introduce the sketches and to get the audience to sing *Trink Brüderlein Trink, Ach du Lieber Augustin* and other ditties from the song sheets they had been given.

Finally we all sang *Lili Marlene* in English, Furlein under a dim cardboard lamp-post in slinky dress and small black hat. The audience seemed intrigued and enthusiastic. No one had shouted 'Disgusting!', and the prisoners were dazed with their success. As we tidied up, the Tooleys congratulated us.

'We must do it again!' they said.

'They liked it!' Zimmermann kept repeating in wonder. 'They liked it!' The prisoners could not believe they had been applauded on this foray into normal life. Afterwards we actually went to a pub. The girls flocked round, and we got drinks and more congratulations. We drove back in the truck under a cold, clear sky, the prisoners chatting about what had gone wrong or gone well. 'We can make it much better,' said Zimmermann. Someone suggested the camp should have a monthly magazine in English with stories and articles. German songs echoed over the quiet English countryside.

'*Die Engländer* after all *sind sympathisch!*' said Furlein in surprise, perhaps forgetting I was there. We turned into the gate and stopped among the dark shapes of the huts. '*Gute Nacht! Schlafen Sie gut!*' Everyone dispersed, like returning Cinderellas.

Christmas was near, and with it my demobilisation. The Germans were sad at yet another Christmas in camp. Every Christmas they hoped they would be free and at home, celebrating with carols and cake and marzipan animals under sparkling Christmas trees. They remembered family celebrations from a time of plenty, the last 'real' Christmas they could recall.

On my last night in the army I had an extraordinary dream. I was in London, near Trafalgar Square, it was 1927, and I was grownup, although I was actually only a few months old then. It was sunny. There were oddly-shaped cars and open-roofed buses, men in waistcoats and bowlers and girls with smooth hats and waistless dresses. There was a sepia light, everyone was cheerful and confident, and I felt very secure. Suddenly realising they must be warned about Hitler, I went into a post office and said I had come from the future, from 1947. The clerk roared with laughter. I took out a pound note. 'That's King George VI,' I said. 'The Duke of York at the moment.' He squinted at the note. 'Beware of Hitler,' I said.

'Who?'

'Hitler.'

'Who's he?'

I reached over and gently hit his chest. 'Hit-' I began, 'Hit-ler. Remember him,' I said, 'he'll try to destroy everything!'

When I woke, the idea continued. I imagined going to India and finding my parents (myself presumably in a cot), and trying to persuade my father to leave the army or he would be killed. I imagined telling people about jets and the atom bomb, and getting them to strangle Nazism at birth.

My thoughts turned to 'civvy street'. Home at last for Christmas. A train to London, and then the usual run down to Torquay. I thought of the prisoners, the mist seeping over the hill, wavering between the cheerless huts, the ghost of the hanged poet hovering over the wet leaves. Perhaps in years to come, travelling through Lincolnshire I would climb a familiar hill to find huts choked with briar and blackberry, grass tufts thrusting through mossy floorboards. This postscript of war would be over. In Bavaria, Neumeier would be tending cars in his garage, Krause a factory foreman with self-important reminiscences about the war and his POW experiences, Koch baking rich cakes in his Munich restaurant.

And Gruber? And me?

PART 3

Putting the World to Rights

14 · Crusade

I collected my last army issue: a striped grey suit, black shoes, socks, a tie, and a couple of shirts, at last equipped for civvy street.

After Christmas at Torquay, I decided to go to London and devote myself to finishing my novel. I would live on my army savings, do nothing else, get so absorbed that I would be pulled over the line into another world.

I found a room in Putney in the house of a Miss Allen whose most worrying mannerism was perpetually grinding her teeth as if sharpening them for victims, one of whom I rapidly became. I was her only lodger and thus her sole social outlet. She was determined to discover anything I might do to violate the decorum of her house: leaving the single-bar electric fire on when I wasn't in my room, shedding little pools of water on the bathroom floor, dropping crumbs from my frugal breakfast onto the tattered carpet. For over a month I saw no one except Miss Allen and people in the cafés where I ate. I felt exhilarated and, saving Miss Allen, free from pressure. But gradually staleness replaced my absorbtion. The alpha obsession still haunted me. Was what I wrote any good? Was I wasting my time? Then there were my changes of mood. I wasn't mature enough to write consistently, but kept darting off on new tracks, lacking the confidence to stick to one developing story and eliminate anything irrelevant. Looking back, I realise half the trouble was that I took writing too seriously. I was too moonstruck by 'streams of consciousness' and pompous descriptive writing, instead of finding ways of expressing my feelings. By temperament no monk, I began to long for girls, for friends in London.

I read about Gandhi's assassination in an evening paper, and wept bitterly under a railway bridge. It seemed such senseless savagery. I read a leaflet about a new political movement called the Crusade for World Government, run by Labour MP Henry Usborne and supported by people like Lord Boyd-Orr, Lord Beveridge and Bertrand Russell. The aim was to rally people in every country and, in 1955, elect a constituent assembly which would hammer out a world government constitution. The idea, that peace could not be maintained if the world were divided into national units with their own armies, appealed to me. Underlying it all was anticipation of an atomic war. When listening to music, particularly Mozart, I felt furious that everything civilised might be destroyed. I imagined all those gramophone records as splinters of radioactive bakelite, music scores burnt up in an immense conflagration, along with all of our flesh and blood. For what? But 'crusade for world government' struck me as a ridiculous name. How could it appeal to Muslims, to the Chinese? And would Russian or Spanish dictators allow their citizens to be canvassed and to vote?

I wrote to Henry Usborne with my objections. He replied, emphasising that his plan would allow individuals to express their desire for peace whether national governments interfered or not. The stumbling block was Russia but, as in all democracies, any political creed could be represented depending on votes. Britain and the US had enormous influence, and strong movements in those two countries would make a lot of difference. Anyway, what else was there to work for? World government was the only way of eliminating the real causes of war. The United Nations was useless because it just represented national governments instead of overriding them.

The internationalism of the idea appealed to the eternal foreigner in me, and I joined the Crusade. I still worked all day on my novel, and canvassed in the evening. I joined a group of young people and we would work a street together. People gave us their names and paid two-and-six, which provided funds. They had more time to argue on doorsteps then. One man in Hackney insisted war was inevitable, 'part of human nature'. He didn't like foreigners, had enjoyed the war, found peacetime boring, and was sure many people felt the same. Another man in his twenties accused me of being a 'cowardly conscientious objector'. 'You don't want war,' he said, 'because you're afraid to fight.' He refused to believe I had been in the army and pushed me out, to show he at least was not afraid to fight. Most people were responsive. I got three or four registrations an evening. The canvassers were mostly in their early twenties, students, local authority employees, Labour and Liberal party members. One was a bus driver. There was an American who had returned to Britain after the war because he had enjoyed himself as a GI.

At Crusade headquarters, the atmosphere was exuberant. People streamed in and out. I met Usborne, in his late thirties and regarded as a guru. He suggested I return to Torquay and create a group there, and another at Oxford later. Without regret, I left Miss Allen to find a new lodger to torment.

Torquay is beautiful, its palm trees and streets winding up its many hills. Splendid houses overlook the picturesque harbour and the sweep of Torbay. From Babbacombe cliffs there is a view of the coast up to Sidmouth. Nearby are picturesque villages, and Dartmoor frowns in the background. In 1948 Torquay had not been modernised for the tourist. In summer months it was given over to northern holidaymakers, in winter full of retired people. Most activity centred on the yacht and tennis clubs, or squash at the luxurious Imperial Hotel.

Olive now lived halfway up Teignmouth Road in her 1930s villa. From here, I launched my campaign for world government, gathering up young friends, new acquaintances, and ladies who lived for good causes. Olive was not in favour. She feared I would use the house for meetings. She did not care for visitors, even relatives, probably because she was not used to cooking and was aware of the contrast between her present home and the large houses of her youth. But she let me get on with whatever interested me, never objecting to my bringing back girls to lie by the electric fire on the living-room carpet and listen to gramophone records. In many ways this was a key period. Gone was the shy introvert of army days. Freedom gave me exuberance. Belief in world government lent me purpose, stimulated my organisational talents. My shyness at asking for contraceptives made me apprehensive of sex. But I became friendly and more at ease with girls, many seeming as eager for it as they would be reputed to be later, in the sixties. I think it was the two world wars, not the pill, which made Englishwomen more open to love.

I canvassed for world government in the evenings, as I had in London. I was joined by Guy Wilson, a friend I had played tennis with since I was twelve, son of a local surgeon and now at Cambridge. The friends he brought in included Pat Arrowsmith, later renowned for her outspokenness in the campaign for nuclear disarmament. We played talks by Lord Beveridge or Bertrand Russell on a gramophone on the promenade. When a crowd collected, one of us would spring onto a box to address them. London sent us Labour MP George Rogers. We hired a hall and put up posters. Rogers spoke persuasively and the meeting was a success. During questions, we were accused of being a communist conspiracy: didn't they too want world government? Rogers handled things fairly convincingly.

I saw my prep school headmaster in the front row, and talked to him afterwards. Accompanied by a small boy on a 'treat', he congratulated me on organising the meeting, and said he had underestimated me and should have put me in for a scholarship to Wellington. Now no longer in his power, I saw just a pompous old man.

The Crusade's surest way of raising funds was through jumble sales, and we were lucky to recruit Miss Toms, known locally as the Jumble Queen, who would raise at least £25 a sale. She was grey-haired with a round face like a cat. Her basement home was like a lair in *The Wind In the Willows*.

Pat Arrowsmith and her brother Peter, perhaps our most unusual helpers, invited me to lunch to introduce me to their many talents. First I was closeted with Pat. She read me a poem entitled *Perverted Love*. I misheard as *Perverted Dove*, which clouded my understanding. Then I went to Peter's room for a short story about a supercilious child refusing to look for Easter eggs in the garden, ending up getting an egg smashed in her face. Downstairs, Pat played *A Sad Moment*, composed at the age of seventeen, on the cornet. Peter played a sonorous hymn on a tuba. Finally we went to the picture gallery, Peter's paintings on one wall, Pat's on another. There was a picture of her in the bath which she wouldn't let me see. I disgraced myself, having misunderstood Pat's poem, reacted uncertainly to Peter's story, and admitting I was colour-blind. Pat asked me if I wasn't tone-deaf as well.

Guy Wilson and I hitch-hiked to the world government conference in Luxembourg. We brought a tent, spending money only on food which, apart from meat and bread, was unrationed in France. We subsidised ourselves by bringing in coffee and selling it. On the way we visited places I had known as a child, and Florence and Rome as well. The whole three weeks cost us £35 each. Europe was recovering fast, at least superficially, without Britain's equality-seeking austerity. In France we indulged ourselves with real cream cakes, unobtainable at home. In Italy we subsisted on spaghetti and glorious breakfasts – a bowl of *caffe latte*, grapes, cheese and bread, and tomatoes! There were no campsites then. We slept in fields and parks, and on the Palatine Hill in Rome, where we were woken by *carabinieri* and asked, with immense courtesy, to move on. Hitch-hiking was harder than in Britain. We had a moonlight drive with an Englishman in a sports car, from Menton along the coast and through Genoa to Santa Margherita, sleeping on the beach and waking to sunlight and lapping waves.

In retrospect, what was most remarkable was the lack of tourism and cars. Florence was as EM Forster must have known it. We strolled into an empty Santa Croce and examined the Michelangelo statues in the tiny, silent Medici chapel. We gate-crashed a reception at the Palazzo Vecchio, and took a horse-carriage up an empty road to Fiesole with my cousin, Francis King, in Italy with the British Council.

On our way north from Rome, hitch-hiking proved impossible. We slept in a cattle wagon, all that was available to third-class passengers. From Florence to Como, we stood in the corridor of a carriage turned into first-class by sticking notices on the windows. The inspector told us to move to third. An Italian Jew who had spent the war in Italy without disturbance tore off the notices. 'We are third now!' he said. The inspector slunk away. In Alsace we got a lift with a horse and cart, on which I tore the seat of my trousers and could not mend them before we got to Luxembourg. We were precipitated straight into the opening reception with the prime and foreign ministers. After shaking hands with them, the tear in my trousers made me retire backwards, as though they were mediæval royalty.

Luxembourg seemed the antithesis of world government, a true celebration of nationalism in miniature – grand duke, guardsmen, royal palace, and such a tiny population. But at least it lent us official support. Representatives came from all nations, even the Soviet bloc, except the dictatorships. The Americans and French were particularly strong. The enthusiasm was encouraging, though there seemed too much discussion on political tactics rather than on the pressing question of how to publicise the movement and rally people. One morning an Indian millionaire announced he would look after all financial needs so long as the manifesto included the words, 'All cow slaughtering will be abolished.' This was laughed away, but made us ponder the danger of an unscrupulous political group trying to take over the movement.

Back in London I tried to telephone Lord Faringdon, a supporter but not at the conference, to invite him to speak at Torquay. The operator said his number was ex-directory, and I only got through by using the girl's snobbishness and calling myself 'Sir John Hay-craft'. Faringdon promised to come for our world government week. When he arrived, those who considered us communists were sur-prised to see an actual lord with us.

The week coincided with the beginning of the 1948 Berlin block-ade and the massive allied airlifts. The Russians only had to shoot down one plane and sirens would scream again, and we would all rush from Lord Faringdon's meeting down into the disused air-raid shelters. Pat suggested going to London and blocking Piccadilly

Circus as a protest. But this seemed aggressive, for an organisation whose raison d'être was world peace. We tried a demonstration in Torquay. Anthony Daw could ride, so he was covered in red-soaked bandages and put on a horse, with placards saying, 'Do we want another war?' and 'Do you want this to happen again?' He rode from Castle Circus to the harbour along crowded lunch-time streets, as we distributed leaflets. At traffic-lights, though, the horse refused to budge. A traffic jam developed with hooting horns, making the horse more obstinate. At the third green light, a policeman tried to move them on. The horse suddenly cantered round the harbour and up to the Imperial Hotel. Amid the Rolls-Royces, the commissionaire couldn't believe his eyes. The climax was a world amity ball at the Grand. We were terrified no one would come. But Olympic sailing week was also on: our ball became an event and we made £50.

Christine, my latest infatuation, was there. I wrote in my diary: 'I love that girl. She is so beautiful that she paralyses me, as if I were a hypnotised bird. She realises this and plays tricks which make me writhe with jealousy. If I weren't so obsessed, I would humour, flatter and make love to her. Why is everything so difficult when you care?'

15 · Fabled City

I was at last to go to my Mecca, Oxford. Nearly four years ago I had come for the scholarship exam, reverent and bewildered as Jude the Obscure. At thirteen I had told myself that when I finally slept with a woman, I should recall that time of unsatisfied lust and realise how lucky I was. Now I remembered the army in the same way – a khaki figure scrubbing floors at Caterham, running thirteen miles with a full pack, sweating up Welsh hills, Sergeant Fram yelling, 'That *useless* man *Haycraft* in the back rank!' Now at last I was free. I lay in bed in my room in Jesus College. It was full moon. Gazing out over the silvered roofs, I calculated the moon had been full 4,497 times since the college was founded by Queen Elizabeth the First.

That first term I sharpened my teeth on the mediæval period. At our first tutorial we received a book list and an essay to write and read at the next a week later. A fellow student, Peter Sawyer, became so excited over the Domesday Book that it could have been Boccaccio's erotic stories. I never found this kind of research interesting. I preferred discussing the consequences of what seemed to have happened, to probing the dust of hidden foundations. Having been away from study for four years was an advantage. At last I had lost the 'alpha mystique'. I made no academic genuflections but answered questions concisely, with illustrations and strictly relevant examples. I liked the system, the solitary struggle with an unfamiliar subject, producing essays condensing new ideas. For it was ideas that counted. Unlike the education system in most countries, here facts were not absorbed for their own sake but were valued in so far as they formed a basis for those ideas. Some lecturers, though, were atrocious. They knew their subjects, but needed elementary communication lessons. They mumbled, made inaudible comments, chortled at private jokes, looked nervously at the ceiling. Lectures were voluntary, with only one or two students at some, generally by dons who regarded research as their real objective and despised teaching mere undergraduates. A few, like the unbearably supercilious Hugh Trevor-Roper (later Lord Dacre) or Lord David Cecil, were brilliant exceptions.

I liked too the chance of doing a myriad other things in term: Union debates, listening to people like Rex Warner, TS Eliot on his conversion to Catholicism, or seeing labour minister Emmanuel Shinwell barracked while opposition leaflets rained down from the skylights. I was at the Writers' Club meeting which saw a change in the idea of authors as leisurely middle-class 'gentlemen' as opposed to working-class 'blokes' with a living to make. Victor Gollancz was lambasted for not paying big enough advances or royalties. Education was anything you were interested in. Multifarious term-time activities were followed by concentrated academic work at home during vacations. During my first term I began canvassing for world government. A 'society' had to invite speakers, hire rooms and print a progamme, financing it all through subscriptions and attracting enough enthusiasts to form a committee. Canvassing from college to college was an excellent way of meeting people.

Our first speaker was Doctor Joad, reserved as ever except on the platform. We organised fund-raising dances and a debate between the economist Graham Hutton and the historian AJP Taylor. I got a lead article on world government into *Isis* and a short story I had written in India into *Viewpoint* magazine. Being published at Oxford was a triumph. Everyone felt Oxford and Cambridge were cradles for success, particularly at this time when undergraduates were older, eager to fill the vacuum left by the war. It was an amazingly élitist group. Among those I met at Oxford between 1948 and 1951 were Robert Runcie, journalists John Ardagh, Alan Brien, William Rees-Mogg, Anthony Sampson, Godfrey Smith and Ken Tynan, politicians Tony Benn, Margaret Thatcher, Jeremy Thorpe and Shirley Williams, the poet Philip Larkin, novelists Kingsley Amis, Nina Bawden, Sue Chitty, Thomas Hinde and my cousin Francis King, the critic Martin Seymour-Smith, John Schlesinger, William Russell, Michael Codron, Alan Cooke, Charles Hodgson, Michael Croft, Tony Richardson, Peter Parker, Robin Day, Robert Robinson and Magnus Magnusson. Government grants for those who had done national service meant there were more non-public-school students. Of 250 Jesus College undergraduates, only five came from public schools.

It was a fantasy world, perhaps because undergraduates were consciously making the most of this euphoric period between the circumscriptions of school and the forces, and the exigencies of a career. One morning Rodney, Rebecca, Janet and I were walking in the Corn, when Rodney suddenly exclaimed, 'It's as sunny as a wedding day! Let's get married!' We bought cakes and wine and told the registration office clerk we wanted to get married at once. I'm sure we would have gone through with it, but the clerk talked firmly about identity papers and giving notice. 'It seems unfair people can't get married when they want!' objected Rodney. The clerk took this seriously and suggested Rodney put it in writing. We celebrated anyway. The rumour of this 'marriage' soon got about. Rodney was hauled in front of the dean and told he would lose his scholarship if he were married – a relic of the times when undergraduates were seminarists.

Rodney was extraordinary with his flowery words and gestures. When I asked his support for world government he roared with laughter, not at the idea but at the thought of actually participating. He did appear as the muscular cabaret artist Anita Gonzalez at a dance we held, though only after getting drunk beforehand. Afterwards we went punting on the dark river with a couple of girls. I fell in and took a bus back in the early morning, clad in a blanket which fell apart as I tried to climb into college without being seen. Rodney said he would never sacrifice a moment of the present to ward off future disaster: anything not sensual was just brittle sublimation. He disliked my 'building sand castles like an absorbed child, getting hollow success on the way'.

We got rid of our tutor, a Welshman and supposed expert on Elizabethan England who made superficial remarks about our essays and then gossiped. We were not 'young gentlemen' preparing for a life of scholarly leisure, and complained to the senior history tutor – something no one had ever done before.

I acted in Magnus Magnusson's *Icelandic Saga*. The audience included the Icelandic ambassador (the only one who didn't have to be prompted to stand for the Icelandic anthem). Magnusson was delighted, proud to be Icelandic, though admitting to a little Scots influence.

The summer was devoted to a world government week in Bedfordshire. A gang of us drove off in a lorry in terrible condition: the steering-wheel was roped to the shaft, top gear didn't connect, the engine stopped regularly. One wag said the lorry, which was a Commer, should have been called a Full Stop. In the end, the police waved us down. We were innocently bewildered; the police were paternal. They brought the lorry to their garage, found thirty-two reasons why it should not be on the road, and repaired it, free, in two hours.

World government week didn't go well. The Conservative MP

talked about Christian principles, lost his temper and stalked out. No one listened to the Labour MP. Other speakers didn't turn up. We had an amateur wrestling display – curious in the circumstances, especially when one wrestler got a bloody nose. We sold helium-filled balloons. One escaped during the children's ballet and got caught among the dancers, crinkling into the tallest ballerina's hair; she danced on with this absurd blue rubber thing on her head. We canvassed in the market-place, where our long hair and posh accents went down badly. One woman shouted, 'Men don't work on Saturday mornings!' Another replied, 'These ones don't never work!' A woman with a crippled husband didn't want to think about the war that had maimed him, and preferred to ignore the dreadful possibility of another. It was easier to live without hope, to drug oneself with the daily routine of insignificant activities. Another one with huge black rings under her eyes talked about the food she would like and the miseries of rationing and queuing. 'Your world government won't cure that, will it? Not for a long time, anyway.' Naively, I wished people would think beyond personal dilemmas. Few people thought world government was a bad idea. If everyone assumed it were possible, it could come about.

It was about now that my relationship with Rebecca developed. We were sitting alone in a field outside a factory in Letchworth, finding ourselves chewing the same piece of long grass from different ends.

In Bedfordshire we all stayed at a prep school run by the Ladds, a gentle, caring couple in their forties. The boys seemed relaxed and happy, were treated with enthusiasm or got cheerful rebukes when necessary. The Ladds were humanitarian non-conformists, part of the postwar Labour middle classes, Christian in sentiment although they never went to church, unassuming except with anyone right-wing or pushy. Reluctant proselytisers, they nevertheless blended pacifism, herbal medicine, concern for others and a benevolent belief that all other countries could be like Britain if they tried. They did everything they could for Rebecca and me. When our week ended, they asked if we would stay on and teach for two weeks until the end of term, for no pay but full board and a lovely little cottage we could share near the chicken-run. I accepted with alacrity. Rebecca was pleased but apprehensive. She had an Italian immigrant grandmother, and was Catholic and still a virgin. Our foreign backgrounds gave us much in common. Rebecca was small and wonderfully lightfooted, with an exuberant laugh; her skirt twirled as she walked.

I produced the old male arguments, but what did I really know about her? It was her life; I had no intention of making it mine as well. The first Saturday, we hitched to Stratford and saw *Henry VIII*. We got a lift part of the way back but were dropped at one a.m. in a little village. We found an unlocked barn, spread some canvas over the straw and slept, entwined, until woken by crotchety chickens arguing in the sunlight. One evening we bicycled to a lake and bathed naked in the dark. Rebecca said the waves were like black serpents trying to reach up the sand towards us. She had once capsized at sea in a sailing boat, and the loneliness of the sky and lights twinkling on a distant ridge reminded her of it. She was happier when we swam close together and the serpent waves gave way, splashing gently in our faces. I enjoyed comforting her. She talked about her Catholic upbringing. The nuns had been ever-present figures of reproach. She sometimes imagined them in our room, prissy voyeurs around the bed, pale faces framed in white looking down while we made love. She said religion had always been her anchor, that she needed a value system which resolved the chaos. Speciously, I said religion and love should be joy. I learned to hold her while she talked, not interrupting, giving her warmth. This made her eager once more, as if she had shaken off a nightmare. Sometimes I thought she was testing my feelings for her, gauging my support.

Autumn back at Oxford, the mornings and evenings misty and drowsy, with a passion that seemed semi-conscious, half-wakeful, reminiscent of DH Lawrence's Bavarian gentians at slow, sad Michaelmas. The punts had gone, the Cherwell a brown, secretive river, overhanging trees dripping and shedding their plumage. There was a different feel to the Radcliffe Camera and working under artficial

light, or listening to lectures with no distracting sunshine outside. It
was dark but not cold, womb-like, monastic, as we worked in quiet
rooms.

I saw Rebecca immediately I got back. I had loved her in June but
didn't want a steady partnership at Oxford. I felt guilty about this.
What was cruel about love was that it had its own life: you didn't
know whether it would carry you down its dark river or up to the
bleak mountain top. We had tea in her warm, comfortable third-
floor room – round cakes, brown bread and the new cork-tipped
cigarettes. She said, 'I think things have changed.'

'Oh, they're bound to,' I said cheerfully, 'Oxford's a busy place.'
I felt falsely buoyant. I was sitting on the bed. Formally she asked
me if I minded if she sat beside me, and things ended as they always
did.

I was becoming disillusioned with world government. Guy and I
had brought in over a quarter of all registrations nationwide. What
were the others doing? Spending the £10,000 donation, furnishing
their new headquarters. I was already suspicious of anything bureaucratic or baroque that distracted from the main purpose. World
government would not be achieved by impressive façades or back-
corridor influence, but by getting people interested. We had done
the legwork, unpaid, while self-important little people sat in offices
supported by our registration fees, sending round tedious circulars
and producing loss-making magazines.

Following an old rugby injury, I had to have a knee cartilege
removed. I awoke to find an X-ray machine aimed at my stomach.
Rebecca told me an electric bulb had fallen off the laryngeoscope
they put down my throat because I was turning blue. I wasn't
supposed to know, so when an electrician came into the ward I said,
'That's the man for me, isn't it, nurse?', and they looked shifty. I
asked why my stomach glowed at night, and said I could focus my
navel on the ceiling. They didn't know what to say. It cheered things
up. Charlie in the corner had a wound on the left buttock and
returned to hospital regularly. Every time he used the loo at home,

the wound reopened. We were visited by a clergyman who did nothing but complain about his bishop and hop about like a sinister crow. He once upset Sister's index cards, and she let him pick them up alone. I caught her eye, and she gave me a broad wink.

Alex, the youth next to me, was dying. His lorry had been sliced in two by a train; he just lay on his back, waiting for death. I visited him after I had left. One day his bed was empty. 'Fraid he's dead!' said a nurse cheerfully, glad to see me. How else could they survive continual bereavement?

I decided to drop world government. I still believed, but was disappointed at the lack of single purpose. Office organisers always managed to take over. Get people into offices and they become maggots, not leaving until you scrape them out. The decision made me unhappier than I had imagined. I felt guilty and miserable. It was the end of a quest, and me one of the first to desert it.

Back in Torquay for the summer vacation, I went to see Rob, the new organising secretary. He seemed displeased. 'Come for an inspection?' he asked, mimicking an 'officer' voice.

'Of course not – why?'

'Hear world government isn't good enough for you.'

'It isn't that . . .' I felt flustered, and after a few pointless exchanges I left. Halfway down the drive Rob came running after me. 'You turd!' he shouted. I stopped in astonishment. 'Going out into your Oxford world!' he exclaimed, 'while I slave away here!'

'Come off it, Rob!'

He stood shaking his fist at me. 'It's your lot that has exploited the working man for hundreds of years . . .'

'Don't be silly, Rob, I haven't got any money.'

'You belong to them, though. There's going to be a revolution in this country.'

'All right, Rob.' My calm infuriated him. If I hadn't walked away, he would have hit me. I wondered what I should do. I finally walked back, uncertainly, but couldn't find him. I went into the house and called. No answer.

That evening I went dancing. In the small hours four of us piled into a car and drove down to the harbour. There was an ageless light, no wind, and only the seagulls awake. We walked along the pier and noticed a man sitting on a coiled rope, looking out at the bay. He said he had lived under a pile of shit since early childhood and, now that he was thirty-two, was at last crawling out.

I hoped it wouldn't take me that long to find my direction.

16 · My Eskimo Grandmother

At Biarritz, Guy Wilson and I met Bruce, a friend from Oxford. Wherever you go there is always someone from school, or the army, or Oxford, or a relative of a relative. Endless cliques. Bruce boasted about his parasitical existence on rich Italian or Spanish girls, charming them at university so they then invited him home for the vacations. He had only 500 francs left.

Hendaye, on a hill above Biarritz, was a village with narrow streets looking over the Atlantic. At lunch we sat beneath vines, the bottom of empty glasses reflecting the blue sky, interlaced with green leaves and little clusters of grapes. Bruce was gullible. Inspired by *Nanook of the North* and exuberant with wine, I invented a tale about my Eskimo grandmother who, I said, had been sent to spy out walruses, when suddenly the ice broke off and she sailed into Hudson's Bay on an iceberg, watched by her tearful family who would never see her again. My grandfather, captain of a Hudson Bay Company ship, saw the iceberg with the girl on it. He was so amazed that he almost crashed into it, the vibrations dislodging the girl who slid down onto the deck and broke her ankle. My grandfather nursed her back to England where they got married, and she was now eighty-four and living in Cheltenham, still revealing her origins by eating all the candles on her birthday cake.

'That's one of the saddest stories I've ever heard!' said Bruce, obviously moved. 'Imagine her floating away onto that icy sea, and her family knowing they would never see her again!'

We crossed into Spain and were instantly on the defensive, ready for hostility, conscious of being in a fascist state. We tried hitch-hiking to San Sebastian. A taxi stopped. The driver said in reasonable English that hitch-hiking was unknown in Spain. There were too many bandits, whom he called *maquis*. San Sebastian, previously the royal summer resort, had an impressive bay protected by an island and a large peninsula. We put our sleeping bags on the beach, but when it started raining moved into a concrete gallery with bathing huts. I was woken by people walking and talking conspiratorially, evoking midnight plots and white-ruffed courtiers with daggers at their hips. I was woken a second time by a couple of tipsy Englishmen wanting us to interpret to two policemen. We couldn't, so they sang *God Save the King* to prove they were British and beyond reproach.

Next day Bruce had found three attractive Spanish girls. Pointing at me, he said, *el Esquimal*! He had told the girls the whole iceberg story, and they too were moved by it. My frozen ancestry got Guy and me invited to a picnic with them. The four girls, Delfina, Lucia, Aurelia and Marina, had all been to England and spoke quite good English. Delfina railed against Spanish conventions forbidding a woman to dance except with her fiancé, and talked of an Irishman who bet a friend he would kiss a Spanish girl before he left Spain. He stayed two months and lost.

We set off in two magnificent cars, through the pine-covered foothills of the Pyrenees. The green bushes, the blue sky, the golden sunlight blended as we swept along empty roads. Villages were collections of small houses where boys loafed in tattered blue clothes who shouted after our cars. We nosed down narrow sloping lanes to a fishing village and parked on the wharf. We bathed off a rock promontory sticking out into a rough sea. On the way back, the tide had risen and I scraped my shoulder bloodily. Aurelia tended me skilfully, pouring a whole bottle of wine over my wound as an antiseptic. For lunch, we had cold tortilla which was delicious, meat in gravy, and oranges and grapes. The girls served us, as seemed natural in Spain. But they wanted to show they had absorbed English ways too, saying they felt enslaved returning to Spain. They equated the Franco government with their authoritarian parents.

We drove back with twilight over the Pyrenees. By a black river flecked with silver, a fisherman walked slowly up the bank. Nearer the town, we saw *Viva Franco! Viva España!* painted red on the walls. The girls invited us to a bullfight next day, refusing to let us pay as we were in their *país*. Franco's daughter was in the presidential box. I felt as if we were at the Colosseum. Trumpets blew. The toreros wore eighteenth-century clothes. The bull seemed incredibly fierce when he came in. There had been a fight between a bull and a tiger here in 1893: the tiger lasted two minutes. I admired the toreros' skill in evading the bull, but it always ended with the bull's dead body being dragged out. There was one pale, brown animal who protested at a persecution not of his asking and was butchered amidst jeers. I loathed the howling, cheering mob, the mothers with their children. A woman in front had a revolting laugh and pendulous breasts, and kept adjusting massive stays. Delfina said that only a few *pervertidos* enjoyed bullfights where the cruelty was evident. What appealed was the conflict between force and skill, a dramatic tragedy played out in reality.

We said goodbye to the girls who had been so kind. Aurelia and I stood in the corridor for a moment, and she said happily that she had never kissed an Eskimo before. She gave me her card. I thought she might come to my Oxford college, whose name no Spaniard could ever forget: Jesus.

At the station, you could not take the train to Madrid without an advance ticket. None were available for several days. So we smuggled ourselves onto the evening *correo*. The inspector was very cross, and said the penalty for having no ticket was prison; he would call the Guardia Civil at the next station. So we pretended to have lost our tickets and went through the pantomine of looking desperately in pockets and wallets. 'What did they look like?' he asked. Hopefully, I described a French rail ticket. 'What colour?' I hesitated. 'Ultamarine,' I said, hoping he didn't know what it was. He nodded wearily and we paid for two tickets.

We had an extraordinary journey on curved wooden benches like whale ribs. A soldier who spoke some English hospitably offered us food and drink. The carriage was full of women chattering all night, two of them arguing ferociously. The soldier said one was married and the other not. The married woman was mocking the other, who retorted that marriage in Spain was slavery and she was proud of her independence. They started grappling, but a heavy suitcase fell off the rack and hit them both on the head. They sat down, dazed. A small woman cluttered the main gangway with piles of luggage and a cockerel thrown carelessly on top, wings fluttering feebly when it crowed. We went into the corridor for a breath of air; when we returned, the cockerel and most of the luggage were under our seats. I lay on my haversack on the floor, and woke to a bare foot with cracked red toenails hovering above my nose.

The journey lasted thirteen hours. The full moon silvered crags and gaunt plains as we trundled slowly through Castile.

Our *pensión* in Madrid was a dark flat with a pervasive smell of cheap olive oil and a lavatory plug that didn't pull. The electricity was off in the day, but the rough sheets were clean and the landlady's daughters ironed our shirts in the evening. They were surprised that we had more than two each. Madrid was then a sad city with paint peeling everywhere, holes in the roads and gaps where bombs had fallen. We went to the Prado, with sun coming through the windows, lighting a feast of Velasquez, Goya and El Greco. A Murillo saint reminded me of a current girlfriend, and I sent her the postcard of the painting. In the evening we went to a fair in the slums and met a drunk who boasted, in broken German, that he had travelled from Madrid to Leningrad to fight the communists. He kept breaking off to say '*Alle Kameraden*' and shake hands, as if afraid he had offended us. The fair was raucous. Naked light bulbs swung on lines. Trams clattered up the road. A bespectacled American drove us back to the *pensión*. He told us in polysyllabic monologues that Franco was good for Spain because 'the Latins' didn't understand peaceful discussion. He thought Franco had achieved more than the republic, and had kept the communists out. With patronising assurance, he spoke of Spain as 'a political experiment', the American way being the universal criterion.

Next day we had lunch at a shabby café, then on to Toledo. On the train we met four Spanish workmen; one spoke some French. I asked what side they had fought on during the civil war.

'Republic,' he said.

'Is Franco still strong?'

'For the moment.'

'What are conditions like?'

'Bad. The poor get a hundred-and-fifty pesetas a week, the rich get thousands, thousands, thousands!'

They felt powerless. They lived with the summer heat and the cold Castilian winter, unable to alter conditions, or to speak openly for fear of arbitrary arrest.

'It was good under the Republic,' they said.

Like Florence, Toledo felt like a separate city-state, though more isolated, mediæval with no Renaissance softness. It was almost an island, with the Tagus tearing through the gorge on one side of the rock. We came through the massive Charles V gates, the double-headed Hapsburg eagle above, and climbed up past the Moorish Puerta del Sol into the main Zocodover Square, with desolate, almost Palestinian countryside below and the gaunt ruins of the Alcazar, smashed in the civil war. Toledo was a city of bell-tolling convents, empty twelfth-century synagogues, and Mudejar churches built by Moorish workmen under Christian architects. The main street was a lane, with glass-enclosed balconies abutting from above. Toledo still reflects most of Spanish history, from the Romans two centuries BC and the baths of Florinda on the river, where the last Visigoth king, Rodrigo, is supposed to have surprised the daughter of one of his noblemen, Count Julian, and taken her. In revenge, Julian is believed to have brought in the Moors who fought and killed Rodrigo at Guadelete in 711, and conquered the whole of Spain in just a few months.

Toledo was the capital of Spain until Philip II lighted on the village of Madrid, at the geographical centre of the country. The Alcazar has existed for centuries. In 1936 the Republicans besieged the Francoists there and bombarded it to pieces.

At night, we explored. There were covered ways and empty, mediæval lanes with dim lights in small houses and glimpses of the rocky, dimly moonlit countryside. I vowed to return and write. Despite Franco, Spain lured me. It was like going back to the eighteenth century with its inefficiency and inequalities. It seemed to have much of the dramatic style of living lost in modern civilisation. It beckoned to the explorer and historian in me.

17 · Brita

I went up a week early to study, the last year before my finals. One morning in the Radcliffe, I decided to work right through without my usual coffee break. But at eleven I changed my mind. On the steps I ran into Peter Sawyer the Domesday expert, and a beautiful blonde girl with green eyes: Brita Langenfelt, from Sweden. We went to coffee, which lasted beyond lunch.

Brita was lovely. Her eyes changed colour with her mood, like the sea. We talked about Uppsala, where she was studying English and French with a dose of Old Norse. At Oxford on a summer English literature course, she lived in Bath Place, part of the labyrinth behind Hertford College. She invited me to tea with cinnamon toast, and a game of shove-halfpenny at 'The Turf' afterwards. I in turn invited her to a sandwich lunch at my little John Street hut. But she said that, everything considered, she didn't think she should; we went to a restaurant instead.

It began as a strangely innocent relationship, Brita ensuring she wasn't seduced. We got on well, with the same interest in languages and other countries and a similar sense of humour. We teased each other in French and German. I gathered she had a boyfriend in

Stockholm, and then discovered she was in love with an Oxford literature don.

We had a ridiculous farewell after only five days, a parody of the end of a love affair – though she seemed unaware of how upset I was. She stood at her first-floor window with a bunch of artificial flowers, not letting me in to say goodbye properly, but dropping the flowers to me. I felt frustrated, but she laughed it off. I had accidentally kept a towel she had lent me, and used it as an excuse to write, beginning a correspondence that would last three years.

We last-year students spent our time making up for work not done in the first two years. The Oxford ideal was to do no work and get a first – that was real 'brilliance'. In the history faculty, success was a question of ordering facts and ideas methodically, and working very hard so that they became familiar. 'Trembling time' soon came, with exams on three years' study of two thousand years of English history and a hundred of European, on constitutional documents, and on a special subject, in my case the French revolution – all that in one gigantic five-day memory test. You remembered best what interested you most, so it was really a test of the vividness of what you had studied. Ideas needed a basis of facts; to express ideas satisfactorily you had to remember the facts. Character came into it too. Would you panic? Still write good essays on the last day? Decide quickly which five questions to answer out of two dozen? Recover if you made a false start? Balance economy and detail? Finish in time?

'Disaster met Queen Elizabeth whenever she ventured abroad – discuss.'

Did 'venturing abroad' include the Spanish Armada, not really Elizabeth venturing but someone doing something to her? Only her forays into France and the Low Countries then, and perhaps Drake at Cadiz and on the Spanish Main? No. Try another question. Mary Queen of Scots? No – quick, back to Elizabeth and the Low Countries.

I knew I would only get a good second. I hadn't worked enough for a first and anyway didn't need one. I didn't want to be a don. I wanted to go abroad and write novels, and an Oxford degree should be good enough to sustain me. The university careers officer advised me against going abroad. 'You will come back at thirty or so, probably with a wife and children, and find you have practically no extra qualifications and no prospects.' Our career ideas changed constantly, perhaps because there was no unemployment. Three years of illusion were being wiped away. We were like railway carriages about to be uncoupled from the locomotive. There were fears we might rust away in a siding. So most people cast about for anything to pull their carriage along.

I did not have to decide immediately, as I had applied for an English Speaking Union fellowship to Yale. While waiting to hear, I had decided to return to Toledo and work as a cathedral guide; I had noticed there weren't many. I enjoyed *Teach Yourself Spanish*, though doubted I would understand a word when I got there. I got posters printed in French and English: 'GUIDED TOURS ROUND TOLEDO CATHEDRAL BY OXFORD GRADUATE'. For the first time since my boyhood in Italy, I had a sense of absolute freedom, of doing what I wanted without let or hindrance.

Early one morning, Peter Arrowsmith and I set out from Paris on his motor-bike to Louveciennes in the soft, bright dawn.

At dinner the next night we met a Spaniard called Manolo who had been on the republican side in the civil war. They were so hungry they attacked a barn full of almonds, which they ate for the next three days. He despaired at fighting for three years, for nothing save his country's devastation. He realised that had the republicans won, Hitler might well have won the war – taking Gibraltar, making the Mediterranean an Italo-German lake, sweeping through Egypt and Persia to attack Russia from the south. What greater futility than fighting a long war against dictatorship, only to find the world ruled by a maniac because you had won! When I said I was going to Toledo, Manolo's eyes filled with tears. He talked about sunsets over the Tagus and the excitement of feeling a new Spain would emerge under the republic. He asked me to go to a tavern opposite the church of San Juan de los Reyes and drink a glass of wine to him.

I was excited because I planned to see Brita in Pau, where she was taking a French course. We had arranged to meet at the Rôtisserie Périgord, but it was closed when I arrived. I located Brita's school, and they gave me her address. When the landlady said Mademoiselle had just left, I felt I would never find her. But suddenly there she was, walking towards me in a white dress, her blonde hair pinned over her ears and her face sunburnt and beautiful. We had only spent about ten hours in each other's company altogether, and almost a year ago. But there was no hesitation, no embarrassment, no need to adjust.

That evening we met a blind man selling lottery tickets in a café, young, good-looking and humorous. We asked him to have a drink. He obviously liked Brita, and laughed a lot as he told us about Pau. Out in the street, he recognised people by their voices. Brita walked between us, arm-in-arm. He suggested we meet again, to listen to the orchestra that played in the square each evening. But '*tous les trois*,' he said sadly, clearly with no illusions about competing for Brita. I was suddenly aware how lucky I was, as if I had been given a precious vase which could so easily slip from my grasp and smash to the ground. The next afternoon Brita and I went up to the Grottes de Bétharram, sitting at the back of the bus and clasping each other shamelessly. We got out and hitched a lift in a big Renault with a happy Parisian family. Two women with handkerchiefs over their hair had baskets from which bottles of red wine and baguettes protruded. Outside the caves we had a *diable au menthe* in the hot sun and Brita, a great nuzzler, nuzzled a wee, fluffy, white Pyrenean hound. Inside we kept to the back and listened only occasionally to the guide, in whose torchlight the rock secretions glistened silver like temples and fairy palaces. We found our own images too: a pillar with a strangely carved body and head which we decided was the god of the cave; a woman looking over an abyss was Brita becoming involved with me. There were dates carved on the roof, one saying 1576, the time of France's religious wars. The cold, dark silence, time measured only by the dripping of stalactites, contrasted with the warmth we felt together.

Afterwards we bathed in the river.

That night Brita's course was having a party, and as Brita's *jeune homme* I was welcome too. She had described some of the course-members: the courteous and eccentric British; two beautiful Romans; a squat young Spaniard of sixteen who showed Brita a scar on his arm, said '*R-regar-rdez! C'est une femme qui m'a mor-r-rdu!*', and told us proudly he had seduced his uncle's wife.

Afterwards Brita had to finish an article on Bernadotte, a native of Pau who became king of Sweden. I have always disliked his betrayal of Napoleon, so suggested Brita add that he died in a welter of guilt one night as an owl hooted 'Waterloo! Waterloo!', a story that may well be in the guidebooks now.

Next day I took the train to Madrid and Toledo. Brita almost came with me, but her father had paid for the French course and she couldn't go gallivanting in Spain with me. I jogged wretchedly south on hard wooden seats. I loved Brita's warmth, her affection and humour, her enterprising independence. There was immediate understanding between us. After a melancholy journey, I arrived in Madrid. I dined at Nuestra Señora de los Correos, on the top floor of the main post office building: soup, wine, a *filete* and as much bread as you wanted for five pesetas. There was the smell of cheap olive oil. Although I missed Brita, it was good to be back.

And so to Toledo: dust and sunlight everywhere, the villages we passed in the plain still apparently not recovered from the armies that had passed this way. I found a whitewashed room in the Pensión del Alcazar, the ruins just outside the window. Everyone ate round one big table, and I imagined Brita smiling at me with that absorbed look, her fair hair swept back. Or I saw her at the window, brown arms on the sill, looking inquisitively out, eager to explore. It was extraordinary living in this unique city, really just a village, with probably more historic buildings for its size, Arab, Jewish and Christian, than any city in Christendom. Four hundred years ago it was the centre of an empire covering much of Europe and South America. Now mules climbed the cobbled lanes, instead of cantering horsemen bringing tidings from Vienna, Ceuta, or Peru. The inhabitants took less interest in the palaces and churches, like the seventh-century Romans who knew nothing of their past except that it had been vaguely glorious. Toledo was the Rome of Spain, with the archbishop in his great palace near the cathedral. People had lived in the same way ever since El Cid took the city in 1085. Modernity had added football, electricity, and a few cars to hoot through the narrow streets. But nothing essential had changed. It seemed a community whose assumptions were different from what I knew.

I worked on my novel in the morning and in the afternoon explored the cathedral, haunted by a few ancient guides who spoke only Spanish. My posters were still in my suitcase but I hoped I would know enough about the cathedral in a few days to take tourists round. Some people at the *pensión* didn't know where England was. The maids were mystified by a £5 note, particularly the picture of George VI: '*¿Quién es?*' they asked, 'Who is he?' I got to know a young officer called Jorge who taught at the officers' infantry school across the river. He had heard of England and reported exultantly one evening that the Spanish boxer Luis Romero had just knocked out Jackie Fairclough. Jorge was fiercely, competitively nationalistic. One evening we played a game with matches. Insisting that Spanish matches were superior, he lit one and held it vertically upwards. My English match would only burn when held head-down. He then tried lighting an English match on the floor: to his great delight nothing happened.

'But English matches only light on the box, for safety!' I said.

'Spanish matches too!' Jorge lied desperately. I conceded that, being made of wax, Spanish matches were probably more flexible. Jorge took on a lofty expression, coming to terms with belonging to a superior race.

Jorge looked through my *Teach Yourself Spanish*, and roared with laughter at the statement, 'It is possible that Norwegians discovered America before Christopher Columbus.'

'This book is all wrong!' he said, 'all wrong!' He helped with my

Spanish, showing me how to pronounce the 'r'. I went around practising it, like gargling, and people looked at me strangely. It was only when I learned the word *burbuja*, meaning 'bubble', that I acquired the knack of rolling my 'r's ferociously. Jorge once confided that he never expected to be friends with an Englishman, as he had always regarded El Drake's compatriots as heretical pirates.

I found Manolo's bar near San Juan de Los Reyes church. There were blackened barrels of Rioja and Valdepenas wine against the walls, a dark, gnarled wooden counter, and Coca-Cola calendars on the wall, doubtless not there in Manolo's day. I asked the walnut-faced barman if he knew Manolo Gutierrez. He didn't seem to. Our halting conversation went something like:

'Did you own the bar before the war?'

'What?'

'This bar, have you worked in it for much time?'

'What?'

'Before the war, were you working here?'

'There isn't any war!'

I toasted Manolo anyway, with a glass of white wine for him and his almonds, and another for the end of the regime.

I took a Dane from the *pensión* round the cathedral for practice. It went well except that the Dane was disapproving: the reredos was dirty, and they should conceal the electric wire, not pass it under the cherub's bottom. I told him the story of the doll-maker who one night stole the cathedral's silver Jesus, covered it in wax, dressed it, and gave it to his daughter on the coach to Madrid. But no sooner were they out of Toledo than the doll began crying and kicking. The theft was thus discovered, and the silver Jesus returned to its rightful place.

The Dane sniffed and said it wasn't true.

'Neither is Hans Andersen,' I riposted.

'But this is religious,' he said seriously, 'They shouldn't tell fairy stories.'

I thought the guided visits would be fascinating, for the reactions of different nationalities alone.

Meals in the *pensión* were excellent for my Spanish. The maids laughed whenever I spoke, quite uninhibited about mocking foreigners. It was good-humoured and made for communication. One morning I explained being late for breakfast by saying I was *casado* (married) instead of *cansado* (tired). I offered one of the girls a cigarette – an insult, as only prostitutes smoke. There were great giggles.

A long-distance telephone operator who lived at the *pensión* asked me who the president of England was. There was a slight, lively, doctor with glasses, who gesticulated with his whole body when he talked and had written a monograph on lung diseases after his fiancée died of TB. There was a caulker from Madrid; when I asked him what side he was on in the civil war, he smiled and clenched his fist. All three lived in the *pensión* because, like me, they had no woman to look after them. I found I could talk to them and understand most of what they said, though it was more difficult when they spoke to each other.

One afternoon I went round hotels and *pensiones* to put up my posters. Some receptionists were intrigued. Others seemed unsure about a foreigner revealing the mysteries of 'their' cathedral. I put a French and English poster at the cathedral door. My first customers were a French lady and her daughter, enraptured at what they saw, though they thought it was less fine than Chartres. They were surprised to find an Englishman interested in Catholic architecture. I guided a fiercely Protestant Scots couple. The sight of the cardinals' hats hanging over their tombs shocked the man, while his wife found the cathedral dark and dingy, not at all a place to worship in. I felt defensive, possessive, as if the cathedral were somehow mine. But I earned 90 pesetas, enough for three days at the *pensión*.

Then disaster struck. I already knew Don Alfonso, head of the tourist office, always charming and helpful. A Catalan, he had an outsider's attitude to Toledo, complaining eternally about the inefficiency and lack of modernisation. Very embarrassed, he told me he had received complaints about me guiding in the cathedral. It was not allowed. You had to be licensed.

'But the other guides aren't licensed!' I protested. He shrugged his shoulders. 'They can't be!' I persisted: 'They can't speak any foreign languages!'

He seemed more upset than me, but said that was how it was. Could I get a licence? He thought not. Without means of support, I would have to move. So I was delighted when he made a suggestion. Why not teach English? He said there were plenty of people eager to learn. The only teacher in Toledo was an elderly Spanish lady married to a German ex-diplomat. Don Alfonso had already talked to a priest, Don Amado, who wanted English lessons in return for board and lodging. Don Amado lived with his mother and sister in a beautiful sixteenth-century house with a dark wooden staircase, great carved doors, and rooms with black-beamed ceilings. He took the Mozarabe mass in the cathedral, a unique service dating from the ninth century, celebrated by Christians under Moorish rule. He was a gentle, bespectacled, tall Basque of about thirty. I can see him to this day, standing in the street with his broad, black clerical hat, the humour welling up behind his spectacles as he made an ironic remark. I was given a small white room overlooking a cobbled *plaza* enclosed by the thick walls of a nunnery, with barred, silent windows and an enormous wooden door that never opened. It took several nights to get used to sleeping through the early-morning bells and the orisons buzzing from the massive building like bees in a hive.

For his daily lesson, Don Amado wanted to translate a little book of witticisms he had published. His questions about English grammar made me realise I knew nothing about it, despite my Oxford degree. Lessons were from five to seven, after which I would roam Toledo, see friends, practise my Spanish, and come back for a late dinner, followed by *tertulia*, chatting in the patio. Priests and neighbours would gather below a tree climbing up one wall of the house. Laughter would flash up the creepers into the darkness. There were anecdotes and gentle teasing, but no malice. Not over-reverent, Don Amado said the Lord Cardinal of Toledo, Primate of Spain, had no sense of humour. His chauffeur drove him between Toledo and Madrid so many times that his secretary said it could probably find its own way. 'What nonsense!' said his lordship, 'A car is not a horse!'

A major pleasure was to go to the Poste Restante to see if there was a letter from Brita. I longed for her. We wrote almost every day. She would soon be leaving Pau for Sweden, and I would probably remain in Toledo. Sometimes I reproached myself for not staying with her. But I couldn't have remained in Pau without working. It was difficult enough here in Toledo, even at Spanish prices. We both had things we wanted to do, like two aeroplanes flying parallel courses. We needed to find our own aerodrome which we could taxi down together.

One day there was a telegram: 'ACCEPTED AMERICAN FELLOWSHIP TO YALE. YOU SAIL QUEEN ELIZABETH THIRTY-FIRST AUGUST. PLEASE RETURN IMMEDIATELY. OLIVE.'

I decided to visit Brita on the way north. I hoped she hadn't left.

I told Don Amado I would return next year. 'You are good friend to the people Spanish,' he said. I was glad. The place and the history fascinated me. I loved the humour and humanity, amid the poverty and resentment at the hateful regime.

I reached Pau after a tortuous journey. At nine on a sunny morning, I went in search of Brita. The first person I saw was the blind man, who recognised me immediately by my voice. 'I'm sorry,' he said, 'but I think Mademoiselle has left. I haven't seen her for days.'

I could see France, Germany and Sweden stretching northwards, Brita somewhere in there. I went to the school and learned that the final party had been the previous evening. Mademoiselle Langenfelt had been there.

There was hope. I ran to the station. The early express had gone, another shortly after I arrived. It was a couple of hours before the next, so I made my way forlornly to the address I had sent so many letters to. And there she suddenly was, coming down the street, looking left and right as if searching. I froze outside a travel agency with Spanish posters in the window and watched her until she saw me. She stared incredulously, and then we were in each other's arms, blocking the narrow pavement.

When we recovered, she told me she had been on her way to the station when the blind man told her, '*Votre jeune homme est ici!*' She had given him a kiss, left her bags in a café, and here she was, her coat over her arm, ready for colder climes.

We took the night train to Paris. The carriage was empty and we nestled together in a corner. Having almost missed her made me realise how precious she was. I awoke occasionally, but not to bells pulled by sleepy nuns. I was warm with my beloved as France passed. I touched her face and hair in delight. We found a hotel near the Gare St Lazare. I bought her a headscarf like those the women had worn at the Grottes de Bétharram.

Next morning it was goodbye again, and again I couldn't believe it: it would be for a year or more. America was too tempting to miss. I was still a solitary hunter, culling experience. But this was like having pieces of plaster constantly ripped off a wound. It ached. An officious ticket collector stopped Brita coming onto the platform because she had no platform ticket and there wasn't time to buy one. We could only wave. The compartment was full of noisy French boys on their way to England. The whole way, all they seemed to say was, '*Dis-donc, dis-donc,*' in time with the joins in the rails.

18 · Porcupines near Yale

On the *Queen Mary* I met a man named Epstein who edited a Harvard magazine with someone called Henry Kissinger and wanted me to write an article on my first impressions of America.

New York was tough. A drunk customs official turned my luggage upside down, a taxi-driver bargained for his tip before taking me. The city seemed organic, buildings sprouting as they occurred:

shabby, haphazard areas, skyscrapers with straight streets like deep, shadowed valleys. Yellow taxis swarmed like wasps. I stayed with a lecturer at Hunter College from the *Queen Mary*, who welcomed me with gin alexanders and endless talk of America. Then I moved to relatives in the suburbs. I had already met the husband in London, a witty US army major. Now he worked for *Good Housekeeping* magazine and talked only of the money he made, like counting beads. He and his cronies worried about the Korean war ending as business was so good because of it. They thought the poor deserved their lot because they didn't work hard enough. Everyone in the neighbourhood was a Christian Scientist. When someone asked me whether I was a scientist and I said, 'No, I'm a historian,' they looked perplexed.

I continued to New Haven, home of Yale, a great gothic 1930s Oxbridge imitation with a huge tower, an enormous gymnasium and a library like a cathedral. A bell chimed tunes on the hour. The room next to mine in the graduate school belonged to a German-American called Heinz Klein. He had eyes that strove to meet, thinning blond hair and a celluloid eyeshade. He spoke threateningly through clenched teeth, stressing every syllable. When we first met, he squinted menacingly and said: 'Oh-you're-one-of-those-foreign-scholars!-Well-you'll-have-to-work-at-this-university!-Don't-think-you-can-just-have-a-good-time!' He showed me his Japanese porno-graphic paintings as if offering a glass of sherry. He seemed bewildered.

The library had plenty of material for my dissertation on French officers in America during the war of independence and how far their experiences affected them during the French revolution six years later. The authorities also wanted me to do an MA in American history. I resisted, partly because I was expecting an automatic MA from Oxford anyway. Instead, I followed courses at the Yale Drama School, probably the best of its kind in the States, and particularly interesting because all activities interlocked. In the playwriting class I adapted Gorki's short story *Tanya*. It was directed, acted, designed and lit by students. Everyone who saw it filled in a form saying what they thought of it. In the end, it was very different from what I thought I'd written. All a playwright does, I concluded, is supply actors and director with situations and dialogues which they interpret in any one of a myriad ways. A play was really an essay in cooperation, everyone creating it together – so different from the loneliness of the novel or short story. It's surprising that playwriting isn't taught at drama schools in Britain. With a novel you create your own structure, but a play needs stagecraft, and you learn it with difficulty, not just in theory but in practice.

Apart from the drama school, educational enlightenment was rare. I followed a history of drama course, where an Austrian lecturer droned out facts and figures about theatre down the ages. We were expected to read 108 plays with regular factual tests (e.g. 'Who was Hamlet's father?'). American universities seemed greatly influenced by German education, at its peak in the 1890s. Even students at our history research seminar preferred regurgitating facts and getting footnotes properly punctuated to seeking new approaches. Perhaps I was being unfair to German education, but I had always believed that, as with learning languages, the individual parts are only valuable if they can link into a whole. What was the value of facts unless they contributed to an idea?

The graduate school was like a European refugee camp, with scholars from all over the world doing their PhDs. One of Heinz's friends was Dr Bromska, assistant botany professor and also of recent German origin. He would go down to the seashore and collect stones shaped like dogs' heads or madonnas, which he polished and sold for fabulous sums. At meals he would take out a jeweller's eyeglass to ensure his salad contained no slugs or grit. He had arrived in England in 1938, causing confusion at his Dover boarding-house because his phrasebook led him to complain that his room had no millpond when he meant 'mirror'. 'But in Germany we have a millpond in every room!' he told the astonished landlady.

Outside the graduate school was the crewcropped, all-American kid, with his football and fraternities, his dating systems and eager uniformity. Both boys and girls seemed brash, healthy, uncompli-cated and shallow – in contrast to Oxford where, misguidedly perhaps, everyone was trying to show how nonconformist and original they were. At Wellington once, during the war, I went to a fancy dress ball as Hitler. But when I suggested the same thing at Yale, there was an outcry about bad taste and the protests there would be. In England, of course, we had known nothing of Belsen and Auschwitz until after the war. It was fascinating, though, to go to one of these kid's homes and find their parents more interesting than them, with memories of pre-1914 Romania under King Carol, or the pig war in Yugoslavia. The friend would be annoyed that I paid him or her so little attention. It was ironic to come all the way to the States for contact with eastern Europe, or at least its past.

Otherwise, Europe seemed remote. After only a few months I felt it might be sliding into the sea, with Britain in a terrible state, although it had seemed all right when I left. Some Americans used me as a kind of talking doll. 'Say something!' they would ask, 'I just love that Limey accent!' They were surprised when I told them I was going back, as if the Black Death still prowled Europe. Some Americans seemed to think they were on Noah's Ark, with everyone else in the world clutching at logs, eager to scramble aboard. But they were benevolent. One weekend I went to Boston and stayed with friends. We drove out to Concord, where the first battle for independence was fought. The trees were red and gold, and there was the same autumnal light you get in parts of England. We met a lady who was 'sweet' about my nationality and assured me the British had shown great regard for private property when fighting nearby.

Some weekends I would go to New York which I loved, and found linguistically so European: Spanish, Italian, Greek, Polish, Yiddish. The subway was so fast you felt the whole train might twist and buckle. There was every racial tint, hair texture and bone structure that Eve gave birth to. New York seemed a microcosmic world – endless ructions, but everyone living together in a kind of tough, open harmony. A friend and I went to Harlem, to see the faith healer Father Divine, a small coloured man who said he was Jesus Christ. He had a large country estate, and could only come into New York on Sundays as he was wanted by the police, who for some reason couldn't arrest him at home, or anywhere at all on the Lord's Day.

Meals were served all day at a great horse-shoe table. You didn't pay, but a receptacle went round for donations which, as everyone watched, was soon filled with jewellery and ten-dollar bills. The air was as stuffy as a sauna. Microphones relayed an endlessly repeated chant: 'Father Divine is Wonderful! Father Divine is Wonderful!'. At the end of a platform sat young women in green, the Holy Virgins, or Lily Buds, with HV embroidered over their breasts. Below sat another group in red with V on their bosoms – the Virgins, or Rosebuds. As the tempo beat faster, both varieties of virgin clapped their hands ever more furiously, while individuals got up and, their eyes closed, lurched and bumped into the furniture and each other. A large, ecstatic coloured woman slumped suddenly onto the table, shoving her elbow into the potatoes, while a little lady in blue twirled round so fast that the black hat pinned to her long hair swung round and round like a flowery discus.

Everyone gradually calmed down again. The Virgins and the Holy Virgins all went to sleep, or perhaps into a trance. The large lady took her elbow out of the potatoes, the little lady adjusted her hat, and all seemed ecstatically exhausted.

I had applied for an interview with Father Divine, and a list was now read over the microphone. Believers had special names, so the list went: 'Miss Divine Grace, Mr Perfect Loveliness, Miss Beautiful Purity, Mr John Haycraft, Mr Holy Ecstasy . . .' I had never been in such celestial company! As we waited outside Father Divine's office, the others talked of his saving them through miracles. One had seen a car coming straight at him, mentioned the holy name, and it swerved aside. Another thought of Father Divine as he fell off a ladder, and landed unharmed.

I was ushered into a big office where the Father sat behind a desk, like a hairless headmaster. On the wall was a photograph of a blonde lady, his chaste consort 'Mother Divine'. We were only supposed to stay for five seconds but I was rash enough to ask him how he knew he was Christ. His voices told him, he replied. But

how did he know his voices were telling the truth? – the devil too
had voices. His face grew darker. The normal greeting and farewell
with Father Divine was 'Peace'. Exasperated, he suddenly stood up
and shouted 'Peace!' at me. 'Peace!' I yelled back. And so we parted.

Outside, everything seemed distorted. On the subway a small
woman sat curled on her seat, eyes squeezed shut, like an embryonic
vole. A beautiful madonna-like girl had her eyes uplifted as though
in ecstatic prayer, until I realised she was reading the adverts.

It was almost Christmas and I decided to hitch-hike to New Orleans
with Dave, a British friend on a psychology research fellowship.

We were soon in Virginia. The sun shone on brown earth and
tobacco leaves like mammoths' ears. People spoke a melodic English
with extended vowels to which you had to adapt. I loved this feeling
of distance. The only time I had felt it before was in India. It must
be part of the American sense of freedom: taking off and travelling
thousands of miles without leaving your own country. EM Forster
said that criticising America was like criticising life: you could find
everything in both. Getting lifts was easy. We made a piece of
cardboard saying BRITISH STUDENTS on one side, YALE STUDENTS on
the other, gauged drivers' expressions and switched accordingly. We
had a lift from a lawyer driving 1,500 miles for a two-day Christmas
holiday, and a dentist who said he was sure our mouths were full of
British socialist stoppings which he would change for a few hundred
bucks. They all spoke freely, indeed wouldn't have picked us up if
they hadn't wanted to talk. As we were unlikely to meet again, they
could get it off their chest. We learned more about America in a
week's hitch-hiking than in months at Yale.

In New Orleans, people kept showing us the Spanish iron balconies
as if they were unique. But the waitresses did speak Cajun, an
eighteenth-century French patois. At night, they lit immense candles
in the avenues and squares, and Father Christmas sledges were

illuminated on the rooftops. Bourbon Street was lined with jazz clubs and strip joints; the girls whirled tassles on their nipples like propellers, as if trying to take off.

We got a job in a garage for three days as we were short of money. I was sorting out screws and bolts and putting them in the right pigeon-holes when I suddenly remembered that Guy Wilson was at that very moment getting married. As I moved greasy bits of metal, it was strange to imagine Guy in tails, a red carnation in his lapel, drinking champagne in the big drawing-room overlooking Torquay bay. At the garage, there was none of the status awkwardness about manual work that underlay vacation jobs in England, and we were well paid by British standards. It was simple: you needed money so you worked; if you didn't work you got kicked out. No one cared who you were, whether you were British, or at university, or even the Prince of Wales.

In New Orleans we had a two-sided existence. We stayed at a seamen's hostel because it only cost $1.50 a night. But our being British involved another element, with people forever telling us how wonderful we were during the war. In other ways, however, we were a disappointment. One lady who heard that we were at Yale and had been at Oxford (me) and Cambridge (Dave) said she must introduce us to her daughter. But when she heard we had hitch-hiked down rather than bringing the Rolls or the Jag she turned away abruptly, as if we had admitted to secret drinking. Another asked us if débutante parties were like this in Britain, and was mystified when we didn't know. Someone else was disappointed we had never met Princess Elizabeth. The débutantes themselves were white-faced and wilting, like flowers left too long in a shop window.

In contrast, there were a lot of poor people on the streets. On Christmas morning, a strangely surrealist thing happened. Across the street, beside a lamp-post, was a pale round object like a large ostrich egg. It was the bald head of an old man lying across the pavement with pedestrians stepping over him. We picked him up. He stank of liquor. We didn't know what to do with him until a passer-by said, 'He lives at number 27.' Slowly we pulled and pushed him along the pavement. The door of number 27 was open.

A man was painting a wall with slow rhythmic strokes, his brush swishing in the silence. As we hesitated, he pointed his brush upstairs, said 'Room three', and went on painting. We got the old man upstairs step by step. It was dark. Dave lit a match. We found room 3 and opened the door. Inside, the walls were neatly papered in pastel colours. There was a bed with a patchwork cover, a washstand with a white jug, and nothing else. We laid the old man on the bed. Just as we were leaving, he stirred and said, 'Thank you, boys,' in a deep, cultured voice. 'I'm sorry I've nothing to offer you and there's nowhere to sit.' Something in his voice reminded me of England.

Downstairs, the man was still painting in the silence. He told us the old man was an English immigrant who worked as a knife grinder. On Christmas Eve he spent everything he had saved on drink. The rest of the year he was stone sober.

We stayed too long in New Orleans and took a Greyhound bus with large, comfortable seats. Once I awoke and thought I was on the train to Paris with Brita. I imagined her green eyes smiling at me. After our unexpected meeting in Pau it wouldn't have been all that surprising if she had suddenly appeared.

Back at Yale, history professor Bemis, a pudgy, innocent man who once spent Christmas in his cellar convinced an atomic attack was coming, commiserated with me over the death of George VI. 'I know how patriotic you English are and how attached to the royal family.' It was touching. I didn't know what to say, but remembered my sentimental feelings about George V's death when I was a boy in France. I didn't feel the American kind of patriotism, with little banners saying things like 'For God, for Country and for Yale!' in their rooms. But I did feel a kind of rooted patriotism, and resented Americans' considering Britain a pitiable shadow of its former self. They had worked hard to make us give up our 'shameful' rule over India and Palestine; and now they condescended because we were no longer so powerful. I also resented America's coming out best from the war and carving up the world at our expense.

In the spring I went down to Washingon to visit the archives. The National Gallery El Grecos gave me pangs for Toledo. I had a pleasant though solitary time. Despite a long list of people I'd been given to look up, I spent evenings lying on my bed in the YMCA reading Isherwood's *Lions and Shadows*. I had had enough of hospitality and kindness.

At Yale there was a third letter from Henry Kissinger enquiring about my article. He always wrote to me as Mr Haycoft, which reminded me of a sheep coughing. I replied that I was too busy to do anything for him, underlined my name at the end, and wrote his as Doctor Kissasser.

A summer job had been arranged for me by a previous British scholar and friend of mine, Tony Thorlby. I was to be butler, log-cutter, chauffeur and porcupine chaser at Mrs Baker's in New Hampshire; her late husband founded Yale's drama school. The poet e e cummings lived on a neighbouring hill with his wife Marion. In my last few days at Yale I handed in my typed research thesis, had a one-act play performed with good results, and took the last of my driving lessons before an easy test. Then I set off by train to Boston to find my way up into the wilds of beautiful New Hampshire.

We lived at Boulder Farm, a large wooden house set on a rock on the fringe of a thick forest, looking down on sloping countryside. There were animals everywhere: woodchucks like painted squirrels, occasional rattlesnakes, a beaver in the lake, and porcupines which got under the house and chewed the foundations. Punctually at nine every evening, a racoon came and raided the garbage can. One night we cornered him with torches and looked at him, growling and switching his long striped tail until we let him go. An ornithologist staying with us was shocked because I had never heard of a whip-poor-will.

Mrs Baker was a New England grande dame, still hardy and independent in her seventies and blind in one eye. She remembered the Spanish fleet appearing off Boston during the war of 1898. 'There was panic,' she said, her scorn implying she had not been part of it. She prepared all the food, and ran the house alone. She abhorred weakness and self-pity. It was all right to sleep late, but to wake up and lie in bed was not excusable. She was frank about everything, and told me the secret of a long life was to keep alive sexually, through masturbation if necessary. Every summer she had different young men at Boulder Farm and, although never intrusive, she obviously enjoyed having us.

In the morning, I worked in a little hut in the woods on my three-act play for submission to the drama school by the end of the summer. One Sunday I heard a chewing noise under the floor. I was mystified until I flushed out a large porcupine and chased him up an eighty-foot tree. At the top, he climbed out along the last branch and sat there raising his quills. We perched there together while he looked at me with his black button eyes, snapping his short tail from side to side and chattering. Porcupines being rightly regarded as pests, I should really have bounced him off. They endanger houses and trees, and you could get a bounty of $10 for each corpse. But I decided one porcupine more or less would make no difference, so we followed each other down again and he scuttled off.

There were four lakes nearby, and every morning we bathed in one of them before breakfast. They were warm, silky, and clear. One was six miles long; in winter they drove cars over the ice at sixty miles an hour and then slammed on the brakes. In summer there were loons, birds with long black necks and a strange, mad cry which would suddenly disappear underwater for minutes on end.

e e cummings and Marion lived on a nearby hill in a wooden house called Joy Farm, lit at night by hurricane lamps. I would go there to drink whisky or have steak dinners. cummings was slight, bald and nimble, with a youthful voice though in his sixties, and mischievous eyes. He never argued. In many ways he was right-wing, and if he disagreed he would release a kingfisher-like phrase to distract you. Pro-Russian intellectuals attacked him for visiting

Russia in the thirties and for his book *Eimi*, which expressed his sense of suffocation there. He wrote the word 'I' as 'i' because he objected to capitalising the ego.

At Mrs Baker's, we had house guests. Dr Hemmer was one, a writer of ponderous books, a large, slow man, with thick-lensed glasses that made his eyes look like an insect's seen through a microscope. One afternoon he lectured Mrs Baker's grandson for over an hour on mediæval European dentistry and the social symbolism of teeth. The poor boy sat helpless in Hemmer's web and just said, 'Yes, yes . . .' the whole time.

There was a woman journalist, dark, with little hairs on her chin, who had been round the world alone. She and Dr Hemmer talked in simultaneous monologues, Mrs Baker peering absently at them through her one eye.

One afternoon the drizzle grew into a violent storm. We watched it come up the slope, a green sea with lightning striking into it. The journalist said she had experienced something similar in Borneo. Dr Hemmer vanished in terror. When the storm reached the house, lightning struck the telephone. A ball of fire bounced out of it, and I watched in amazement as it hovered in the kitchen and then sizzled into a glass of milk Dr Hemmer had poured himself before he fled.

He reappeared and drank the milk, then started hiccoughing. I didn't want to alarm him by telling him what had happened. He hiccoughed helplessly through dinner and apparently all night. The next morning, though, he shaved with his electric razor and the hiccoughs stopped – which unfortunately meant he could start talking again. Despite his sleepless night, he told us about his war. He saw little fighting because when he landed on the beach of an island captured from the Japanese, he removed his helmet to scratch his head and got hit by a falling coconut. It knocked him out for five hours, during which he caught sunstroke and had to spend six months in hospital.

I escaped to visit Marion and estlin Cummings afflicted with bats in their attics. Armed with tennis rackets, we opened up a wall and smote them as they came out. Unfortunately estlin hit himself on the head, and Marion and I had to carry him downstairs and restore

My paternal grandparents, John Berry Haycraft and Lily Stacpoole with my father William (top) and his brother John (p.14)

My maternal grandparents Lucas King aged 50 and Philomene von Fischer aged 18, married in 1887 (p.18)

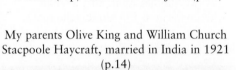

My parents Olive King and William Church Stacpoole Haycraft, married in India in 1921 (p.14)

My mother with me in 1927 (p.15)

My brother Colin and me in Alassio (p.26)

My mother, right, after a tennis
tournament in 1934 in Rapallo (p.23)

Play up and play the game. With my mother
in 1936 (p.35)

In the Queen's Royal Regiment in 1945 (p.58)

Marriage to Brita in Stockholm, 1953 (p.161)   Brita's father Gösta Langenfelt (p.162)

Christmas in Hampstead 1957. (From left to right: Olive, Anna, Colin with William at 7 months, Suzanne with Katinka at 6 weeks, me and Brita) (p.238)

Exuberant in Cordoba, 1953–9 (p.168)

Shapely casks of
Montilla for our
bar (p.174)

Beginnings of
International
House (p.176)

(Above) Stockholm archipelago in 1968:
me, Katinka, Jimmy, Richard and Brita

(Left) Katinka at 1 in her Sevillana dress (p.175)

(Left) Katinka with her son Merlin in 1985
(Below) Richard and Jimmy in 1990 (p.284)

Open classroom seating. Teaching with real objects in Shaftesbury Avenue
in the early 70s (p.193)

The English Teaching Theatre in 1974.
Centre: Doug Case and Ken Wilson compèring (p.211)

Using the National Gallery as a classroom (p.265)

Paco Peña with Harold Macmillan inaugurating our Piccadilly premises in 1977.
Behind: Colin McMillan and Anthony Sampson (p.291)

Ausonio Zappa introduces Ann Mills and me to Pope Paul VI (p.246)

Researching for my book on Italy, *Italian Labyrinth*, in 1983 (p.246)

With our chairman Norman Reddaway at the Budapest Directors' Conference in 1987 (p.294)

him with whisky. estlin gave me $100, he said for my birthday, although it wasn't until December. In Spain, $100 would last me nearly two months!

Mrs Baker's grandchildren were lovely. Twelve-year-old Betsy and I built a hut in the garden with branches and straw. The sun shone almost every day and we would all drive through the woods to bathe in one of the lakes and lie in the sun. There seemed to be no one anywhere, just the painted squirrels, and the loons sticking their heads out of the water when you least expected them with their mad cry. I felt crazily healthy and contented. I could see the grandchildren looking back on this time, as I did with Italy.

estlin told me he had once been advised to see a psychiatrist but declined, because he felt that if the sessions were successful he would no longer want to paint or write. He said he would rather be a neurotic poet than vegetate. He was sprite-like, sensitive, free and absorbed, with Marion to protect him. It was partly his humility that made his poetry so good. He had been invited to lecture at Harvard about himself and the poetry that influenced him, but was reluctant, feeling people wouldn't understand him. I said it was unfair to deprive them; after the initial shock he would enjoy it. He saw himself as a young poet who would be ridiculed, failing to realise he was now a mandarin.

He joked that he didn't like England because it had never appreciated him. When his collected poetry had appeared in Britain in the thirties, it had sold only one copy!

I finished my play but didn't think much of it. It was about the first world citizen, frustrated by vested interests as the bomb growled distantly. It was all too forced, my same old problem: linking ideas to fiction, creating what Olive called 'a pot of message'. The dominant feeling was indignation at living under the shadow, and the fear that a hysterical politician might suddenly press the button. But I hadn't expressed it properly. Too many porcupines! I had episodic ideas on other themes: a poet's widow who detested him but now idealises him; two chess players competing for an inheritance day and night, while porcupines chew at the foundations until the house finally collapses; three lonely sisters living by a dangerous corner where cars constantly crash, with dashing young men carried away to special recovery rooms designed to reflect marital bliss – all this set, of course, in a wooded part of America with a picturesque non-hero to link everything.

As August ended, I decided to return to Spain. After months of indecision, it was pleasant to reach a conclusion. I liked America but sensed the trap of living in an exuberant cloud where everything was too easy. At almost twenty-six I didn't want to be a student any more, although estlin and a Yale professor had kindly guaranteed an extra year. I wanted to find a lair and start my novel, supporting myself again, I hoped, by teaching English in Toledo. America seemed frothy. I preferred the poverty, the beauty, the dilemmas, and the spiritual heritage of Toledo. In America I felt the absence of distant history.

It was a good time to be going, with autumn gilding the leaves. I said goodbye to Mrs Baker, to estlin and Marion, and made my way down to New Haven and New York.

On the *Queen Elizabeth* I shared a cabin with some Americans going on a tour round Europe. An attractive girl called Gracie working for the tour company suggested I take a group of Americans round Europe the following summer, to see if I liked it.

At Southampton, the cars on the dock were like small toys after their American counterparts. I phoned my brother Colin, and was appalled at how affected his voice sounded, and could only presume mine did too. I wrote to my beautiful Brita telling her I wouldn't be going to Stockholm for the time being as I was off to Toledo. It was only a postponement, I wrote. I hoped she wasn't disappointed.

PART 4

Taking the Plunge

19 · Attraction in Toledo

I could see the signs from the bus: Toledo 70, Toledo 50, Toledo 15. The familiar outline brought a jolt in my stomach. I was on my own now, with just enough money to get back to England if need be.

It was overcast, the bus trailing clouds of white dust. Suddenly we were driving past the gate with the double-headed eagle, up by the Moorish arch of the Puerta del Sol, and into the Plaza Zocodover where we stopped. I felt I was coming home to this mediæval city. I looked about me, like a bird scanning for a twig to perch on. My old *pensión* had been engulfed in the rebuilding of the Alcazar. I found a couple of rooms in a central street called Alferitos, 'little pins', with a shrine to the Virgin where girls wanting a husband said a prayer and put a pin into a jar. The rooms were ideal – a bedroom and a larger room with a long table for classes. The landlady, Doña Maria, charged what today would be 50 pence a week. There was a washstand though no hot water, but I could always have a bath in a hotel. I had breakfast in a café, lunch and dinner in a *pensión* for today's equivalent of £2 a week, providing contact with tourists. All I needed now was students.

Don Amado and Don Alfonso welcomed me warmly, surprised to see me back from America. Don Alfonso promised to recommend me to his guides and tourist staff, and Don Amado to anyone he could. They advised me to charge 100 pesetas a month for a daily one-hour lesson for a class of six, all my room would take, and advertise with a notice in the local bookshop. Gradually my classes filled up. I got down to my novel in the mornings, the maids singing as they washed shirts in the patio. In the afternoons I worked on my Spanish and roamed Toledo. From six to nine I gave my lessons, and then the usual late Spanish dinner.

It was bliss. I had never felt so independent and self-sufficient. A door had opened onto a fascinating, creative life where I was free to do what I wished. If I felt lonely, there was conversation with sociable people in cafés and tavernas. I got to know more people, including the lady married to the German diplomat. Having abandoned the German embasssy in Madrid in 1944, he was captured by Spanish fascists and sent to Dachau with his wife just before the war ended. Now she gave English lessons.

Toledo was full of people bruised by the past. Don Amado introduced me to a Scotsman called McPherson, slight, solemn, bald with glasses, and unable to pronounce his 'r's. He invited me to lunch and I met his Irish wife. They were fiercely Catholic and lived in Toledo because they disliked modern civilisation. Their two small children went to a Spanish school. He translated at home, and had a book coming out in English on bullfighting. In the middle of the *tortilla* Mrs McPherson suddenly said:

'Whenever I hear an English voice, it makes my flesh creep.'

I didn't know what to say. McPherson looked embarrassed, and we continued talking as if nothing had been said.

I met a disagreeable German who had been in the SS. He looked just like Hitler, who had commented on this when inspecting his unit. 'It is natural, *mein Führer,*' he had replied, 'You are the father of the Reich and I am its son!' By day he seemed meek and tolerant but by dinner he would be drunk and give Nazi salutes and goosestep about.

At my embryonic school, my favourite class was the intermediate level, with two army officers, a bank clerk called Paco, Isobel, whose husband owned a tourist shop, a prettily dark girl called Elvira, and Juanito, who brought melons in every day on a mule and was saving to buy a tourist shop. Other classes had more people from business and shops. One student, a guide, was learning flowery phrases by heart from a Spanish guide book: 'In Toledo, is the whisper Moor you can be hearing with the sound of falling fountains!' We sat around the long table and used the only textbook available. I had a blackboard and devised practical ways of teaching, rather than use the book too much or do exercises of the kind I remembered sending me to sleep at school. Every morning, I woke knowing I would be doing precisely what I wanted. Ideas flew, and I typed page after page of the novel.

My landlady, Doña Maria, was worried because I didn't go to mass. She told me where the nicest church was, and on Sunday mornings would ask me archly if I wasn't going for a walk. After the material dynamism of America, the pessimism of Britain, the resentful bitterness of most of Europe, recently occupied and defeated, it was extraordinary to live under a regime where the pursuit of holiness was an official aim. There was of course always the clenched fist and *Viva la República*. But underneath were over twelve hundred years of intense worship dating from when Spain was a few Christian kingdoms launching crusades against the 'Moors'. It was only when this creed began to clash with new commercial and industrial values that Spain began to decay. That was why it was so fascinating to someone like me, brought up on tenets which gave Britain prominence and power it was now losing because its world, too, was changing.

At the *pensión* where I had my meals, the landlord's penetrating eyes made him look like a gaunt monk, lost in spiritual speculation. One day I asked what preoccupied him. The increasing cost of everything, he answered. He was planning yet more rooms for tourists. He was also an expert on brothels, or where to find a willing widow. His hard-working wife was very pretty; but when you're married, he said, you get tired of 'the wind always blowing in the same direction'.

Toledo had its behavioural rites. The most obvious was the *paseo* at the end of the day, when everyone walked up and down the Plaza Zocodover, boys sticking together, girls preening and giggling. Families strolled too, mother and father in the middle, giving perpetual greetings, 'Adiós, adiós,' or pausing to gossip. The community was thus welded together, the local news disseminated. The sexes were like opposing armies: the boys discussed the girls, the girls appraised the boys. The boys sent scouts to find a weak point in the enemy lines, to be attacked by each in turn. The girls abandoned any outpost penetrated, and reformed. They laid traps and when these were sprung, there were two more *novios* strolling the plaza, beamed on by their elders. Antonio, one of my pupils, had a pretty sister of twenty-three whose fiancé had left her; now no one would take her out. She sat at home and moaned, 'I sit here and grow old!'

McPherson invited me home for chess. He had been a Mosleyite and a great friend of William Joyce, 'Lord Haw-Haw'. He thought fascism was the last chance for the 'old civilisation', predicting Russian invasion or atomic disaster. He was really mourning his upper-class tribe and its privileges. He wore a monocle on Sundays, had been interned on the Isle of Man in 1940 as a fascist, fled to Spain in 1945, and used prewar upper-class expressions like, 'He's not quite a gentleman, don't you know?' and, 'He's not quite, quite!' I liked him, but could see him in Gauleiter's black, dispensing brutally dogmatic judgements – though he wouldn't have lasted long: 'Nazis aren't quite gentlemen, don't you know?' Me being a 'Brit' as she put it, his wife remained hostile. She once asked me what I disliked most. 'Fanatics,' I said. She demurred: 'I like things to be definite.'

In my English classes, Isobel was very intense about learning the language. There was no obvious commercial reason, as her husband was rich. She was spurred on by her *amor proprio*: a poor lesson gave her a sleepless night. Juanito learned fast because he wanted to sell enough melons to buy his own *damasquino* jewellery shop. At his melon stand, I taught him to sell with sentences like, 'Excuse me, would you like to buy a melon? They're very sweet and juicy. Would you like to try a piece?' This technique seemed to me highly relevant. I trained Isobel to sell *damasquino* at her shop counter, with me the customer and her greeting me politely. I asked her about all the objects she stocked: ear-rings, a sword, a necklace, a brooch. To start with she just said 'Very beautiful' about everything, but I helped her be more subtle. I also took Enrique, the guide, round the cathedral and had him describe it in English.

Elvira learned fast because we were mutually attracted. She had bright, dark eyes and a full but not excessive figure, called in Spanish *bien puesta*, 'well-formed'! I found classes dull if she wasn't there, almost blaming the others for coming without her. They noticed how we looked at each other, and Juanito told me they were betting we would be *novios* soon. I only had to take her to the cinema once, for Toledo to consider us engaged. But when I left no one would want her. So, reluctantly, I behaved impeccably.

I once asked everyone for sentences using 'each other'.

'We like each other,' said Juanito.

Paco, learning English mainly to approach foreign girls, said loudly, 'They kiss each other.'

'They love each other,' said Elvira, holding my eye.

'They fuck each other,' mouthed Paco silently at me, telling me later he had learned the word from an Australian girl he had bedded.

'They sell each other,' interrupted Isobel seriously.

'Good, but not quite right,' I said gently, remembering Isobel's sleepless nights. 'They sell *to* each other.'

I hadn't heard from Brita for three weeks. Had she found someone else? The thought appalled me. She had written that I was like a phantom, constantly by her side but never there. And she didn't want a ghost for company. At least I was enjoying myself. My novel absorbed me. I even wrote in the small hours after supper at the *pensión*. But supposing I had lost Brita? The thought appalled me. I would go to Sweden when the book was finished.

Toledo's electricity supply was unreliable, and I often wrote by candle-light. I thought of Cervantes, who also wrote in Toledo, filling the pages of *Don Quixote* with a quill-pen in the wavering candle-light, a ground olivestone-burning *brasero* warming his shins beneath the tablecloth. The *brasero* gave the girls dark streaks on their legs in winter. But it kept the family together as everyone had to sit round a single table for warmth. With personal independence, there was always the itch of sex. Self-sufficiency necessitated the final ruthlessness of seducing women. Two English sisters lived at a *pensión* down by the station. One had separated from her Brazilian husband and brought her baby to a place they could live cheaply. Both sisters were attractive and fiery-eyed. But it would be difficult to avoid entanglement in their complicated cat's-cradle. I wasn't really ruthless, and wanted to be free of encumbrances when writing.

I imagined a world where women just took a pill to be 'safe', able to take their pleasure like men. In Spain this would probably destroy the regime rather quickly. But it might mean less love and more lust. As Aldous Huxley wrote, love is like an aeroplane: it needs resistance on its wings to take off.

I decided to go to a brothel. The crowded waiting-room had benches like a railway station, and a chirpy Madame who hoped my pocket dictionary wasn't a breviary. But the idea of queuing to follow in other men's footsteps dampened even my lust. Perhaps I should have asked the *pensión* landlord for one of his willing widows.

It was getting cold in Toledo. Swathes of mist rose darkly off the river. The narrow streets disappeared and the silent buildings were like palaces at the bottom of the sea.

Juanito now had a good English patter for selling melons. Despite the cold, he had sold dozens to tourists. He suggested I take Elvira round the town, with Isobel, and do the same thing for tourist shopping. So we went wandering down the main street, Elvira and I only too aware of the overcharged nature of gestures, looks and incorrect English, the only outlets in the classroom for pent-up passion.

At an art dealer's, Elvira proudly began, 'Those are . . . ,' and then we recalled simultaneously that 'picha', which is how a Spaniard pronounces 'picture', is the Spanish word for 'prick'.

'Not interesting,' said Isobel quickly, moving us rapidly to an ironmonger's where we were safer with 'hammer' and 'saucepan'. She must have realised that all Elvira and I wanted was to go off and do the impossible. Having coffee together was too compromising, so we wandered back to the plaza having an execrable English conversation, me intent on corrections in a desperate bid for neutral ground.

Gracie Williams from the American tour operating office had been working on my behalf, and I was asked to go to Nice to meet a Mr Robeson. I took the yellow bus to Madrid and then flew to Nice. What a contrast, between the Swissair passengers and those on the bus, with their black tobacco, rough clothes and bristling chins. It was my first flight ever. I was glad it wasn't Aviaco, the domestic airline. As Spanish friends said, 'If you want to see this world, fly Iberia. If you want to see the next, fly Aviaco!' On a bridge near Madrid much favoured by suicides, was scrawled: 'Don't do it here! Fly Aviaco!'

At the luxurious, almost empty Hôtel Negresco on the Promenade des Anglais, the old ladies had face-lifts, not black skirts, and glass handbags and little dogs on decorated leads. I spotted the bulbous spires of the Russian church, where the priest had cried 'Bogi! Bogi! Bogi!'

Robeson was intrigued that I was English with an Oxford and Yale background, but writing a novel in Toledo. We went to parties in sumptuous villas, presumably to test my sociableness. One was owned by an Englishman in his sixties married to a girl of 27, the daughter of a bankrupt peer. There was an immensely fat English girl, married to a French count, who smoked cigars and talked only about her age. A Swiss banker's wife was unbearably obsequious to Robeson, praising American ice-boxes and television and cars as if they were the only symptoms of civilisation. At the casino, Robeson pointed out the 'richest and tightest man in the world' and a Polish countess, who had been Goering's mistress and got her head shaved in 1945. Robeson flashed 10,000-franc notes, and flunkeys touched their toes with their noses as he passed. I had little regard for the wealthy. Most of what they did seemed ostentatious. Perhaps it was because I have never really cared about money. Just then, I was doing what I wanted on £19 a month.

I got the job, to start in June. Seven countries in six weeks, all found, $6 a day and a hefty commission on watches bought in Switzerland. Returning to Toledo was a relief. Although I had only lived there for three months, the city was part of me. I found a wonderful letter from Brita, inviting me to stay with her family when I had finished my book.

Marzipan was first made by monks in Toledo. Christmas almost on us, the shops were full of ornate marzipan snakes in cardboard boxes and succulent little cushions filled with honey. Christmas was also lottery time. The radio broadcast a sing-song voice interminably chanting winning numbers, listened to by millions of Spaniards all trusting the Virgin of the Lottery to smile on them. Christmas Eve, *Noche Buena*, is strictly a family feast and I felt solitary. At ten o'clock, Toledo was deserted, everyone eating and drinking at home and even the bars closed. Christmas can be a great test of a foreigner's self-sufficiency, though my students had given me a marzipan snake and a bottle of *Cuarenta y tres*, a sweet liqueur.

One evening in the New Year no one came to class at seven. As a teacher I had theatrical anxiety; if people dropped out I worried there was something wrong. Had I offended them? The door opened and Elvira came in. She smiled, then looked surprised.

'Where is everyone?'

'I don't know,' I answered shamefacedly. We looked at each other in that hungry way we had, and I moved to help her take off her coat.

'No,' she said suddenly, 'there's obviously no class today.' She turned to the door. With it half open, she smiled and said, '*Adiós, guapo*. I'd love to stay but you'd teach me things the rest of the class would miss. So till tomorrow.'

Juanito told me everybody had decided to stay away, without telling Elvira, determined to marry us off, but I said it was unfair on Elvira. The *machote* convention presumes a girl and boy alone together will automatically make love. Juanito said they wouldn't tell anyone; and anyway Elvira had rushed immediately to see Isobel to show we hadn't spent much time together. Another student, Luis, was worried about me. 'Look,' he said, 'you've been to all these universities, you're twenty-five, and you haven't started your career. You can't earn enough money teaching English.' I told him I wanted to be a writer, but this seemed inconceivable. 'You might as well say you want to be a thinker!' he mocked. I was struck by how these social pressures impinged even on me, a foreigner. It was touching that they cared. The theory seemed to be that if you delayed too long you would never save enough to marry, and sink from your scratching middle-class status into the misty world of the labourer earning half-a-crown an hour.

After class one evening, Juanito brought out his conjuring set and gave us a show, producing coloured handkerchiefs from a silk hat and coins from Isobel's ear. Each class was a small, pleasant community with a common purpose. Everyone was speaking English more confidently and beginning to experiment, instead of regarding it as a series of dead formulæ, prison bars forged by grammar rules.

Paco was obsessed by his virility, and said he was trying to transfer to the foreign currency section in his bank. He regarded foreign girls as much easier, and anyway would never dream of seducing a Spanish woman. Like most Spanish men, he distinguished those who do and those who don't. There were virtuous women you would never touch, and *putas* whom, if foreign, you didn't need to pay. He claimed to get through fifty black-market French letters a month, admittedly on whores. At a dance at the casino he sat among the men, throwing confetti balls around. He was an amiable Punch, with black-rimmed glasses and a perpetual smile, a moustache bristling in the gulf between prominent nose and chin, overshadowed by the need to show machine-gun potency.

Spring was coming. The streets were damp, the trees in the Plaza Zocodover still bare, the countryside desolate and rocky as ever. But there was a golden light on the river, the arches of the Alcantara Bridge and the ancient chains of San Juan de los Reyes. There was warmth in the air, a feeling of excitement, of people waking and preparing for the hot summer of fiestas and bull-fights and evenings spent in patios, which that year I would not share.

My novel finished, I was now revising and rewriting it. The worst thing was the doubt. Was it any good? Gone were the soaring ideas, the intoxication, the release. I cut whole passages, only to restore them next day. Somebody might actually read what I had written.

Alone in the Plaza, I met Elvira and we talked, separated by the low wall around the main square. With people passing, she was self-conscious. Anywhere but in Spain our meeting would have led to a walk, or coffee, or the cinema. But *hablar*, speaking, also often implied making love, as if you couldn't have one without the other. 'She spoke with a boy in her *pueblo*, and now she's pregnant.'

Elvira said she was sorry I was going and English lessons would be over. I asked her if she liked Toledo. She said it was very boring. What about a job? Her parents wouldn't like it. Although she didn't say so, it would seem as if they were too poor to support their daughter. English lessons were the only distraction in winter. In summer it was different, with outings and the Feria. Had I been Spanish, I would have expressed myself with flirtation, compliments, challenges and humour. Elvira would have responded like a flower in the sun, and we would have created a floral bridge between us.

Assuming Sweden would be cold, I bought some extraordinary longjohns and very thick vests from an underwear shop which embarrassed Isobel and Elvira on our 'English shopping' walk. For our final lesson, everyone brought red wine and sausages and bread and Manchego cheese. Isobel unwrapped a cake crowned with a white frothy mixture of whipped eggs and sugar, in place of cream. Paco brought an old gramophone with dance records. Elvira looked ravishing in white. The spring sunlight just reached the window sill of that, my first classroom. We pushed the long table to one side and danced and talked and drank. Dancing with Elvira was intolerable: so much lust. We edged into a corner and brushed lips quickly.

Doña Maria sat near the window like a chaperone, her cat on her knees, frail and smiling, the eternal Spanish grandmother, part of the family which English classes had brought together. It was difficult saying goodbye. '*Adiós! Adiós! Adiós!*' Clasping, *abrazos*, the embrace between men, shoulders touching while you thump each other on the back. With women there was only the hand clasp, shorter or longer, brushing, pressing, or of course the more formal carrying of hand to lips.

I left next day. I couldn't afford to eat in the dining car, and stuffed a bag with boiled eggs, cooked sausages, bars of thick, crumbling chocolate and bread. I took the familiar bus to the Atocha Station, and travelled for days. In France I shared a carriage with a hungry girl who had tried being an 'artist' in Portugal and was returning to England, having found life too 'difficult'. She consoled herself by shamelessly devouring half my food. In Germany, I met two Danish trick cyclists who had demonstrated all over southern France and Italy, and had made enough to keep them alive for two months. In Copenhagen, I stayed with the Dane who had been 'hygienic' in Toledo cathedral. He was a baron and had a portrait of his ancestor, the first king of Jerusalem, on the wall.

And so I crossed the straits to Sweden. Brita met me at Stockholm station, wearing the same beige coat as that first time in Oxford. We looked at each other incredulously, then drove into the snowy forest to a wooden coffee-house which to me, in my ignorance, looked Russian.

20 · Love in Sweden

There was no disappointment, no wish that Brita be different in any way, just delight. Brita is still beautiful today, with thick blonde hair, deep green eyes and a warm smile of enjoyment, shared when our glances meet. In Toledo, I had imagined her standing at my door, her welcoming smile in the sunlight.

One of the things I liked best about her was her habit of nuzzling things. She nuzzled a tulip in a café in Uppsala, like a playful deer, and 'nuzzler' became one of my names for her. Used to displays of affection and tenderness from childhood, she now lavished them on me. After the warmth of my own childhood, I could never have really loved a remote woman, however attractive.

Apart from the pleasure of resuming our love after over two years of letter writing, I also took in Sweden. It seemed less intriguing than Spain and was mostly guided by common sense. One obsession was alcohol, rationed and therefore more desirable.

Sweden in March was remarkable, the world melting. Green patches appeared in snow, ice slabs disintegrated into floes on the lakes, thumps of falling snow accompanied forest walks. Most dramatic was the silence, compared with the crowds and blaring radios of Spain. Only eight million inhabitants lived in a country which, if pivoted from its southern tip, would reach Naples. Swedes did not drop in unannounced, retaining much prewar formality. They lived in comfortable wooden houses, receiving for tea or dinner parties and family celebrations. Drinking was controlled by the hostess, who had to say '*skål*' before you could drink. There were a few coffee houses to meet friends at, but in the long winters the streets were deserted from early evening. Drunks stayed indoors or they might freeze to death.

I had a room in the attic looking over the woods with sparse houses dotted about, in Bromma. Every so often the distant rumbling of the electric tram to Stockholm entered my double-glazed window. The silence made me restless, though it led me to speculate on the Swedes' reserve, perhaps the need for drink. Suzanne, Brita's mother, was mystified when I asked to have a bath every day. I learned that Swedes had a daily sponge, and a bath once a week.

I found the men monosyllabic, the girls lively and talkative. Brita's father Gösta was an exception. He and Suzanne were cosmopolitan and spoke French, German, and English.

Gösta had always been poor. His father had spent his savings buying iron-rich land near Mount Kiruna in the far north, only to find he had been sold small plots, inaccessible without trespassing on others. He took the family north twice. His daughter called her cat Kiruna, after the mountain. When the town council was debating what to call their new town, the daughter suggested it too be called

Kiruna. And so it was. Gösta was an ebullient, talented academic with a great love of England and an amazing capacity for work. He only slept three hours a night which meant he had one-third more time awake than others. He would take daytime cat-naps for as little as five minutes, waking up to wonder where he was. I was asked to give a lecture about India at Bromma high school. Gösta introduced me and then snored through most of it, waking up to thank me warmly and ask the most apposite questions. He learned this trick while studying at Uppsala, working as a station-master at night and cat-napping between trains. The job also gave him free rail travel throughout Europe.

In 1912 he abandoned an impulse to take British nationality, loath to abandon his elderly parents. He turned to research and journalism instead. He spent 1916–17 at the Swedish diplomatic mission in St Petersburg. Neutral Sweden representing German interests, he travelled throughout tsarist and revolutionary Russia visiting German communities who, brought in by Catherine the Great, still lived on the Volga until Stalin transported them to Kazakhstan.

In the twenties, Gösta was *lektor* in Norse languages at the Humboldt University in Berlin. Then, at forty, he married and took to schoolmastering, which provided more income and stability than university posts abroad. From 1938 as head of English at the new Bromma high school he was a great success. In his autobiography the Swedish writer Lars Ardelius, educated there, says the only really good teacher was the vivid and encouraging Gösta Langenfelt.

I found him fascinating. In a foreign country for the first time, one needs a Gösta. He could answer any question on Swedish history, not to mention relations with Russia, Britain and Germany. Suzanne, a piano teacher and writer on music, had also travelled extensively in pre-Nazi Germany, Britain and France.

We spent a week in Stockholm and then went to Uppsala. In the train we found a place between two carriages where we could stand wrapped together in the open air, looking out at the cold, mottled countryside. We were in love, the wind blowing in our hair, and free, at least for the week that remained. We slept in a borrowed flat in a bed set into a wall cupboard, as in ancient peasant homes. I fell more in love; the prospect of leaving for England, of separation, became unbearable.

I had to leave to take my first American tour group round seven countries in six weeks. This summer earning would give me financial freedom for the whole year.

The group was small because it was early in the season; later there would be up to thirty-five. We toured England, Belgium, Holland, Germany, Switzerland, Italy and France. Time was tight, but we saw an amazing amount with superb local guides, from Stratford to Waterloo, Florence to Nice, the perfumes of Grasse to the Paris Concièrgerie. The great enjoyment for me was language practice. My job was to ensure that everything ran smoothly, that guides and buses were punctual, that we caught trains on time with all our luggage, to make everyone feel comfortable, suggest exciting night-life, and deal patiently with eccentricities of which there were many.

In 1951 Europe still seemed battered, from the bullet-holes in Aachen to tales from the young German guides who had fought in Russia. To most Americans, the war had been a glorious procession of 'our boys' laying down their lives for those scheming Europeans who were now ungratefully flirting with 'commies'. Why, said my tourists, even Britain with its half-American Churchill still owed them money from 1914–18. Their isolationism and lack of inter-national press made them chauvinistic, assuming it was a national inferiority complex that made me say television had been invented by a Scotsman, the internal combustion engine by Germans, cinema by Frenchmen, radio by an Italian and the helicopter by a Spaniard. This first tour became the model for later ones, except that I was especially impatient for it to end so I could see Brita again. We met in Paris and flew to an embryonic Heathrow consisting of Nissen huts, where to avoid customs you opened a door and walked across the grass.

We rented the London house of a respectable schoolmaster away on holiday. So as not to shock the neighbours we bought a wedding ring in Piccadilly Circus for £1. Brita hated the deception of pretending we were married. She had muddied my clear waters, though. I didn't want to return to Toledo alone. I tried to persuade her to come to Greece as my girlfriend. But her father would never accept the interruption of her academic career for what seemed a mere 'fling'. Grateful for all the efforts he had expended on her, she loved him too much to defy him in that way.

But I didn't want to get married. I thought of marriage as a shackle, so easily losing its freshness. However much in love I was, I didn't want to be dependent all my life on someone else's moods and impulses. My friend Guy Wilson was enchanted by Brita, and told me that if I left her, even for a short time, I was sure to find her married to someone else. I brushed my negative thoughts aside. The overwhelming thing was not being separated from Brita. We would get married in Sweden, then go back to Spain, to the south where neither of us had been. We would learn Spanish, then perhaps return to England to work for the BBC Spanish and Scandinavian services. Brita suggested I teach English in Sweden, but I wanted to return to where I could live amid drama and history.

In the end, everything was arranged from London. I became excited at the prospect. The wedding was fixed for October 17th. The banns were read on three successive Sundays. My new relatives whose language I didn't speak were invited. Few spoke English with ease, Swedes learning German at school until switching in that decisive year of El Alamein and Stalingrad, 1943. I remember a stunted conversation with a farmer about how many pigs, horses and cows he had, after which we lapsed into silence.

Olive arrived. She was too eccentric for the Langenfelts; they couldn't understand her delight in living alone. We went for a long walk in the pine forest. She said this would be a greater separation than anything before, school, army, or university. Of course I said that was nonsense.

Suzanne worried that I had nothing smart to wear except my striped de-mob suit, so we went and bought a new one. My shoes, too, seemed down at heel – more cause for concern.

The morning arrived. The service was held in Bromma church, a lovely twelfth-century building whose Reformation plaster had been removed at the turn of the century to reveal mediæval frescoes. That church means a lot to me, as a monument to those times: Gösta was buried there in 1965, Suzanne in 1971, everyone leaving a rose on her coffin, in the Swedish way.

We assembled outside the church. Brita wore blue, feeling it dishonest to wear white. She wept on her way to the altar, which worried me. Was she having regrets? Was it something to do with Lennart, her previous boy-friend, now married and in the congregation? But she assured me afterwards it was just the emotion. Everything ended exuberantly: none of that British standing about with drinks, wondering how long you should stay. There was dinner, with a string orchestra and exuberant dancing. Then we went to the station and everyone threw rice into our compartment. It got into our bunk, like gravel between the sheets.

We started our long journey to somewhere we did not know, in southern Spain.

21 · Cordoba Honeymoon

I had money from the American tour, but there had only been one and most of the money had gone in London and Stockholm. When we reached Madrid we had about £60, much of it Brita's. But living was cheap in Spain and the exchange rate helped.

We were economical. I already knew the restaurant at the top of the elaborately decorated cathedral-like post office, nicknamed 'Nuestra Señora de los Correos'. Lunch, with soup, bread, *filete* and fruit, plus wine, cost five pesetas, the equivalent of sixpence. We were regulars.

In Toledo, I introduced Brita to Don Amado, Don Alfonso, the McPhersons and some of my students. Juanito reproached me (in Spanish) for what he considered letting Elvira down.

Then we took the night *rápido* to Seville, our goal. At Cordoba at six in the morning, we woke to singing. Hunching our cramped limbs to the window, in the carriage alongside we saw a group with a guitar, singing a popular Seville song about a girl who throws an offered carnation down a well, wanting no gifts from any boy. As the train moved slowly out of Cordoba, we saw white houses shrouded in mist, part of a cloud city in the first wispy rays of sun.

Seville was a large city with trams and a flowery Moorish quarter with narrow streets and whitewashed houses. We called on the director of the British Institute, Brian Kelly, and said we were looking for a town to teach English in, with as few other foreigners as possible.

He suggested Cordoba.

'Seville doesn't seem your place, although there's plenty of work here. Perhaps Malaga or Granada? – though they're usually full of tourists.'

So we got the train back to Cordoba and found a *pensión*, once a coaching inn. Called *Alegría*, meaning 'joy', it was full of children and a grandmother who beamed and said it didn't matter that we had no children yet: we would soon have as many as them – 'if God wills,' she added, crossing herself.

The town was full of winding streets and smaller than Seville: 250,000 inhabitants compared to Seville's 400,000. The Guadalquivir river ran through it, spanned by a solid Roman bridge, with views up to the Sierra Morena, with olive trees outlined against the sky. On the slopes lay the ruins of the splendid Moorish palace, Medina Azahara, built by the powerful caliph Abderrahman III for his love Azahara, which means orange blossom. There had been fountains of mercury and, according to Gibbon, five thousand loaves every day to feed the fish in its ponds. Arab poetry compared Medina Azahara to a Nubian girl in the arms of an Ethiopian. It was destroyed when the Berber mercenaries rebelled in 1010.

Cordoba's real jewel is the mosque. After Damascus it is the second largest in the world, a forest of pillars under a low roof, beside a patio full of orange trees, symbolising the powerful Cordoba caliphate. While northern Europe slumbered in unhealthy dark-ages mists, Cordoba was civilisation – architecture, poetry, music, geometry, algebra, astronomy, medicine. There is an entire Renaissance cathedral inside the mosque, erected by jealous Christians after five hundred years of Muslim rule. I suppose we must concede that without it, the mosque would probably have become a quarry. The city had chunks of walls and columns from Muslim or late Roman palaces. House-fronts hid great patios full of palm trees and decorative tiles, cool refuges from the broiling summer sun since Moorish times. We learned that house-restoring was a risky business. You might easily find a Moorish bath or Roman tesselated pavement in the basement, and be officially prevented from building further.

We felt exuberant, free and in love, delighted at the thought of living and working in this intriguing, historic place. In a bar, eating *tapas* and drinking a morning glass of *fino*, was a *corredor*, a runner, who worked as an ambulating house agent. He took us to see his aunt, Doña Carmen, and her tailor husband, Don Manolo, tenants of a dilapidated but beautiful old house with two patios near the mosque. There was a room with a double bed large enough, said Doña Carmen, to be a *campo de futbol*. The room was lit by a grating high up in one wall. When we explained we wanted to start a school of English, Doña Carmen let us another room giving onto the patio, and promised another in a week or so. There was a tin bath which one heated on the stove, and a wooden loo flushed with a bucket of water in a rear patio beneath a fig tree.

We took the rooms and looked into advertising on the local radio and in the *Diario de Cordoba*. We got a poster printed, advertising English classes at the new Academia Britanica: 50 pesetas a month for an hour's lesson three evenings a week, in small groups. Doña Carmen taught Brita Spanish cooking and language at the same time. '¡*Ésta es una sartén – repite!*', and she would brandish a frying-pan. Brita already spoke English and French, and quickly learned to 'defend herself', as Spanish puts it.

Then began one of the most painful parts of starting a school – waiting for students. Someone would knock at the door, but it was for the people upstairs. A youth would hover expectantly, but wanted to speak to Doña Carmen's son. We waited, plunged into doubts about our advertising. We counted the forty pounds we had left, just enough to get us back to England. We decided we could wait one more week. One evening there was a sudden rush of people, all asking for '*la Academia Británica*'. We enrolled so many that, until we got the third room, we had to use our bedroom, curtaining-off our washstand and the *campo de futbol*. New students wrote a short composition and we tested their speaking. Most went into beginners' classes, including Eulogio Cremades who would one day become director of the Academia Britanica.

We had to take great care over 'intermediate' students, as differences could be large. Sisters or friends would want to stay together, whatever their ability. I resisted this firmly, even if it lost us students. I knew from Toledo that different levels could wreck a class. What was important was a pleasant yet thoroughly studious atmosphere. Although largely unused to language learning, and only too happy to chat away in Spanish in class, our students really did learn English.

By Christmas, we were amazed to find we had sixty evening students. Cordoba was one of the most isolated towns in Europe, eight hours train journey from Madrid, three from Seville, and nothing but small towns in between. There was no apparent reason to learn English – although in that same year, 1953, the USA began aid to Spain, a dictatorship being OK provided it was vociferously anti-communist! We had not anticipated the novelty of English. 'I am learning English at the Academia Britanica!' a girl would say proudly, clutching her Eckersley textbook, originally written for Polish coal miners during the war. It also provided a unique chance for boy to meet girl in innocent circumstances, and made a change from the endless round of cafés and censored films. Later, before starting a school I made it a point to find out if people got bored in the evenings. English, too, was a forger of dreams, leading to Britain or even the USA. With English, a young Spaniard might meet a

British or American traveller who would bring romance, or at least escape from parental control.

Our pupils told us they found us *simpáticos* and therefore didn't want us to roast in hell. But as Anglicans, could we be Christians? One class brought us a Spanish New Testament, hoping to convert us. Their own biblical knowledge shaky, they were unsure how many apostles there were and thought Gethsemane was a prophet. Getting to know our students was a fascinating introduction to Cordoba. Life seemed an endless series of fiestas with quiet periods beween. As well as Christmas and Holy Week celebrations, there were two *ferias* a year, a *Romería*, some saints' days and the Day of the Dead.

When the Queen visited Gibraltar, friends warned us. But that evening we went to a party anyway. There was flamenco dancing and when Brita danced the graceful *Sevillana* there was wild applause. '*Viva la inglesita!*' they cried, '*Viva la Reina! Viva Isabela Segunda!*' We avoided politics and religion in class. One group had both a hotel porter and a marquis's daughter improving their English together; socially they ignored each other, having obviously supported opposite sides in the civil war. But there was a casual side to all this. I was once summoned from class by the *Policía Secreta*. The secret police! – what on earth had we done?

'I'm sorry to disturb you, *señor*,' said a small man with glasses. 'But would you take out an advertisement with us?'

'Advertise?' I said, 'Where?'

'In our magazine.'

'Do the *Policía Secreta* have a magazine?'

'*Naturalmente, señor*. Here is our football team!' He proudly indicated a group of grinning policemen.

It was the same at a cockfight. A burly Guardia Civil was there too.

'Aren't cockfights illegal?'

'*Sí, sí.*'

'But then why are you here?'

'Ah well, someone has to keep order.'

We made many friends. Dr Celestino Infante owned a blood

bank, had a Norwegian wife, and sent his sons to England to perfect their English. Anastasio Perez Dorado was a well-read and omniscient veterinary surgeon, French teacher, provincial tax inspector and father of seven children. The poet, painter and antique collector Julio Aumente looked after the office of an absent American. Eulogio Cremades was a railway clerk and chemist's accountant, fervently patriotic over Gibraltar. Most people had several jobs as salaries were low, often also working at night. Until recently, the sun in this agricultural society had been more important than any official clock. We too learned to be twenty minutes late for appointments; the system worked so long as everyone observed it. Punctuality was known as *la hora inglesa*, 'English time'.

Another friend was Pepe de las Morenas whom I met teaching English at the Circulo, formerly a monastery, now a club in the centre of town with splendid patios, dining rooms, and a vast baroque lecture hall. Over a drink, Pepe handed me his card: 'Marqués de Aguila de Campoo'. He had come from Madrid to start a modern garage, spoke excellent English, and in the civil war had been captured by republicans who were going to shoot him and his companions. 'Well,' said Pepe, 'we may as well have a last cigarette.' This cool bravura saved them all. Pepe was now in his mid-thirties, very entertaining and generous. He would drop in late after classes and invite us to a *tapas* bar or dinner up in the Sierra. He would also promise to lend us a book, or to take us to Madrid at the weekend, and then seem to forget all about it. He taught us not to take things too seriously, or reproach Andalusians for failing to follow English precepts.

We seemed to know half Cordoba, saying *adiós* the whole time. We got to know painters and 'literati'. Many writers could not be published for the time being. A friend organised an *homenaje*, a tribute, for Antonio Machado, a well-known Castilian poet who had taught at a secondary school in the area. Like many Spanish writers he was a dedicated republican, and died escaping to France from Barcelona in the last days of the civil war.

*

We had many women students. We became good friends with Emilia Amian, whose vast family had a New Year reunion – ninety cousins, aunts and uncles, some of whom she didn't even know.

Redhaired Blanca Rosa Poyatos was the voluble, eccentric daughter of a leading lawyer. Our first English teacher, Shaun McCarthy, a friend of mine from Oxford, had met and fallen in love with her at a fancy dress ball at the Circulo. She was Mary Queen of Scots, her father hoping she wouldn't meet a similar fate. There were rumours that Shaun might be married already. One evening Blanca Rosa found some letters from another woman and spent the whole night translating them with a dictionary. Until then her English had been nil, but this episode motivated her. She is the only person I know to teach herself English via someone else's love letters. She and Shaun later married and had four boys, one red-haired graduating from Oxford like his father.

Less fortunate was Alberto Maura, who fell in love with Pilar, daughter of a rich landowner. Both came to class in our Academia. Alberto was certain Pilar's father would never consider him, a mere veterinary student. They linked converting us to Catholicism with their chances of success in love and assured us they prayed for us every night. We were somewhat embarrassed. They were making their plight somehow our fault. It wasn't long before Pilar's father heard about it and exiled his daughter away to a fierce aunt's farm near Granada. For a while Alberto would not speak to us.

Brita, particularly, got to know the señoritas well, several of them brilliant students. Asked why they were not at university, they said their fathers would never permit them, as they wanted them to find husbands. We settled in. Every spring we thought of returning to England. But things seemed to go better, and made us decide to stay just one more year. Doña Carmen's premises became too small. We rented a flat the other end of town, by the open market, in the eighteenth century a bull ring. The new rooms were spacious if ancient. There was a fountain in the patio. But after only a few months, the ground floor below us was taken over by a sausage factory, and we had placards of cheerful piglets prancing beside the whitewashed entrance. We protested, but the sausage-maker just flirted with Brita and gave us *salchichas al infierno*, highly spiced sausages which he said were *muy muy buenos*. Eventually we became friends and he removed the cardboard piglets.

We started to organise Spanish courses and sent our prospectus to university Spanish departments all over Europe. There was doubt about whether Andalusia was the place to learn, although I didn't find it very different from Toledo, where they also pronounced 'y' and 'll' like the English 'j'. We emphasised that Andalusian Spanish was a better preparation for South America than the 'clear' Castilian of Madrid. We wanted our course to be different – lively, conversational, throwing light on contemporary Spain. It would last a fortnight, during Holy Week. Students would stay with Cordobese families. Brita and I would take the beginners, our educated Spanish friends teaching the others. I stressed it would be classes, not lectures, our aim being to get students talking in Spanish.

Our first course had twelve students: a German girl, a French mother and daughter, and nine British students from mainly Cambridge and Durham. Classes were in the morning, conversation with our Cordobese students in the late afternoon, then lectures in Spanish on Velasquez, the Arabs in Cordoba, Lorca – and flamenco, given by a professional orator called Pedro Palop who looked like an Edward Lear drawing and captivated his audience.

When Cordoba realised these courses would actually happen, it wanted to take part in welcoming foreigners on the city's first such venture; it was a question of pride, of helping visitors feel at home. The mayor gave a reception. Pepe Cobos invited everyone to his bodega in Montilla, for a wonderful meal with excellent wine. The Circulo offered its splendid Moorish courtyards for classes. It was a great success, marred slightly by the British girls' sunbathing: one displayed herself on the rooftop and got shouted at by the woman opposite for trying to steal her husband; another hitched up her skirt to sit in the sun at the Circulo, bringing members and stewards to the windows for a look. None of this stopped us having twenty-eight people the following year and fifty-six the next, by which time we had new, larger premises, almost inside Cordoba's ancient city walls.

Our new school had a solid glass patio above a furniture shop, central heating, and a space under the stairs which we filled with shapely casks of delicious Montilla wine for the bar. There were eight classrooms and a library/lecture-room. We lived upstairs. Reception had straw-topped tables decorated by Brita with hotel stickers from our American tours. I heard the British Council was jealous – they couldn't open a bar without questions being asked in Parliament!

22 · '¡Prohibido de Entrar en España!'

We bought a Vespa in England in the summer, and Colin and I drove it down to Cordoba. It took five days and felt like a mechanical horse, as France and Spain unfolded slowly beneath us. The spires of Chartres were like the horns of a distant deer. The grim workers' houses and chemical discharges in the river in San Sebastian smacked of a word not yet in vogue – pollution. Then the baked tablelands of Castile, arid after the stifling *tres meses de infierno*, 'three months of hell', shifting colours under the vast sunset. Every peasant seemed a friend because he was human. We slept in a whitewashed *pensión* in Val de Moro, an El Greco in the small church and bullfights every Sunday in the sixteenth-century wooden-arched plaza.

The Vespa meant the countryside was ours, with its olive-trees and swirls of dry multicoloured earth, though the potholes meant reinforcing the springs. The garage was surprised: they assumed everything foreign was superior. We roamed the villages: Lucena, Linares where the renowned bullfighter Manolete was killed, Cabra with its great *sima*, or chasm, gaping over 100 feet down into the earth. You could easily fall in; there was no warning apart from a notice on painted tiles, which said the *sima* appeared in *Don Quixote*. You could drop stones and marvel at the time they took to reach the bottom. Some lethal gas was supposed to prevent a rope descent. I imagined Roman armour, Moorish helmets, Castilian swords – the whole history of Spain lying down there!

The Vespa was great publicity. We had adopted a black-and-white stray puppy and graced it with the august name of Califa. All Cordoba knew us as *los extranjeros*, the foreigners, with their Vespa, the pretty blond wife and their black-and-white dog. They expected us to add children, asking intimate questions directly (as they also did about how much we earned). Women scrutinised Brita's stomach and asked: 'Is there nothing new?', or simply, 'Nothing?' Then, turning to me with an accusing laugh: 'And you, what are you doing, eh?'

When our daughter, Katinka, and then Richard arrived, we had a maid called Micaela to help. She had a broad face, deep wrinkles, a hoarse voice and grey hair. She had never learned to read or write and did not know how old she was, but reckoned about sixty. She lived with her daughter and son-in-law, their baby daughter and her bachelor son, all in a single room with a leaking roof by the river.

Her son Rafael had fought for the republic and escaped to Vienna in 1939, staying right through the war. Micaela visited him once, travelling free because her husband had worked on the railways. She was very eloquent about her journey: 'I know France and Italy, Germany and Belgium!' Unable to warn Rafael she was coming, she was let in by his wife. When Rafael came home, Micaela leapt on him from behind a door. All three wept; they had not seen each other for fifteen years. '*¡Ay, qué pena!*' Micaela kept repeating, wiping a tear from her eye with a corner of her apron. She would not go again; she had other sons to look after in Cordoba. One had just been arrested for peeing in the street outside a bar. She asked us to help get him out of prison. Micaela was a no-nonsense republican. When the Saudi king visited Cordoba, his motorcade roaring down our street, she went on scrubbing the floor with supreme indifference, muttering, 'Who cares for kings, anyway?' She was an expert cook of *tortilla a la española* and lentil soup, producing them at no notice.

Our more central position brought us visitors. Miss Popham, retired head of Cheltenham College for Young Ladies, looked around and said, unforgettably:

'It's jolly sporting of you, producing a school like this!'

Our students thronged to any talks given by passing travellers. Peter Smithers MP talked about Addison to bewildered students, who found him hard to understand and had never heard of Addison. Walter Starkie, director of the British Council during the war, gave a magical evening on gypsy music, illustrating it on the violin. The star event was a talk on Christopher Fry, which was packed.

'I understood everything,' announced Enrique proudly, 'except one word, 'fry'!'

We now had three hundred students and had to get teachers out from England. It seemed odd: we had chosen Cordoba precisely because there were so few foreigners. We met people of other nationalities, too. Eolo Viale, who had fought for Mussolini, noticed pieces of frieze on our book-case from Medina Azahara, the ruined Moorish palace.

'Where did you get them?' Eolo asked.

'In a field.'

'Ah, the British!' mocked Eolo. 'They find everything in a field! – Australia, Canada, India, and almost the whole of Africa!'

Estlin and Marion Cummings arrived in Gibraltar on a warm spring day and we went down to welcome them. We offered them our flat above the Academia, but estlin had arthritis and felt continually chilly and so they moved into the new Cordoba Palace Hotel looking down on the Moorish rooftops. estlin said his only worthwhile experience was watching a small boy trying to jump onto a donkey and falling off every time.

Through them we met Gerald Brenan, the English authority on Spain, and his wife Gamel, who became warm friends. They lived in a house near Malaga with old peasant furniture and primitive paintings, and a garden that was a forest of tropical trees and plants.

We held 'weeks' devoted to other countries, with films or talks and crates of exhibits embassies cared to send. The city invited the ambassador and provided a sumptuous lunch, usually in the Calahorra, the mediæval fortress which appeared to weigh down the end of the Roman bridge over the Guadalquivir, after which he would inaugurate our week. The Dutch were first, sending cheese, photographs of flowers, sets of Volendam blouses and trousers with wooden sabots and some Spanish-speaking lecturers. We borrowed a film projector from the American consul in Seville. Next came Sweden, with a talk on snow and forests by Brita, then Britain, then the USA, whose ambassador was the former film star John Cabot Lodge. The Cordobese called him 'the dancing ambassador' because he did a brief twirl at his reception. We were starting something that lasted throughout our careers: the idea that international relations is a limitless field. Word soon got around Cordoba of our international visitors. The events paid off by attracting ever more students.

In many ways our life was ideal. We would leave Cordoba in June, when it became intolerably hot for teaching, and go to Lysekil on the Swedish coast to teach on an English course organised by Gösta for Swedish primary school teachers. In July and part of August we made money taking Americans round Europe, often on parallel tours. The rest of the summer we were at Torquay with Olive or with friends in London. We would return to Cordoba at the end of September. We thus kept in touch with those closest to us, and at least dipped into the countries closest to us.

I had been spending the mornings writing a book on Cordoba called *Babel in Spain*, and sent it to Gerald Brenan. He liked it, offered to write an introduction and sent it to his publisher, Hamish Hamilton, who accepted it. When it was published, Hamish and his wife Yvonne came out. We took them to Cordoba's only nightspot, a brothel *La Primera*. Some students at neighbouring tables kept sending over complimentary bottles. Hamish was thrilled by the unusual outing.

Babel in Spain touched on politics only marginally. British readers found it an exuberant, positive picture of an Andalusian town. It got a quiverful of favourable reviews. But what would the Cordobese think? They might expect a foreigner to stick to the gaiety, the splendour of the city and the beauty of the flamenco-dancing women – but I had written about how they lived. I had showed the manuscript to Vicente, a friend, who had been guarded though not outwardly negative. I made some small changes but still detected unspoken disapproval. Then I realised Spaniards were unaccustomed to uncensored opinion. Only a few of our best students of English could read the book accurately; perhaps this was how the rumours began, brewing up while we were away for the summer.

We were uncertain about returning to Cordoba because we now had two children. But reports indicated Cordoba was seething, and I could not run away from people among whom I had lived so long, my tail between my legs. Cordoba was part of my life; I could not crumple it up like paper. So we returned.

That year, 1959, was our last and most painful. Student numbers fell; old friends did not come back; people cut me in the street. The Spanish courses and national weeks had made Cordoba consider electing me *hijo predilecto*, its favourite son. But no longer. My book was denounced in *El Cordobés* in an article full of lies, misunderstandings and mistranslations. The law gave the right to answer a newspaper attack with a reply the same length. If I sent in my answer, the editor was obliged to publish it. I did, bewildering the Cordobese who mostly couldn't read my book and now didn't know what to think.

Forty years on, the Academia still exists. It has grown to 1,800 students. We sold our last half share to Ned Thomas, an Australian teacher and our son's godfather. The very next day, we heard from our friend Basil Potter at the British Institute in Seville that he was retiring, leaving the institute to our Academia Britanica in Cordoba. If only we had not just sold up, the lovely, prosperous Seville institute would have been ours! Instead it was virtually given to Ned, it being British Council policy then to sell off its institutes in Spain and Italy at a minimum. Ned promptly sold his Cordoba school on to Eulogio Cremades and installed himself in Seville, uninterested in any further links with us.

My book continued to reverberate. Six years later, with three children and a Swedish au-pair, we returned to Andalusia on holiday. We took the ferry from Gibraltar to Algeciras and sat at a café, revelling at being back and waiting for the bus to Fuengirola, where we had rented a villa. Suddenly a policeman appeared.

'*Señor Hykraf?*' He beckoned and took me to the police station, where they had a replica of my passport, overprinted: '*Prohibido de entrar en España*': 'forbidden entry into Spain'.

I was to take the next ferry back, though my family could stay. I protested. Couldn't they ring Madrid to see if it was a mistake? But it was Good Friday. The offices were closed. Precisely, I argued: it was scandalous to separate a father from his family on Good Friday! And what of Spanish hospitality? The policeman agreed, but it was not his affair; he was following orders. I must take the two o'clock ferry. At ten to two he came to accompany me to the boat. I was furious and considered causing a scandal by jumping overboard. At Gibraltar, I tried the La Linea border post, but the Spanish official wagged a finger and grinned, '*Prohibido! Prohibido!*'

I flew to Tangiers and heard some Scandinavians were flying back to Malaga after a day-trip. There were nine of us. It was already dark. I sat looking out at the lights ringing the Costa Blanca, still livid, vowing that I would get there, whatever happened.

Malaga airport was deserted because of the holiday. I stood in the middle of the passport queue, reckoning that was when the official would be the least alert. I got through. There remained my suitcase. The others were day-trippers; I had luggage. It did not arrive. A white-bearded policeman was walking up and down, reading documents with concentration. I remembered the delay in noticing I was *prohibido* in Algeciras, and asked the porters to hurry. The tour guide said they had to leave. My case arrived just in time. In the bus I imagined the Spanish police in pursuit, scrutinising every car that overtook. But we reached the plaza uneventfully. I took a taxi to Fuengirola. I told the driver I was Swedish, so had to listen to his disapproving stories of the British.

Brita and the children were at the villa. To cover my tracks further, I was her German 'amigo' for the next fortnight.

23 · Bricks in Blackheath

We had taken a mortgage in London for a house we had never seen, largely owing to an enthusiastic recommendation by a friend, Russell Enoch, the actor William Russell. We had already considered sharing a large house with Russell's family and that of Robert Shaw, another actor – large houses being much cheaper, especially if divided.

Russell had been demanding with the houses we had seen, so when he wrote about a wonderful modern house in Blackheath made by a company called Span, we thought it worth the risk.

The sun shone as Russell drove us through early-morning London from Heathrow to Blackheath.

We had never heard of Blackheath before. It seemed an oasis. Acres of grass gleamed in the early sun, with a glimpse of Wolfe's statue in neighbouring Greenwhich Park.

'Imagine Henry V reviewing his army here before marching to Dover and then Agincourt!' declaimed Russell. 'Or Londoners crowding here to welcome Charles II after fifteen years' exile. Or . . .'

'Where is our house?' I asked.

We drove through the village, turned left along Blackheath Park and down Pond Road, ending up at what must have been a vegetable garden, piles of bricks fringing a concrete path.

'We've arrived!' proclaimed Russell, and pointed to some bricks. 'That's yours! With ours next door!'

I had never heard 'next door' used so imaginatively.

As the house would not be ready for months, we spent the sunlight of that splendid summer of 1959 at Olive's. I earned just enough to support us with occasional *Observer* articles, talks for the BBC Spanish service and odd work for 'Panorama' (once in quest of the most attractive barmaid in London). It cost £20 a week to support the family, mortgage included. But what about my career? I remembered the Oxford advice about not teaching abroad because it would be so difficult when I returned. I tried and failed to join the BBC and was shattered. It destroyed my naive illusion that once I had published a decent book, everything would fall into place. Americans seemed to accept such rejections. But the British are mortified, their self-respect wounded. I had more bounce than that, but in the end chose the patchwork of freelancing. The American tours aside, I had never had a boss and didn't like the idea. And I still wanted the mornings free for writing.

The house was finished at last, and we moved in. I was toying with starting a language school in London. It seemed logical after Cordoba. There seemed to be few decent schools in London, apart from the London Education Authority and a couple of private ones. There were few places where foreign students could go for advice. Embassies couldn't be bothered with their student compatriots. Au-pair girls had no regulations about their hours or how much they were paid. Many were not at all on equal terms (which is what 'au pair' means) with their families, often eating alone in the kitchen. All this made me impatient. I still felt the international sympathy we had known in Cordoba, with world government, and in my childhood. I detested the stuffy obliviousness of those who still believed Britain was superior to other countries. True, Britain was still wealthy – all the more reason to make foreigners and students feel at home.

Tentatively, I looked round for premises. Several were not central, too expensive, or not easily divided into classrooms. But there was something reasonable in Endell Street on the borders of Covent Garden: only £6 a week, near tubes and buses, with space for reception, three classrooms, and a tiny teachers' room. A lecture room downstairs belonged to a film company called The Grass-hoppers and could be rented. The rooms were on the top floor, up fifty-three steps. But surely we, and our students, were all young and healthy! It was a two-year lease. How would I finance equipment and furniture and pay the rent? Was there really a market for English lessons in London? People in Cordoba had been bored, and we were a novelty. We had financed much of it from our American tours. Now we had about £500, mostly due from Ned Thomas for what he still owed us for the Cordoba school.

The owner rang early one morning to ask if I really wanted the premises. Still in bed, I said: 'Yes.' It was one of the most significant decisions of my adult life. I doubt I would have looked for other premises. I would have abandoned the idea, launched into writing novels again, hammered at the BBC's door once more or gone into politics – in any case, something more 'respectable' than a language school.

We were almost the only university graduates in the field. Teaching English to foreigners was usually something undergraduates did for minimal pay. Having taught only in Spain and Sweden, we didn't realise we were entering an area which most British people, respecting neither foreigners nor languages nor teachers, regarded with scorn. Now we had premises, we needed to equip them. We contacted anyone who might send us students. This produced little. I remember the Iranian embassy, then representing the shah. Knots of restless people who looked like protesting students were loitering on the pavement outside. I was ushered in to the cultural attaché.

'Could you send us students?' I asked. He hesitated.

'I don't have much to do with students.'

'Where can I contact them?'

'Probably outside on the pavement!' he bumbled.

We found October the worst month to start a school. The summer rush was over. Students taking the Cambridge exams had already registered elsewhere; ILEA classes were under way. We went into partnership with a couple from Gibraltar, Pepe and Maruja Brew, who wanted to create a travel agency to send students to Cordoba to learn Spanish. Maruja became receptionist, and got very bored because we only had two Portugese waiters planning to emigrate to Canada. A cat would walk across the skylight above her desk, or lie on it and obscure what little light it gave.

I got an ILEA job, teaching an adult class of thirty-two girls of different nationalities, and one male Turk, all intermediate, able to follow a general conversation. Because of their mixed languages, I could only use English, without translations. The size of the class called for techniques familiar to experienced teachers: quicker tempo, repetition drills, pictures or mime to introduce vocabulary in a way I hoped was vivid. With a wall picture, I pointed at items, named them and had students repeat them before writing it down. Next day we revised them and introduced new words and grammar, until they could describe the picture coherently. Topics had to stimulate. There was little point in talking about car engines with a class mainly of girls. Variety was essential in keeping everyone interested, involved, even amused. The atmosphere had to be relaxed. Trying to speak another language can provoke laughter, perhaps mockery. Encouragement was therefore vital. So many had studied English for years at school and couldn't even ask for a sandwich. Grammar and translation were the easiest options for most teachers and lessons were rarely practical. Schoolchildren were seldom given a chance to speak the language and were often bored.

I realised the importance of not being ponderous, of approaching classes with lightness of touch, of getting students to talk about their adventures, in our case in London. I went to the shabby ILEA school every afternoon, the walls outside scrawled with fascist slogans. Wealthier students could also join these subsidised classes: ladies in expensive shoes, stout diplomats, Covent Garden tomato merchants – sitting beside au-pairs and waiters. There was no common room, no hot drinks. At breaks, students crowded into corridors and teachers to a gloomy 'rest room'.

Our Endell Street school continued empty, the cat still on the skylight. Near Christmas we decided to give a party – I always do when things are going badly. Up the fifty-three steps came a procession of people who had been to Cordoba, old friends, ILEA teachers and students, new Span neighbours, about thirty altogether. They transformed the forlorn atmosphere, crowding classrooms, reception area, teachers' room. They drank wine and ate peanuts. Some were surprised to see such drab premises after exotic Cordoba. Others were delighted we had opened in London, asked about our plans and how many students we had. Afterwards, Pepe was enthusiastic:

'What a party! I'm sure they'll help.' It wasn't clear how, except by sending occasional students. Maruja looked round at the empty glasses and pools of spilled wine. 'Nobody seems to care!' she lamented. Why should they, I thought.

After Christmas, a Spanish priest called Don Arturo called at Endell Street. He was about fifty, had lived in London as chaplain to a Catholic hostel, and appeared unable to speak a word of English. How he got around, I never understood. But we were delighted to speak Spanish again. He had no time for English classes but wanted to see what we could offer the young Spanish students in his care. 'They need help so much,' he said, 'with English, and for their moral welfare!' He was surprised our school was empty, and began recommending us to every Spaniard he met, even strangers on the tube. A trickle of students came, mostly Spanish waiters and some Italians, in a new 3:30–5:30 beginners' class, the only time they were free. Brita found them determined to learn, despite their exhausting work schedule. Most spoke only a little English, and this was their big chance. If they went home speaking English, they would have no problem getting jobs connected with the new tourism wave. They could earn well, with tips, and perhaps save for their own restaurants, at home or in London. They did their crumpled homework, probably early in the morning, and painfully absorbed phrases to use with customers. Brita helped them learn restaurant requests, tableware vocabulary, complaints, apologies. They fell in love with her, which countered their tiredness and made them attentive. They would slip her *billets doux*. 'You the joel of my hart!' wrote a poetic Colombian, 'alway i you luv!'

I had lunch with Christopher Dilke from the BBC, who had been at our party. He wanted me to write an intermediate book for BBC English by Radio, initially for broadcasting, then to become a teach-yourself textbook. Each lesson would have a recorded dialogue, new words translated as necessary, followed by grammatical explanations in the student's language and exercises. We needed a topical story to bind it all together. I felt dubious: it would interrupt my novel – but it might increase my reputation as a teacher of English to foreigners, and help our school. Brita suggested a foreigner coming to England to sell his new invention, instant whisky, a kind of alcoholic Nescafé. He would have adventures and visit different parts of Britain before finally launching his product in a blaze of glory. I suggested it to Christopher Dilke; he accepted it promptly. I started on the first dialogue, about foreigners' amazement at how, in mid-Channel, the British will start queuing to get off the ferry at Dover.

Our student numbers grew, and in April I gave up the ILEA job to teach at my own school. I became increasingly interested in teaching techniques. There were few inspiring or instructive text-books. Practical teacher training was largely unexplored. No university courses told you how to teach a class of beginners all of different nationalities. The British Council taught hardly any English except in capitals like Rome or Madrid, having sold off most of its overseas institutes for a pittance. It put literature studies above language learning. They forgot it was pointless studying Shakespeare when you could hardly say 'good morning'. I remembered being 'taught' Russian at Wellington by a cheerful chemist who made us read Pushkin's *The Captain's Daughter* aloud. We distorted the sounds and learned nothing useful at all. The British Council did not really go in for English language teaching until Sir John Burgh became director general in 1981.

Teaching English to foreigners was not a profession. It was about now that a friend told me his brother was slightly off his head but not dangerous, and could I possibly give him a job as a teacher? Good grammar books were rare. The best was *Living English Structure* by Stannard Allen, a long-time teacher in Czechoslovakia. He explained English grammar for foreigners concisely, with scores of sentences with gaps for the student to fill in. Eckersley too had a concise, full grammar, but without essential rules of thumb. I became inspired by the tape-recorder, which in Cordoba I hardly knew existed. The audio cassette had not been invented, and the machine we bought was bulky, with reel-to-reel tapes and complicated switches. We began taking it round our three classrooms in turn, and advertised it. 'Special English classes with tape-recorder,' proclaimed the poster which, as in Cordoba, we persuaded shop-keepers to hang in their windows.

Meanwhile, we settled into our Span house. Earnings from summer teaching in Sweden, American tours and occasional articles just about kept us, while our school brought in nothing. Nevertheless, we bought a 1929 T-Ford for £20. Katinka and Richard were dropped at a crèche every other day, when Brita rushed off to her classes. It was accepted that Brita was largely responsible for her 'area', which included the children, not to mention cooking, household chores and her teaching. To eke out our earnings, she also started a translation agency called Transinterpreter – partly to help the polyglot Moroccan fiancée of a friend who once flew me from Cordoba to Barcelona and back in his Tiger Moth. Once married, they moved abroad. Transinterpreter carried on until we left for Italy in 1967.

One day in the Blackheath train, after a year of giving the Covent Garden school life support, I bumped into Rodney Forsyth, a friend from Oxford, now in the British Council. He asked hesitantly what I was doing. As we approached my station, he said he would ring me about something 'rather special'. Next morning, he rang to ask if I would teach English to President Kekkonen of Finland. It involved spending four months at the Helsinki presidential palace before he came on a visit to England, hopefully with good enough English to broadcast, make a speech at the Guildhall, and discuss the world with Harold Macmillan.

I talked it over with Brita. We were both in favour. We had taught in Finland one summer, at a place called Lahti by a beautiful lake. My cousin had been in Helsinki with the British Council and introduced us to some entertaining university people. I still remembered the Finns' dual bathing system, everyone naked but the sexes separated by a wooden barrier. I once dived under one of these barriers unawares, and had been screeched at by a lot of bare-breasted women like hens disturbed by a fox.

Forsyth was anxious I should accept. He said Kekkonen got drunk often, was a womaniser, and perhaps a closet communist, being a crony of Khruschev. I accepted, provided I could return to London for a fortnight half-way through and would earn enough. I would be paid a handsome eighteen pounds a week, all included, starting in January.

24 · English for a President

I flew first-class to Helsinki in a Finnair Caravelle. Dusk set in over the North Sea. I saw Stockholm five miles below, surprisingly small yet spread out, like a collection of incandescent villages. It was my last view of the familiar. I felt lonely as we dived through the dark sky and landed in the snow at Helsinki.

I liked the president: a slim, athletic 62, bald, with glasses, thin lips and clear, determined eyes. He seemed cordial and considerate, and spoke enough English for us to communicate. His wife, who seemed older, had published stories about Karelia, her native province, occupied by the Russians after the 1940 winter war, then overrun by the Finns pushing to Leningrad in 1941 in alliance with the Germans.

Next day we began a routine involving about six hours a day of English lessons. We started with an hour's walk round the lake after breakfast; then lunch, two hours tuition, supper, and a final chat with tea at nine o'clock.

The house, on an island, was a comfortable villa with the bodyguard's lodge beyond my window. My room was furnished in 'boudoir' style with a flower painting, a gift from Molotov. Downstairs, where we had lunch and dinner, reception rooms led into each other. The garden doubtless looked cultivated in summer but was wild in winter: a frozen lake, snowy paths and slopes, trees and bushes sparkling. All around stretched the ice, smooth and white.

On our morning walks round the lake, a bodyguard puffed

behind, out of earshot. We discussed politics, recounted our lives, our travels, the people we had met. I told him what I knew of England and Franco's Spain; he told me about Finland, independent only since 1918. For centuries it was under Swedish rule, then, after the 1809 war, Russian, with little history of its own, just the *Kalevala*, mediæval legends of giants and magicians, some of which Sibelius put to music. Kekkonen seemed frank about his difficulties, maintaining friendship with Russia while not letting it absorb Finland, trying to control his communists without alienating Moscow. His enemies called his policies communist – but he had fought against them in 1918 during the war of independence. The world seemed starker than in Britain. While I was in Finland, there was war in Congo, the Bay of Pigs, the generals' coup in Algeria. I realised how protected Britain was, compared to little Finland, exposed on the Russian border.

The president's real language problem was confidence. I encouraged him as much as possible. We used Stannard Allen, and it was strange having a President give a sentence illustrating the difference between 'make' and 'do': 'My boy friend Cyril made love to me last night.' I also used books specifically designed for Finns, and readers by Alan Beasley, a brilliant teacher I had known at Oxford who now had a language school in Helsinki.

My life at Tamminiemi was solitary. To begin with I was invited out, particularly by some Helsinki university people I had known at Oxford. My salary did not stretch to Finland's inordinately expensive restaurants, and I had nowhere else to go. People hesitated to call the president's residence, a bit like telephoning Buckingham Palace. Kekkonen sometimes took me to unexpected places. At the opening of the House of Representatives I talked at length with a white-haired gentleman whom I later discovered was the prime minister. At the sauna, the cream of Finnish political life sprawled naked and sweating, drinking beer. No wonder Kekkonen and Khruschev got on well in such relaxed surroundings. I met a young-looking man with excellent English who had been ambassador to London. At the opera to see Prokofiev's ballet *The Stone Flower*, we were received with courtly flourishes and led to the royal box, everyone looking up at their president. Two images clashed: my fumbling student who thought he was no good at English, and this decisive leader of four million people.

I busied myself with my BBC series, *Getting On in English*, now being broadcast. I had to send at least one lesson a week for checking by one of the driest, nicest and most critical of the English by Radio team, René Quinault, who appeared to think encouragement unnecessary among grown men. He never said what he thought of my lessons, just wrote comments like, 'No!', 'Is this really true?' or 'Write "usually" to cover yourself!' I tried learning Finnish with a teach-yourself book, which presumed no one would get beyond lesson four as everything collapsed there. Anyway, Swedish was taught in the schools and would do for everyday use. Indeed some Finns hardly spoke Finnish at all. Alan Beasley asked me to write a book on Finnish jewellery and silverware. I knew little about it but felt sure I could find out, and spent time with jewellers and silversmiths. Most design was taken directly from nature. Börje Rajalin designed gold pendants and necklaces studded with tiny gems. The silversmith Bertil Garberg transformed a leaf or a concave pebble from the lakeshore into a candlestick or a silver bowl.

My old rugby knee had made skiing difficult, but the disappointingly warm winter spoiled an excellent opportunity to learn. Every April the president went to northern Finland to spend a week skiing fifty kilometres a day; I wondered if I could learn fast enough to accompany him. His ADC kindly telephoned all over Finland for somewhere with snow, coming up with a sports centre. I slipped and slithered on a practice slope where a woman had died ten days before. I turned out not good enough for Kekkonen's skiing week, but enjoyed the speed, the grace and the healthiness of it all.

Brita wrote regularly. The family was flourishing. The school had fewer students in January and February, but thanks to my salary and advances on my BBC and silverware books, we had our nostrils above water. Brita had found empty premises in Shaftesbury Avenue, just above Piccadilly Circus. The snag was that it was part of the new Piccadilly scheme and we might only get a year's lease. Was it worth the risk? What would happen when we had to leave? My two-week break was approaching, so I could see the place too.

London: noise and rush, after the quiet months in Finland. But there was playing with the children, seeing old friends, making love, independence, the theatre. We decided to take Shaftesbury Avenue. It was roomy yet shabby, pigeons lurking in rooms with peeling paint, a stained stone staircase overlooking a vast gloomy courtyard full of scrap. One wall had an enormous portrait of the queen, slowly disintegrating in the rain. Even if we were only there for a year, the central position should attract enough students in summer for us to become better-known and move anywhere we wanted. Also, the shop-owners either side reassured us that they too had one-year leases, and had been there since 1949.

Back in Finland, we geared up for Kekkonen's visit. He had written the Guildhall and radio speeches, and we rehearsed them, he at one end of the room, I at the other. I was audience and director:

'A bit louder, Mr President!'

'You're telling a joke, Mr President. Let it show in your intonation!'

'Good, but try to avoid an even tone. Express your feelings as naturally as you can!'

I corrected mistakes gently, suggesting what I felt were more evocative phrases. Teaching was becoming theatre, with rehearsals and encouragement. When he had put everything he wanted into them, I recorded the speeches on a tape with as much expression as I could, so he could rehearse alone.

Spring set in; Helsinki revealed itself. The sun shone, the lake became a stretch of water, leaves and flowers burgeoned, the lawns recovering.

I acted as Macmillan for Kekkonen, though he said he always used interpreters with foreigners because it gave him time to think. We discussed current world politics and I asked him the sort of questions I imagined Macmillan would ask. Kekkonen did valiantly, his English accented but fluent. I remembered being told he was a communist and a drunk. I saw no evidence for either. We had one cognac after dinner. While I could see him getting on better in his sauna with Khruschev than with the aristocratic Macmillan, I found only warmth for Britain and America.

Departure. Crates were boarded up. Kekkonen asked me if I would like the Order of the Finnish Rose. When I said it wouldn't make much difference, he gave me a Finnish hunting knife with our names inscribed on it. We left with Mrs Kekkonen's maid, body-guards, staff from the London embassy, a few ministers and civil servants, and the foreign minister. At Gatwick we all stayed on board save Kekkonen, who descended to receive the honours. I watched through a porthole as he trod a red carpet and inspected the guard of honour. I was worried: people speaking another language under stress sometimes freeze. But Kekkonen chatted cheerfully with the air-marshal who welcomed him. At the Admiralty that evening he chatted exuberantly with Harold Macmillan. He used my tapes to rehearse before going to sleep and, thank God, his broadcasts and speeches were clear and intelligible!

25 · Shaftesbury Avenue

It was not sad moving out of Endell Street, and we carried desks and chairs down fifty-three steps and loaded them onto a hired lorry. Teachers helped: Sam, the bilingual Gibraltarian, Martin, who had absurdly been sent down from Cambridge for making his girl-friend pregnant, Colin McMillan, a student from London University who had taught a sabbatical year in Seville.

We spilled furniture out onto the Shaftesbury Avenue pavement before carrying it up to the second floor. In the larger classrooms, our sticks looked pitiably sparse. We put down some discarded cord mats from a room upstairs. Mr Peters, a carpenter we used occasionally at home, covered the basins near the front door with plywood so the entrance could be a reception office, any money we took concealed inside the basins. Brita and I bought prints in the shops off Charing Cross Road. They didn't make our school any more respectable, but at least it was welcoming. It was all we could afford and, as I repeated defensively, a school should be judged not by its furnishings but by its teaching.

Despite the fact that we had so little to steal, we kept on being broken into, presumably from neighbouring Soho. So I had a large notice painted above the door, which said:

ROBBERS!
WE ARE A SCHOOL OF LANGUAGES WITH NOTHING TO
STEAL! SO PLEASE FIND SOMEWHERE ELSE AND DON'T BE
A NUISANCE BY SMASHING DOWN OUR DOORS IN THE
MIDDLE OF THE NIGHT — WHICH MEANS WE HAVE TO
CLEAR UP THE MESS IN THE MORNING!
ALSO, IT GIVES A BAD IMPRESSION OF THIS COUNTRY TO
FOREIGNERS WHO ARE THE MAJORITY OF OUR STUDENTS!

The effect was miraculous. The robberies ceased. We had already bound our tape recorders to their stands with heavy black chains — after I found several by one of our exits on Rupert Street, lined up and ready to be taken away.

Then there was the prostitute and her clients in a flat visible from one classroom. Until the police evicted her, she was a useful visual aid: 'Right, she's called Sarah and he's called Bill. What's her name, Fernando? That's right! And his name, Maria? That's right! And what are they doing, Rodrigo? You don't know! Carlo, then? Yes, quite right! Well done! What is Sarah pulling, Carmen? Giuseppe? Anyone? Yes, she was pulling the curtain. Repeat! Sarah was pulling the curtain! Good! What was she pulling, Hildegard? Yes, the curtain! Quite right! Repeat! The curtain, the curtain . . .'

Drug addicts came much later, trying to use our loos, leaving syringes on the floor. But most were scared off, like moles coming to the surface, finding their hopes of a dark, private refuge dashed by the bustle, the footsteps passing, the laughter, the burble of foreign languages. They were a sad part of being at the centre of one of the biggest cities in the world.

In the evening, through our Shaftesbury Avenue windows, the lights of three theatres flashed their neon lettering into our class-rooms. Down on the pavement the whole world strolled up and down, and students soon began to flock to this newly-opened school. This posed a problem. How could we get hold of reliable teachers more quickly? There was no agency supplying teachers, and university departments had no such service. Was there such a thing as a qualified teacher of English for foreigners? Did any real training exist? The answer was no. My Oxford MA had little bearing on teaching my own language to foreign students. Brita was better qualified with her firsts at Uppsala in French and English, covering grammar, literature and phonetics.

All I could do was observe new teachers, give them advice, and hope they would turn into reasonable teachers after three months. What was required was a short practical course. My BBC course *Getting On In English* gave me a starting-point. At least those attending would already know English. We were uncertain how many would pay for it, so it lasted only a fortnight. We charged eight guineas. Anyone could enrol, even if they had no degree or teaching experience. A single classified advertisement in the *New Statesman*, inserted for three weeks, brought the twelve people on our very first course in June 1962. From tentative beginnings, in tatty premises in the heart of London, was born a significant activity that was to grow into the specialised training of over 35,000 teachers, in Britain and abroad.

The crux was to suggest ways of teaching a beginners' class with different nationalities, in English. Without translating, new words had to be taught with pictures, mime, or blackboard drawing, or real objects brought into the class. Practice was done through repetition drills and acting out little situations. Writing came last. The problem was very different from the ordinary secondary school, where a subject could be talked about at once. The only parallel was primary school level, where teachers talked less and used visual teaching and games more. At least our course started from the right end, being desperately needed and free of traditional academic fat. Tuition was intensive, partly to give value for money, partly because I felt it would be more effective if absorbing.

Theory occupied the morning. We produced pithy teaching formulas that trainees could use to tackle the foreign students' common problems with English grammar, introduced stage by stage. As the only people not to study their own grammar at school except for parsing, the British had only the vaguest idea of English grammar, especially from a foreigner's point of view. In her pronunciation seminars Brita showed the trainee teachers ways of helping students adopt English sentence stress and intonation and overcome problems with sounds. On the methodological side, we dealt with the platitudes of clear teaching techniques: neat blackboard work, not going round the class in a predictable way with questions but keeping the unexpected and thus students' attention. The object as I saw it was to ensure that students got sixty minutes' learning' out of a sixty-minute lesson.

The course started with a Swedish lesson by Brita, to prove it was possible to teach without using a word of the students' language – an idea from Lionel Billow's excellent book *Practical Language Teaching*, one of the few 'modern' works then available. The retention level was amazing. It only lasted fifty minutes, but months or even years later we had former trainees greeting us with '*Hej! Kan jag få en kaffe?*' or '*Tack så mycket.*'

The core of the course was the live teaching practice, in the early afternoon. Monday morning's discussion was the basis of a lesson prepared that evening and taught on Tuesday. After each trainee had finished his or her ten-minute lesson, everyone discussed how it had gone and how it could be improved. The 'guinea-pig' students, who after all were the ones being taught, were also asked what they thought, though they tended to stick to how well the trainee had communicated: 'He not speak well,' or 'She write bad on blackboard,' or, pointing, 'She is best! *Molto viva!*'

The mini-lessons were commented on without aggression or malice, although as the course progressed trainees became more eager for negative criticism too, if it would help their teaching. It was best to start with positive comments and then talk encouragingly about what was not so good. Knowing their turn was coming, the trainees were seldom brutal. From 3:30, they observed our own classes, in pairs so they could discuss what they had seen. I believed observing a mediocre lesson was just as valuable as observing a 'good' one, because it made trainees analyse why. At the end, we did not give a 'certificate' but a report summarising the ability the trainee had shown, and awarded one of four frank grades: Oustanding, Good, Moderate and Below Average. When criticised for having only two weeks' training, we replied that ours was the only practical EFL (English as a Foreign Language) course we knew of.

As the number of courses grew, we needed more teacher trainers. We now had two particularly talented teachers on the staff, Roger Gannon and Ian Hammet. I got them to sit in on one of my courses, and then observed them. After all, we were essentially teaching obvious things about communication, not difficult to understand, only tricky to apply. These training courses added to the atmosphere. The staffroom buzzed with teaching ideas. Soon everyone had gone through the course, and most had become far less touchy about criticism, actually asking to be observed rather than regarding it as an ordeal. We all began to observe each others' classes regularly as an excellent way of maintaining standards, sharing information, and getting to know one another.

At first volunteer students paid nothing. But this meant irregular attendance and lack of commitment. So we started charging a small fee, meaning more lessons for very little extra, which also attracted new students. The British trainees were anxious to get to know the 'guinea pigs', as it might help them teach better. So our students got extra conversation practice with English people, something they often felt could never happen in cold, bustling London.

In 1962, teacher training became an essential part of the new International House, achieving indirectly my longheld aim of mixing nationalities by making them do things together, rather than just meeting with glasses in their hands. Interestingly, the outline of the course has remained the same over more than thirty years, with the same proportion of input, observation and teaching practice, while absorbing new attitudes and technologies, both 'functional' and 'communicative', and use of the language laboratory and video. It soon grew to four weeks. One enormous advantage was that we could keep the very best trainees for our own school, many later becoming trainers themselves.

As more and more new teachers were hatched, a new problem arose. We had always emphasized that we couldn't promise a job to all who had taken the course. Many wanted to teach abroad and we had only Cordoba to send them to. At the end of summer, when teachers were most wanted overseas, we gave lists of jobs available to trainees who had done well on our courses. This worked fine until the Sardinia catastrophe. A trainee who had done quite well on our course agreed to go to Cagliari. A bare month later she was back with a long list of complaints, just as a letter arrived from Sardinia complaining about her. Fortunately, we had stressed in writing that employment was not our responsibility and that a precise contract should be signed – which had not happened in her case. Something had to be done. We should have special links with reliable schools abroad to send teachers to. We had to know standards were reasonable and teachers well treated. And so, as a direct result of our teachers' courses, began our system of affiliated schools which was to spread all over the world.

PART 5

The World Our Oyster

26 · Algeria

Just at this time I met Michael Donelly, who had a large match factory in Tunisia. Idealistic about helping developing countries, he wanted to invest in newly-independent Algeria. This was close to my heart: it seemed common sense to help in every way possible, especially in the case of a French-speaking country which also needed English to trade and communicate. Through Neville Barbour, a specialist on North Africa, who had attended our course in Cordoba three years before, I had already met the unofficial Algerian ambassador in London. Michael Donelly and I agreed he would provide the finance and we the know-how for a school of English, sharing any profits 50/50, although it might be better to plough everything back in. Donelly, a caring, wealthy man, was among the first to read Arabic at university. If Algiers went well, he thought we might try Libya and perhaps even Jerusalem, then mostly Jordanian. I found this intoxicating. Prospects suddenly seemed limitless, particularly as we could now provide competent teachers. We might open up all over the developing world.

In April 1963 Air France took me from London to Algiers. During the two-hour stopover at Orly I had a delicious lunch, the prospect of which made my mouth water on every subsequent trip: *Omelette Parmentière* with *petits pois à la française* and half a bottle of Algerian wine.

To my surprise Algiers seemed very modern: tall buildings climbing up from the busy docks, the appearance of a Mediterranean French town, with small iron balconies and painted wooden shutters, like Nice or Menton. Although Algeria was now independent,

many French people had stayed. The streets and cafés seemed as full
as they presumably had been, the city alive with new-found liberty.
An *enseignant* was welcomed everywhere, in contrast to England
where saying you were a teacher usually earned a sniff. Taxi drivers
often refused my money when they heard I was going to start an
English school. Many walls had been painted white in a city clean-
up, and some had *Vive l'Education!* painted in large green letters.
This first trip was for reconnaissance. I had the address of a
journalist, Margaret Pope, from Neville Barbour: 'She'll be a great
help, knows the Arab world like the back of her hand.' Margaret
took me to a press conference where Ahmed Ben Bella, who had
started the rebellion in Oran in 1954 and was now president, talked
of the future like an excited child while Boumedienne, who commanded the army, said very little and looked round furtively as if
expecting assassination. Then we went to a reception where they
served only fruit juice. Margaret took me to meet the press, who
were interested in the prospect of an English school. The task now
was to find premises. Prospects were excellent. 'Why are the
Algerians so keen to learn English?' asked parochial Englishmen,
failing to realise that with our language we were sitting on a fortune.

My next trip, in the summer, almost felt like coming home, so
intrigued was I by this new post-colonial experiment, the sunshine
and the Mediterranean once again. I began to meet a lot of
Algerians, many immersed in the new tasks thrust on them by the
fleeing *pied noirs* who had left even the trains without drivers. I met
the man in charge of telecommunications, his qualification being
that he had once worked with a French telephone engineer, but only
on wires outside houses, an Algerian not having been allowed into a
colonial French home. While I was establishing the school, there
was all the improvisation of a novice government taking over from
experienced administrators. I went to see the Chef de Cabinet of the
Minister of Education in a low, modern building without an
appointment, and got a document giving my school official approval
before it had opened. I also became friends with the Chef de
Protocol, a red-haired Kabyle in an old tweed sports jacket, just
back from a Pan-African conference in Addis Ababa with a potent

honey liqueur which he insisted on sharing one evening in the Préfecture. In the vast empty hall with very little furniture, once bustling with colonial administrators, we found two chairs and a small table. The liqueur was foul. Rarely have I met such an ill-tasting, explosively alcoholic liquid, blurring the senses at a sip, tasting of fermented acquavit. Joseph repeatedly refilled my glass and drained his own. There was no way out but guile. I poured some of my glass into his, and left him snoring in the vastness of the Préfecture, while I stole away swaying gently.

I found a big flat half-way up the hill overlooking Algiers. It seemed very suitable, with potentially four or five classrooms, a large reception area, teachers' and students' common rooms, on the second floor above the Rue Mohammed V and, on the other side, Algiers and down to the gleaming sea. After much discussion about not so much the rent as the inadequacy of Algerians and the way the *pieds noirs* had been betrayed by De Gaulle, everything was agreed. 'Le Centre Anglo-Africain,' as I called it, was born. I ordered classroom furniture from a carpenter who to my surprise was Jewish, typed out a brochure one night in my hot room right under the roof of my hotel, and arranged for advertisements to appear in a month's time.

This was done on the assumption that we would come out ourselves and repeat the Cordoba experience. But when I got back to London, difficulties arose. Among other things, our third child, little Charles, had been stillborn, having died of water on the brain only two days before his birth. As Brita was rhesus negative, it seemed essential to run no health risks. Who, then, would be a suitable director? I was considering advertising when our old friends, Guy and Angela Wilson, returned from a year's teaching in the States looking for a job. They seemed eminently suitable, having been with us for a while in Cordoba before starting their own school in Salamanca. We met in a pub in Shaftesbury Avenue and I sounded them out. They were very enthusiastic. All that remained was to find teachers.

This was where our training courses came into their own. We had actually seen candidates doing teaching practice, revealing much

about character and ability. I was fortunate never to interview with
only references and a CV to go on. Looking back, I think it would
have been impossible to select good teachers for schools all over the
world by talking to candidates 'cold'. In turn, the candidates knew
something about us from the course, and had little of that suspicion
which a job abroad can so easily engender. We also knew they had
got 'outstanding' or 'good' on the course, although they only knew
the basics after just two weeks. At least they had some general
knowledge of techniques and problems and the confidence to get up
in front of a class on their first day, and some were surprisingly
good. There were also those who seemed promising but got miserable grades; sometimes I would suggest they do the course again
without paying. I can think of two who did, one now high up in
BBC English and another one of our school directors. We got the
cream ourselves – although, as we gradually found out, short courses
favoured the bright extrovert but could be unfair to the slower,
more reflective trainee.

Back in London, I prepared the things needed for a new school –
text-books, tape recorders, cork boards and posters. They would
cost a fortune to send by air, so the Wilsons and I went to Marseilles
by train, and thence on the three-hundred-mile sea journey to
Algiers. When we told Algerian customs we were starting an English
school, we were waved through with our mountain of equipment.
Guy employed Margaret Pope as school secretary and registered an
amazing 400 students in three weeks. When the school was inaug-
urated in October, the Wilsons invited all the local celebrities and
hired some Ghanaian dancers to start off in true international style.
In London I found the extra teachers they needed and sent them off
post-haste.

Following the Algiers success, Mike Donelly was anxious to
explore possibilities in Libya, and I reconnoitred. I dropped in on
Algiers on the way, observing classes and holding teacher seminars.
The staff occupied some one-room flats, and the Wilsons had settled
in on the third floor, reached by a wheezy lift which, perhaps
symbolically, could be made to move only by inserting old-fashioned

five-franc coins left behind by the French, which had to be hunted
high and low and could be bought back *en masse* from the landlord.

27 · Lebanon and Libya

Unlike the Algerians, few Libyans lived in cities, being essentially a
desert people. Libya was colonised by the Italians only from 1912,
snatching it from the Turks, until 1943 when they were expelled by
the British Eighth Army. When I arrived, Libya was still under
British 'influence', and there was the big American Wheelus air base
not far from Tripoli. Desert campaign veterans came to re-visit. The
Italians had left fewer traces than the French in Algeria. There was
a cathedral, a good restaurant called the Romagna, and the magnificent Roman remains at Leptis Magna and Sabrathra. Tripoli consisted of an old Turkish fort near the main square, masses of shops
and houses, and newly-built villas for the Europeans with dusty
gardens choked by bougainvillea. The streets were covered with
yellow, sandy dust which the cars raised in clouds. Oil discoveries
were only just beginning. Libya had until recently been one of the
poorest nations in the world. There was a whole area of shantytowns just by the sea front. Ships lay at anchor beyond the palm
trees in the colourful bay. The hot wind blew sand from the desert
into one's mouth, to be ground between the teeth.

Tripoli was more obviously Muslim than Algiers, with veiled
women and very few Europeans. One Sunday morning, I watched
men standing in line for a brothel. I also visited the British Council,
whose scant English classes were run by a biology professor at the
new University, assisted by David Wilkins, later well known for his
'functional' approach to learning: by adding situation and mood to
grammar, he would revolutionise English language teaching in the
1970s. I ran into yet someone else from Oxford, Harold Sykes. He
taught in a secondary school where half the class had trachoma and

took turns in front, to see the blackboard properly. The disease was spread by the masses of flies which crawled over children's eyes in the villages, and would be cured by Gadaffi's oil money in the 1970s. I noticed that many adults had white marks on their eyeballs, the scars of trachoma.

To get permission for a school, I contacted an agent recommended by the British Embassy. Ali Majdani was a clever, voluble Palestinian, taller than most Libyans. Both a fixer and dignified, he flourished on bribes and what I presume were seedy deals. We would meet in a little patio outside my hotel. Once, I asked him which nationality he thought were the best businessmen. 'The Italians,' he answered unhesitatingly.

'And the worst?'

'Probably the Swedes.' I was puzzled until I realised that, to him, willingness to bribe was the true criterion of effective business management. He was well off and owned a house in Kensington. I asked him how much he would charge to get permission for our school. He waved his hand. 'Nothing! It's easy! The Director of Private Schools is a relative of mine. His son is married to my daughter!' Nevertheless, permission didn't come through. I returned to Tripoli several times and looked at possible premises. I found a couple of good directors in London, Ann and Derek Risley. They had both done the teacher training course and had taught in Cyprus. They were young, with three small children.

Permission still did not arrive. I told Majdani I would see the Director of Private Schools personally. He blanched.

'Actually – ' he began hesitantly, 'I've been meaning to tell you . . .'

'What?'

'Well, you see, we've had a quarrel.'

'What about?' I asked, irritated myself now.

'Well, he had the nerve to tell me there were too many flies in my daughter's house. When I told him it was none of his business, he said that if there were flies in a married woman's house there were also lovers. I got furious. We shouted at one another. I threw an ash tray at his head, and I haven't seen him since!' So our school was up against flies and putative lovers! I went to see the Director myself. He was dumpy and amiable, with a stubble beard, as if he had just got up.

'No problem!' he said, and signed the permission there and then.

I showed the document to the landlord of the building I liked best, a new, sprawling house, with rooms set round a tiled interior space. There were two floors, with enough room for the directors and some teachers to live there too. It was both cheap and central, although the road outside was being paved and new houses were going up all round. I went through the usual processes, though this time I got books and tape-recorders from a local supplier. The school started with three hundred adult students in the first few weeks, although the Risleys had to wait for furniture. When they were visited by Norman Reddaway, the Foreign Office man in charge of cultural relations in the Middle East, there were only orange boxes to sit on.

Mike Donelly now suggested Jerusalem. This meant advertising for a director. Nick Dobree and his wife Chloë were intrigued by our project, although Nick was hesitant about leaving his job at Aldermaston. He later told me that he thought the whole scheme seemed crazy. But gradually, after an initial interview and over dinner in Leicester Square, it began to seem more rational. Nick had taught for a year at a secondary school in Amman and enjoyed it. He had taken a first at Cambridge in mathematics and maintained that the best age for maths was before 24, after which the brain cells began to decay. He was in his late twenties, shrewd enough to see through bombast and self-deception, and not reluctant to speak his mind. There was also, underneath, a quick temper, particularly if an area he felt was his was threatened or invaded. But he had great humour and integrity, made his mind up very quickly, and then went ahead whatever the odds.

In Jerusalem we stayed at the YMCA, then on the border between the Arab and Jewish quarters with barbed wire below our window. I was enchanted by the Holy Places, the narrow streets, the underground reservoir, the Mount of Olives. But Nick had been there before and was not interested in tourism. I was rushed off my feet by his determination to get everything finished as rapidly as we could. We did visit the Armenian quarter, with its narrow entrance which one swordsman could defend alone; but there was not even time to see the Dome of the Rock.

As always, there was great interest in English classes and we found perfect premises, central, roomy and cheap. But the education minister, whom we both knew, told us the Jordanian cabinet had decided to prohibit investment in Jerusalem. A firm applying to invest massively had turned out to be Jewish, and the public feared the whole of Jerusalem would be bought up in this way; even an English school might arouse suspicion. But we could certainly go to Amman or Ramallah. We were too disappointed to be really interested. We phoned Mike Donelly and he felt the same. Nick returned via Beirut, which we had passed through on our way out, and met Mary Zeine. Her husband, Zeine Zeine, was a history professor at the American University of Beirut. Mary was an alert middle-aged woman with a Scottish grandmother of whom she was very proud. She had a small English school and might agree to combine it with Nick's if he started one.

I went to Beirut again. It was, then, the playground of the Middle East. In April, you could swim in the sea in the morning and drive up to the mountains to ski in the afternoon – although Nick didn't allow much time for such things. We chose a building which was ideal: we could have the whole ground floor, seven rooms, set back from traffic noise in a little courtyard, with an attractive gallery on the first floor. The sheltered situation would also protect it in the civil war which was to break out twelve years later, though of course we could not know that. We signed an agreement with Mary Zeine who, cautiously, would only agree if our London school would come in with Nick. This was fine by me provided we had no liability and sufficient profit to cover the costs of servicing the Beirut school centre and supplying teachers.

28 · Deep On the EFL Trail

My idea was not only to develop a language school but also to have all the facilities which blended naturally with it. These included teacher training, a canteen, a bar, a lecture-room, a bookshop, an au-pair bureau, a travel agency, and a social office to organise theatre and concert outings, excursions, and talks. We also needed a library and a welfare, information and advice bureau. I saw International House as the name of the overall organisation, the International Language Centre being part of it, teaching both English and other languages. We gradually added new activities: a teachers centre for monthly talks by EFL pundits; the magazine *Modern English* which we took over, with Charlotte Eastwood as editor, an energetic young woman who had worked for the *Economist*. She also designed International House Christmas cards and more stylish prospectuses. She generated the first teacher training magazine, *Modern English Teacher*, edited by an experienced trainer, Helen Morwood, which proved a good repository for our own new teaching ideas.

40 Shaftesbury Avenue, a vast empty building in the heart of London, gave us the opportunity for all this. We burrowed like mice from floor to floor, even from house to house in adjoining Rupert Street, chasing out the pigeons and employing our students to clear up and re-paper the rooms, while we installed off-peak central heating in massive steel cases in each. Jane Glover, one of our teachers, painted an imaginary cloud city on the wall of the canteen. By 1970 we had rented ninety rooms, just a few hundred yards from Piccadilly Circus. We were constantly demolishing or constructing partition walls, with the help of Manny, the electrician with a shop downstairs, our carpenter Peters, and Mr Bestavachvili, the builder, who spoke English without using 'the'.

When we took the top floor, I came up against a fire-brigade requirement that nothing could be over forty-two feet from the ground, the length of their ladders, without a separate fire-escape. The fire officer and I solemnly measured and counted the stairs: eighty-four of them, each six inches high, making exactly forty-two feet.

Our first canteen was started by one of our first teachers, Colin McMillan. When he went to Lisbon to start a school, it was taken over by Salvatore Fugallo from Palermo and his English wife Kate. Salvatore was a brilliant cook and organiser but had fierce Sicilian pride, expressed in gruffness and a perpetual frown which frightened even our Italian students. Salvatore would lurk behind a multi-coloured bead curtain while the charming Kate would deal with the students. But he would often catch an opinion or snatch of conversation, particularly if it was a complaint. The curtain would tremble and he would leap out like a leopard in the high jungle grass. 'What you say?' he would growl, while the wretched student, or sometimes teacher, looked terrified.

I had been best man at their wedding, and Salvatore was very loyal. 'You are the father of this school,' he said once in feudal mood, 'and I am a son!' When I told him my old watch had cost me £3, he looked at it with scorn.

'You were married when you got that watch?' I did not see the relevance.

'I don't think so . . .'

'And you get your wife with that watch?' he asked incredulously, as if marriage depended entirely on the riches one could display.

Salvatore once went on strike, despite the blandishments of Tony Thompson whom I had appointed school director as I was so often abroad. We had a weekly meeting for department heads and Salvatore was supposed to provide lunch. One week some idiot met him on the stairs carrying a tin of Kit-e-Kat and said 'I hope that's not our lunch!'

No lunch appeared. Tony Thompson went to investigate. He came back looking pale and mumbling about 'Kit-e-Kat' and 'refusal to serve lunch'. I went in to see Salvatore and persuaded him it was only a joke. He gradually calmed down and provided lunch, very late and served not by him but his assistants.

We allowed Salvatore and other entrepreneurs a moderate profit. They paid what their premises cost us in rent and rates, and made what reasonable surplus they could. Some people thought that with all these separate activities I should have used a single company, to make more money. But I favoured the Spanish expression, 'every owl to its own olive tree'. I didn't want to run a complex firm with endless financial intricacies. Britain at this time was the richest country in Europe. I was interested in not charging people from other countries too much, and at the same time having a top-quality school. This may have sounded tremendously virtuous, but it gave me little credit. I took only a small salary because I had sufficient royalties from *Getting On In English*, and I didn't want to pay 65% in taxes. Better to plough it back into the school when I could. My background had given me little training in business: my father in the army, grandfather in the judiciary, my uncles and cousins and Brita's relatives all journalists, teachers or writers. My brother and I had been educated as 'toffs', virtually free. This gave me the feeling that almost anything could be done without money. We now lived in a world that was socialist in ideas if not in practice.

The history of post-war Britain will surely be recorded as the battle between state and private enterprise, politics reflecting this in all sorts of complicated ways. As our fringe organisation grew, we found people envied what they imagined was our wealth. They were indignant that as a private firm we claimed to be making a large contribution to English language teaching and expected to be considered in the same breath as official organisations such as the British Council and universities. Other private language schools jealously refused to think us different from them, although they were happy to upgrade their staff from our training courses. Now extended to four weeks, they gave a hundred hours including forty of teaching practice, with class observation on top. This made them a concentrated equivalent of most postgraduate university courses. As we grew, people swarmed in off the streets. The more facilities we provided, the more students we attracted; this covered the costs of new ventures, which in turn generated more student fees.

Brita met Ann Mills, at her small travel agency and accommodation bureau in Greek Street – just what we needed. We invited her to rent an office on our third floor. Ann was a member of the famous Forbes-Robertson theatrical family. Her sister was married to Ralph Richardson, the celebrated actor, reputed to have come home with a loaded revolver, fired it into the ceiling and shouted in his inimitable crabbed tones, 'Someone's been fucking my wife!'

Ann was beautiful, about forty, with gorgeous blue eyes, and married to George Mills the film director. Near her office was Vera Traill's au-pair agency. Vera was Russian, the daughter of General Guchkov, one of the two officials who accepted the tsar's abdication in the imperial train. He had been Kerensky's hated war minister in the provisional government that succeeded the tsar, only to be swept away by the Bolsheviks. Vera had been saved from the revolution being very thin, and had been sent to the Crimea to live in the sun and drink goat's milk when she was eleven – with her mother, who was such an optimist that when chased and finally arrested by the Red Army, she just roared with laughter. Vera remembered her chortling in amused disbelief, 'But you're not going to shoot me!' In the end, the soldiers hadn't the heart to harm her. She moved to Paris, where she crossed streets with contempt for motorists until one finally got her. Despite her father's imperial monopoly on glass, Vera was very poor, existing entirely on her agency. She was half-blind, and had to hold everything up close to her thick-lensed spectacles. She was madly possessive of her grandson, and tried to kidnap him from her daughter when he was six, at one point involving an International House teacher in a break-in plot. She was a frantic worker, interviewing au-pair girls and telephoning families while she puffed away at Gauloises and chain-drank Beaujolais.

This was London in the sixties. I heard my first Beatles record when I came back from Algiers in 1963. Metaphorically, the sun shone. Students of all nationalities streamed in. I think now that we charged too little. We were in central London, we offered some of the best teaching available, orienting tuition to students' linguistic need.

One preoccupation was to get the right atmosphere in class. We started a minor furniture revolution. Instead of the traditional rows of tables and chairs which blocked communication by giving students only the backs of each others' heads to look at, we got chairs made with small side-desks, placing them in a semi-circle towards the teacher, so that everyone could see and talk to each other directly – allowing for more movement. It also made handling of books, and especially writing, less convenient, which meant students raised their heads and listened and spoke more. We brought this more flexible, informal arrangement to schools all over the world.

It struck me one day that if we used theatre so much in the classroom, why not actually teach English in a theatre with an audience? Our Christmas parties had become too big to have in the school. We hired Chelsea Town Hall, which seemed a good place to try out the idea. A group of volunteer English teachers worked to create sketches containing common idioms or grammatical structures. Our audience of predominantly foreign learners would be asked to repeat phrases from these sketches by the 'major domo', a role filled by a talented teacher called Jeremy Harrison. On party night the experiment proved a great success. Christopher Dilke, now publishing my *Getting On In English* (the inflatable umbrella replacing the instant whisky as the Arabs and Scandinavians objected to the whisky), was interested in getting the sketches broadcast. I found a theatre to rent of the right size, belonging to the Conjurors' Magic Circle in Gower Street. Christopher Dilke delegated an able young man he had just taken on called Piers Plowright as theatre director of the new venture. Piers had already written a book called *Talk English* with sketches for learners of English. It had a surrealist, Kafkaesque approach which appealed to all nationalities alike.

The English Teaching Theatre, as I christened it, opened in the summer when there were the most students. We charged for entrance, and it was packed. Piers wrote most of the sketches, but I wrote one which had a strong publicity effect, about a striptease. It practised two tricky structures in English: 'going to' and 'have just'. A girl I called Mimi came on, overdressed with a jumper and a skirt. The music struck up and she held up her gloved hands. 'What's Mimi going to take off?' asked Jeremy, and answered himself: 'She's going to take off her gloves!'

Mimi took off her gloves. Jeremy asked 'What has Mimi just taken off?' 'She's just taken off her gloves!' he answered.

The process was repeated with the audience answering, as Mimi's jumper, skirt, and blouse, each of which she indicated in turn, came off. Finally she stood there in bra and panties, while the music throbbed. Then came the roar of a voice from the back of the hall: 'This is disgusting!' Everything came to a halt and a 'policeman' came up and said the show was closed for indecency, just in time for the interval!

A few days before the first night, I called the press to announce our new experiment in drama and English teaching. I sent them programmes. The *Daily Mirror* rang back to ask if they could take photographs. A cameraman appeared at rehearsal. He seemed particularly interested in the striptease. The first night went well, although none of the newspapers came. But next day a *Daily Mirror* page two headline said the BBC was organising a 'teaching strip-tease', with a picture of Mimi in her underwear writing on a blackboard and Jeremy supervising with a mortar-board. Christopher Dilke was mentioned, as director of English by Radio, but International House was not. We were bombarded with phone calls from newspapers. Canadian television came to a show, of course interested in nothing but the striptease. Christopher was under a cloud with the BBC. But it passed, and his already rakish reputation was enhanced.

The English Teaching Theatre became part of International House. Jeremy's group got an office in the 90-room labyrinth and, with the addition of two other teachers, Ken Wilson and Doug Case, went from strength to strength. We insisted it become self-supporting as soon as it could, so it toured schools abroad as a paying attraction. Mimi was a professional actress. But we generally preferred to employ people with English teaching experience who could understand the language problems and be teachers as well as actors. Without this, we found, there was an element missing.

Variations on the drama theme involved sketches for students to act in English, as part both of the social programme and of a new beginners' book, *Action*, which Brita and I were writing. Speaking another language is a form of acting. One changes, one tries to become a person of the other culture. Acting out scenes seemed an excellent means to this end. Later at the new IH school in Madrid, Roger Hunt got the students to write a play in English as well as direct rehearsals and video it, each student given a copy to keep. Students seldom resist this colourful and varied, yet challenging activity. Only once did I have a group – some Japanese – who thought it was 'not real' work. The teacher must give rein to his or her dramatic talent. Many are too self-conscious, worried about losing control, about making too much noise, about a process they think has no ordered syllabus or proof of what students are learning. They may find it 'childish', or too 'experimental'. In all of this, my slogan was always, to use a facile expression, that 'English is fun', and I have never seen any reason why it shouldn't be – or indeed why any classroom situation shouldn't be. There are always a few disapproving souls, perhaps 'sound' teachers with excellent results but bound by the masochistic idea of western education that you only learn if you toil, sweat and weep. Our educational backgrounds had marked us all.

29 · A Further Touch of German

'Of course I feel guilty – '
'Why should you? You had nothing to do with it. You were too young. You're only twenty-eight.'
'Maybe. But I can't forget!'

I was talking to Trudi Wacht, a student from East Germany. Her parents had been active Nazis from the start. She had lived in Danzig, towards the end of the war bombed ceaselessly by the Russians. She remembered the shelters, the people committing suicide during the perpetual bombardment, the trees used as gallows for deserters, a man hanging from each with a placard saying he had betrayed the Fatherland. Trudi got a bomb splinter in her thigh. Her father, head of the local seaborne fire brigade, fled with his family to Lübeck. Trudi ran away when she saw her first British soldiers, and was later surprised that they weren't 'bogeymen' but kind, with smiles and sweets. We met Trudi in 1962. Most of our German students were aware of their horrific Nazi heritage. As Brita once said, it was terrible to think that a civilisation with such culture and history and beauty could do such injury to itself. It sometimes made our Germans aggressive, contrasting their bright new Germany with Britain's strikes and industrial problems.

The endless war films on British television were irritating. The German soldiers – who looked like our students – were still the 'baddies', although the war had ended twenty years earlier. Interestingly, German au-pairs were popular with Jewish families – certainly not the work of Vera Traill who was very careful in this respect. Perhaps it was because the families often had German-sounding names, and language and cultural similarity drew them together. But living in the same house could be a strain. A German girl called Waltraud lived with an edgy Jewish lady, who finally exploded and called her a 'bloody German'. Waltraud also lost her temper and called her a 'bloody Jewess'. They looked at each other for a moment in horror, aware of the taboo they had broken, and then collapsed in tears, saying they hadn't meant it, and got on famously thereafter.

The Italians, not remotely concerned with their country's role in the war, were our most lively students. We called them 'pepper and salt', as they would invariably liven up a class, endlessly talkative and cheerful abroad. (Later in Rome, we found students more formal, perhaps worried about making fools of themselves in front of people they knew.) All the 'Latins' were obsessed with grammar, taking it down laboriously instead of actually participating in a class. The French and Spanish complained if they didn't get enough grammar. The French demanded the rules on the blackboard, and only when they had copied it to make it 'theirs' could you get on with the lesson. I love the French, was at school in their country, and find it sad to try and remove a French girl's pretty accent. Yet our French students were more sullen than most. People accustomed to imposing their own culture, rather than absorbing someone else's are not the best language learners. We found the British, French and Spanish the worst linguists, and the Italians, Germans, Dutch and Swedes, their imperial experiences at best fleeting and remote, among the best. The French seemed trapped, perhaps because of the centuries-old rivalry with English in diplomacy and culture. They often called English 'commercial', although seldom actually added 'a nation of shopkeepers'. They were rarely inventive, reluctant to embark onto unknown seas. French culture is dominated by abstract ideas – one reason for their obsession with grammar rules. They wanted to speak 'good' English, which often meant they didn't speak at all.

Through our Algerian school we had some seventy Algerians, sent by the John Brown Group which would then employ them on the pipeline at Arzew. They just saved us from bankruptcy, as we had invested in one of the first language laboratories, built and marketed by a Welsman called Conn-Evans. The cost, including the masses of tapes necessary, and the tiny salary of Alan Wakeman in charge, was more than our overdraft would stand.

'You're just trying to grow at our expense!' accused my grumpy bank manager, apparently still living in a pre-industrial age.

'Of course I am! I'm trying to borrow more money for a very worthwhile venture!' I responded icily. 'What else do you think banks are for?' The John Brown Group said the Algerians would come for five hours a day and promised an advance. I thanked them heartily and changed banks with delight.

The Algerians were better at learning English than their recent masters, the French. For one thing, they already had two languages to feed on, Arabic and French. This first group included one of my best-ever students, Rayan. Starting as a beginner in October, he passed the Cambridge Proficiency exam in June. He and others had confidence, and no sense of being 'colonials', automatically inferior to westerners. A more timid soul told me, 'If I hear someone laughing, I always assume they're laughing at me.' We also began to have Libyans, including a sheikh who spread his prayer mat outside the classroom to pray twice a day. They were less excitable than the Algerians. The English families they stayed with complained they were difficult to talk to, even if their English was good enough. They radiated benevolence rather than expressing it and saw no point in discussion or small talk, partly because there was little common ground for discussion. They were unused to criticism. Two of them got only moderate reports and the comment that they had not done enough homework: the row went right back to Tripoli. A Libyan newspaper was fiercely critical of the London school and its 'racist' course reports, and called for the Tripoli school to be closed. 'Please, please,' wrote Derek Risley from Tripoli, 'never criticise a Libyan. Say they are wonderful, are excellent at English, have made fantastic progress! Anything to avoid them feeling hurt.'

By the late sixties we were getting every nationality. No sooner had I said our students came from every country except Andorra, than I met one at the next new students' party. It was a boom time for IH. Although no teachers, including Brita and me, made much money, there was a sense of things going well – the English Teaching Theatre, new schools abroad, and our language laboratory experiments. The amazing Alan Wakeman produced *English Fast*, a pioneer course for use in both classroom and laboratory. There was a sense of breaking new ground and improving quality. I still taught and observed classes, but delegated a lot of supervision to directors of studies, responsible for planning morning, afternoon and evening classes. There was a very open atmosphere: anyone with a new teaching idea could demonstrate it during the weekly teachers' meetings.

Around now we had our first Japanese student, precursor of the masses we would get ten years later. This man, a kamikaze pilot, had been due to divebomb an American aircraft carrier, samurai sword at his side, on the very day peace was declared. From fanatic willing to sacrifice his life for his emperor, he had come to think like a civilised individual. 'Sometimes, I list in my mind all I would have missed if the war had lasted a day longer!' he told me emotionally. 'The friends I have made, the places I have visited, the things I have learned! All would never have existed!'

Our first students from red China came at this time, to improve their English before going on to Birmingham University. They missed the Trans-Siberian Express and arrived a week late. As all twelve were at the same level we put them in a class together, enabling their teacher to concentrate particularly on Chinese difficulties, and help them adapt more easily. Next to them was a class mainly of Italian priests, who gravely paced the corridor during breaks as if they were at a Curia. From behind a door, suspicious Chinese faces would peep round and then withdraw resentfully. Thinking them unwilling, perhaps unable, to break through this phalanx of ideological enemies, I invited them to take coffee at Salvatore's en masse. Up we went, a whole procession. I ordered coffee for all and reached into my pocket.

'No,' they said, 'We must pay! We do not accept gifts!'

I was put out. 'Not even hospitality?'

'Not even hospitality!' they insisted gravely. Even a cup of coffee could be a bribe. Who knew what might follow? Demands for the atomic potential of the Great Wall? Further complications followed. Students were supposed to do homework, and to write a letter or a composition. Despite continual blandishments, the Chinese did neither. They took offence easily. After a week, we split them off to different classes. One teacher asked whom the students most admired, and the Chinese of course said Mao. Why? They talked about the Long March and everything Mao had sacrificed for China, and said that he was very fond of swimming, which they pronounced 'wimmin'. This made the teacher and the other students laugh, and the Chinese felt their national honour had been impugned.

Their leader came to see me, furious. Not only had their Leader been insulted: another class had been discussing nuclear power and someone had said the real menaces to world peace were France and

China. How could people be allowed to say such a thing? Perhaps it was true of France, but China was well known for its peaceful attitude to other nations. I tried to explain that ours was a free country, that we often criticised even the royal family, that people could say what they wanted. He dismissed this with a sweep of the hand. 'We are not British,' he said, emphasising the obvious, and added, 'Peking is more important than London.'

'Yes, yes,' I placated him.

'I want all political discussion stopped in this school!' he barked as if addressing a political minion. 'We are here to learn English, not to be insulted!'

I looked at him pensively. We were now into negotiations. 'Very well,' I said, 'I will forbid all political discussion in the school – but only if you do your homework regularly and hand it in for correction.'

We both knew why the self-important Chinese did not write compositions: they imagined their masterpieces being handed over to MI6 and culled for secrets. They probably got their instructions from Maida Vale, where I knew they lodged and received indoctrination.

His expression changed, wooden rather than triumphant. 'Yes . . .' he began.

'OK? We agree.' I held out a hand and he shook it limply. We only met once more, on Primrose Hill when we were playing piggyback with our children Jimmy, Richard and Katinka. We saw a group of Chinese coming down the hill, the women separate from the men. We smiled and waved as they passed.

Our only other communist country students were at Westfield College, at the summer course we ran with the BBC and the English-Speaking Union, where Longmans and other publishers gave scholarships to Poles, Czechs, and the occasional Russian. I remember best a Czech, who later sent me a book about his escape from the Eastern bloc. At Westfield he fell in love with a French girl. Sent on a trade mission to Algiers, his one idea was to escape to France and marry her. He stole a pedalo from the beach, to pedal across the Mediterranean to Spain. He set off one evening with what he hoped was enough food and water, a blanket, a torch and a compass, and pedalled through the night, past the lights of fishing boats. He pedalled all the following day and rested a bit the next night, drifting, wrapped in his blanket, till dawn.

On the third day he saw a steamship making straight for him. He waved and it stopped to pick him up. To his horror, it was Polish. To disguise himself, he said he was English, which seemed to explain everything. 'Who but an Englishman would try to pedal across the Mediterranean?' he heard the crew say in Polish. When the ship reached Genoa, he rang the French consulate and explained his situation. They picked him up at the docks, gave him some money, and paid his rail ticket all the way to his beloved. She was amazed to see him again, and married him soon afterwards.

Another picturesque student was Kisoon, a Korean student of Brita's, typical of someone swirled between Orient and Occident. She could still speak the Japanese she had been compelled to learn as a child. Wounded at nineteen in the Korean war, she was rescued by Chinese forces and taken to Peking, where she enrolled at the famous art college and met a Czech sculptor who swept her off to Prague. Her large poetic tapestries became celebrated. Now, years later, in her English class in London, her enforced Japanese worked magic when she comforted a timid girl from Tokyo in her own language. They became firm friends. When Brita organised an exhibition of Kisoon's works at International House, the Japanese girl brought her tycoon husband and a South Korean friend from Korean Airlines. He was so bowled over by Kisoon's art that he flew her and her Czech husband to South Korea and laid on a nationwide exhibition. He also helped trace two of her sisters in Seoul from whom she had not heard since the Korean war.

We must have taught some twenty thousand students in the sixties and seventies in London alone, many from tumultuous backgrounds. They studied for an average of four months, going home, we hoped, a little richer, in both English and tolerance. The number of political refuges increased in the seventies, and we gave free classes to anyone recommended by an official refugee organisation.

It was because of one of these refugees that I met Margaret Pope again. She rang to ask if we had a class with no Algerians. She was looking after an Algerian refugee called General Sbiri, who had bombarded Algiers with jets in an unsuccessful coup against Boumedienne. I found him a beginners' class with no Algerians and he turned up one afternoon, a short, serious man of about forty. Margaret came too, and we all went to a pub before Sbiri's next evening class. He hadn't done his homework, and sat stubbornly revising *English Fast* while we talked. It was strange to think that this small, earnest man could so easily have taken over a whole country, instead of preparing for an English beginner's class and sipping warm beer in a London pub!

In many ways, International House was the place to get to know the world. If you were learning or teaching, there might be several nationalities in your group, all of whom you could get to know well. There was a magnetic atmosphere in any class. There were no discipline problems because the students were adult. The teacher was their one dependable safety line, their source of advice in a puzzling land, their fount of English. This could be a great ego stimulant for teachers but also brought responsibility; professional and personal contentment depended on students' progress and satisfaction. People were often perplexed that I never seemed to tire of EFL. Rules and explanations might not change, but the students were always different – varied personalities, countries, and experiences.

Although things were better for our students than when we had started in the early sixties, the welfare bureau at the entrance was always crowded. In true international style, it was manned by a Canadian girl called Gill, a French student called Mauricette, and an English volunteer, Liz Prince. There was still a sense that most students were poor, needed English for their careers, and could be swindled by incompetent amateurs. At International House, they came to feel safe.

30 · Allies in Italy

One of our first affiliated schools was in Italy, run by Dottore Ausonio Zappa, an Italian of about thirty with thick hair combed back, a Roman nose and a beaming expression. He came to us one summer with a group of his pupils in Rome. He improved his own English in a class of Brita's.

Ausonio was playful and easily moved, and we became good friends. From near Turin, he regarded the Romans with mistrust, and discussed leaving the school he worked at and starting an independent English school in Rome. Could we help? Perhaps we could send him English teachers, give a teachers' course? I went to Rome, looked at Ausonio's school, and three classrooms in the Via Appia Nuova became part of our international organisation. Brita and I gave a fortnight's course to a group of highly talented British trainees there.

Ausonio then started bringing in his family as traditional Mediterranean-style school owners, although they had never taught in their lives. His sister started a school in Seregno, a small town near Milan, which flourished with the help of a good director of studies, Marcella Banchetti, who had lived in Liverpool when young. I had to object when Ausonio's aunt started a school in Erba, another small northern town. She spoke no English, had no idea what a language school was all about, was tight-fisted, and infuriated the teachers we sent her. I told Ausonio I would have nothing to do with his aunt. When she came to London, I refused to see her. She roamed the corridors for days, disconsolately looking for me. She did not know what I looked like. We actually met in a corridor and she asked me to direct her to 'Signor Haicraf's office'. Strangely, I didn't know where it was!

I started writing an official affiliation agreement. It stressed that no teacher could be employed by an affiliated school without at least a grade B on the teacher's course. A school could only affiliate after a visit by an IH London representative. A teacher trainer would visit annually to observe classes and give seminars. A yearly meeting of all affiliated school directors would discuss the non-profit fee, to go towards the expenses of what we began to call the central department. The idea was to ensure teachers were employed honestly and fairly, and taught well. Failing either of these, a school would be warned, and if necessary disaffiliated.

We became increasingly involved with Italy. We needed a larger building in Rome for a proper IH school with teacher training and Italian classes. Colin McMillan already had a splendid building in Lisbon, whose inauguration I went to. He had started teachers' courses, for teachers of both adults and children, and offered Portugese classes too. In September 1967 Michael Williams, director of studies at the Via Appia Nuova school, rang to say they had found a wonderful building near the Termini railway station. I flew out with Donald Biddle, a partner of the Smith & Williamson accountancy firm, a good friend and ally, sound ballast for my more impulsive ideas. We stayed in a private house recommended by Ausonio, where we were kept awake by an illuminated religious picture on the wall, and a cockerel which appeared on the balcony to crow lustily at five each morning.

The building thoroughly deserved the name *palazzo*. There was a spacious entrance, with windows giving onto a small garden. The white marble staircase went up three floors to a roof terrace. The large, elegant rooms with parquet flooring would make ideal classrooms. There was even a small theatre in the basement, and a fully-equipped cinema. Living quarters were at the top, with small rooms giving onto a terrace. The only problem was that the premises had to be taken quickly, or someone else would snap them up. If we wanted to open that year, we had to start immediately, the main months for enrolment being September and October. We asked Ausonio to rent the house, agreeing to share the expenses of setting up the new school.

Back in London, I got Brita enthused. Quixotically, we decided to go ourselves, as we would never find a suitable director at two weeks' notice. This meant letting our house and taking our two eldest children out of school. We would drive out, with our new, pretty Angolan Portuguese au-pair, Maria Alice. She was amazed to realise she would be studying English in Rome rather than London. But she reckoned we were presumably coming back and was intrigued. We rented our house to a doctor from Aden who proved extremely reliable, and were soon speeding across to Calais, where we put ourselves and the car on the overnight train to Milan. I recalled my earlier delight with the American tourists, when leaving the staid, rainy north, to spring through the Alps to Stresa and the first Italian lakes. This time we stopped at Florence, had grapes and great bowls of coffee for breakfast in the sun, and then went round the town with the family in a horse carriage.

We reached Rome on a gorgeous autumn evening, long shadows interspersed with splinters of sunlit gold. Inevitably nothing was ready, so we stayed at a pension with hard beds. Brita went out to buy furniture and mattresses. The only problem was getting Jimmy, our youngest son of three, used to the marble staircase. He would insist on climbing the banisters over the fifty-foot drop. I told him he would be killed if he fell, but he just said, 'What is killed? If I fall, I shall be mended in hospital!'

'No, you will be dead.'

'What is dead?'

I decided not to mention heaven: it might make death attractive.

'It means you sleep for ever.' He looked mystified.

'Everything is finished,' I added, 'it hurts and everything is black. No Mummy, no Daddy, no Richard, no Katinka. Alone. Just everything black. For always.' Of all this, I think he understood 'alone' and 'hurt', and above all my tone. We had no more banister climbing. He seemed no longer interested in them, or in death.

We gradually settled in, advertised classes, and ordered classroom furniture and a language lab from England. I employed Jane Glover, a London teacher who had also worked in Turin, as receptionist and spare teacher if student numbers swelled. Richard and Katinka went to the Lycée Français in the Borghese Gardens and didn't much like it – too formal compared to their London primary school, no celebrations, no nativity plays at Christmas. Jimmy went to a nearby Montessori school, dressed in a little white gown. As we walked him there, even grown men would stroke his blond hair, murmuring '*Biondino, bellino,*' as they passed, repeating the experience Colin and I had had in Alassio with the Arighettis. Jimmy became so popular, particularly with local shopkeepers' wives, that we became known as *il papà e la mamma del biondino*, the parents of the fair little boy. He once escaped Maria Alice and appeared stark naked, like a cherub off the wall, in reception, where some new students welcomed him enthusiastically.

By Christmas we had three hundred Roman students learning English and forty foreigners learning Italian. We could hardly get to our bathroom on the floor below for the crowd of students waiting for the language lab. Ten-year-old Katinka in her red dressing-gown became a familiar sight as she waited to wash before going to bed. We had once lived alone in this beautiful building. As we got more students, they began to cross the borders of our temporary home. In the cinema we showed a new English-speaking film every week, taking advantage of the fact that foreign films were always dubbed in Italy. In the theatre, we had teachers reading/acting parts in well-known plays, largely Oscar Wilde but also *Look Back in Anger*.

We had some brilliant Italian teachers – Giancarlo Luciani, Bruno Giuliani, Giancarlo Romano. I observed their classes and they mine, and they ultimately became Italian teacher trainers. At our first directors' meeting in the new Rome International House, we made observing Italian classes part of the programme, for I realised how much our teaching techniques had 'Latin' origins. Bruno and Giancarlo took to them naturally, in a way few Anglo-Saxon teachers did, at least regarding the personal, dramatic and situational approaches. It was as though we had absorbed a Cordobese approach to life, London-honed into a modern teaching methodology – or perhaps mine went back even further, to subconscious assumptions acquired in childhood in Alassio.

We built a bar in the basement. I wanted a plain one made of wood, but Ausonio insisted on one made of steel for a million lire, which I thought could be better spent on teaching aids. But Ausonio claimed, 'No one will come to a bar made of wood! – and in any case, wood is not *bello*.' I gave way. The gleaming structure, with resplendent basins and taps, certainly attracted a lot of custom. At least it served to balance out the language laboratory from England, delivered with Roland, a serious-minded expert provided by Cybervox to put their lab together. It arrived late one evening, helpfully unloaded but nothing else by the lorry driver, who left us and the crates standing on the pavement. We needed manpower. Hadn't Jane Glover complained about being endlessly pestered by men? I turned to her and asked,

'Can you go and find some men?'

She was soon back, with a young man whom I asked to carry a crate upstairs with me. Surprised, he did so without demur. When we came back down, Jane had lured another man. He and number one carried a second crate up. Jane produced yet more panting men, who ended up carrying the entire language lab to the third floor. We thanked them all warmly and they left, while Jane felt she had been revenged! Roland was delighted the equipment had arrived because he was getting bored. I had suggested he go sight-seeing, but he said he had taken new language labs all over the world and never visited anything. 'None of it's a patch on home!' he grunted, summarily dismissing the beauties of Rome for those of Wigan.

Christmas approached. The sun gave way to dull, cloudy skies. In the Piazza Navona, shepherds came in from the country to play their bagpipes. There were services for *il Bambino Gesù*, a tiny sacred doll. Brita fell ill the day term ended. And when we drove up to Roccaraso, a ski resort, Richard and I went straight to bed with flu. I had reserved late, so we only had a gloomy basement where Richard and I lay in bed attempting to play chess. As Brita said, we had worked too hard and only had time to be ill in the holidays.

Guy and Angela Wilson came out to replace us. They had bought a third of the new school. Ausonio owned another third, and the rest was owned by a company we had formed in London with a new wealthy name, Colonel Tom Hall.

31 · Bangkok and Osaka

Tom Hall was no doddering old colonel. Now 37, he had been the youngest colonel in the British army. He was very handsome. His pretty wife, Mariette, once claimed he was the best-looking man in London. They were both immensely rich. Each an only child, they had inherited their parents' fortunes. She was linked to WH Smith and Hornby toys, he descended from someone who had been a bank clerk in Johannesberg, when a man came in and showed him a nugget of gold. He left the bank and opened up an incredibly rich mine in partnership, from which his fortune originated. Mariette and Tom had a Georgian house at Chiselhampton near Oxford and six children with two sets of twins. Tom said he was determined each would inherit as much as he had. He struck me as totally honest. His father had steadfastly refused to allow his accountants to find ways of legally reducing his enormous tax bills. Tom was a client of Smith & Williamson, and Donald Biddle had asked me to meet him when he left the army. I remember sitting alone with him in the bar at International House while he told me what sort of thing he would like to take up next. I talked about how IH worked, and the projects I had in mind.

I suggested that IH put in the know-how if he contributed to any project on a 50/50 basis. He agreed to visit Japan with me, provided we went via Thailand, whose queen Mariette had known since school. We got advice from my cousin Francis King, who had lived in Japan for several years and written novels set there, as well as a man from the British Council who had once taken part in an official inspection of International House. He had the cheek to tell us, seriously, not to forget blackboards in classrooms in Japan. We boarded a Britannia turbo-prop, nick-named 'the Whispering Giant' by the press. It chugged over the Gulf and India, then up over

Burma to Bangkok. We slept most of the way, waking only for food like babies.

Bangkok was immersed in a sticky cloud of invisible steam with open canals called 'klongs' by the side of the roads. We went sightseeing, and were taken down the river in the royal barge. Prospects for an English school seemed excellent, although fees would have to be higher than those of other Thai language schools which used local teachers and sometimes had fifty students in a class. I insisted on a maximum of fifteen, to allow conversation. We would also have to pay the return air fare for teachers and give them British-scale salaries.

The only government organisation teaching English to adults was the American USIS. They were in the throes of applying 'behaviourist' dogma, teaching everyone through a rigid system of mechanical 'drills' and endless repetition. The students had to recite one exercise after another, everything 'pre-determined' to make all classes equally long, personal idiosyncrasies totally excluded.

'It's strange, but it works,' commented an American I met from the USIS, 'at least it has in Iran where we have a really large enterprise.'

We visited the colourful temples and shrines, painted in blue and gold. We were told how criminals were executed: by being shot at from behind sheets and hit at random, Buddhist principles forbidding the intentional killing of any creature. The majestic British embassy building stood in the middle of a great lawn, a splendid echo of imperial days. There we met dozens of princesses related in some way to the royal family, who promised to help our English school.

Accommodation looked like being easy and cheap. We found an ornate wooden building with eight potential classrooms and a palm tree in the garden, at low rent.

Then we flew on to Japan, landing at night, the best time to arrive in an unknown city. Tokyo was vast, clustered round the green island of the Imperial Palace with its broad moat. The impression was partly of shabbiness – low buildings, often made of paper, with no postal addresses, grouped on unpaved roads in the suburbs. The contrast was the offices, neon-lit and bustling, often in daring skyscrapers, the sun reflected on surfaces of blue and red glass. We did not linger in Tokyo, staying only to see Verner Bickley, the British Council reperesentative, who was most supportive. Then to Osaka in the 'bullet train', which seemed a miracle. Drivers who ran late were reputed to commit suicide. The speedometer in each carriage showed a steady 125 miles an hour. This was before the French TGVs or the modern TALGO. The bullet train seemed a symbol of Japanese modernity and enterprise, as did the long caterpillars of plastic greenhouses we could see in the fields, later imitated all over the world. We went to Osaka because of the 1967 Expo. It seemed a good opportunity to make available the English the Japanese might need. Remarkably few seemed to speak English. There were a reputed thousand English teachers in the state education system, but we found later that most of them could not speak a word, teaching being limited to reading and writing.

Osaka was a big industrial town whose only unusual feature seemed to be a gigantic mediæval castle out of a Kagasaki movie. I have never known industrial Britain, but Osaka was one of the most depressing cities I have ever seen in the rain. There was little smoke or dirt: it was more the greyness, unbroken slabs of concrete, alleyways between tall buildings, all smoothed to featurelessness by the dribbling rain. In the damp streets, uniform black umbrellas contrasted with the white nose bands of those who had colds and considerately avoided breathing their germs on others.

I had already corresponded with the director of the Chamber of Commerce, and we went to see him on our first day. He was enthusiastic. Through an interpreter he told us our school was just what Osaka needed now. He had always admired the British Empire, and seemed to think it still existed. He said it was good to send British people to teach their language. He even had premises ready, and showed us three classrooms, with office and reception areas, in the Chamber of Commerce building. It seemed fine for the time being, and we said we would confirm by Christmas. With many smiles, he invited us to a geisha show that evening. We didn't really know what Geishas were: not prostitutes, but perhaps 'courtesans'? We never really found out. To me they seemed like Egyptian mummies in kimonos, playing games with scissors and stones with staid business men in suits who suddenly cavorted around them like little boys. Perhaps they were for men who could not afford mistresses. In Japan, we were told, there was little guilt about sex, or getting drunk.

Nearby lay Kyoto, the capital of the emperor of Japan, formerly considered a sacred figure descended from the sun goddess. In Kyoto we stopped at a place where you caught and cooked your own fish. There were tanks with beautiful carp. You selected the size and price, and were given bait and a rod, with which you caught your fish without much trouble. You then roasted it yourself. Carp is the sacred fish of Japan because it shows neither fear or agitation. If you put one alive into a pan to fry, it does not move, unlike the excitable shrimp which jumps all over the place before a cruel death in boiling fat.

I found Kyoto interesting. Its temples and palaces seem too unfamiliar to European eyes. They form a complex of wooden beams enclosing small pebble gardens, with sacred stones. I remember once wondering, in Toledo, how some Japanese looking at El Greco's apostles could appreciate his mysticism. In Japan the symbols of Shintoism, with their geometric patterns and soothsaying charms, seem enigmatic to an outsider. In the same way, I felt no real sense of history in the United States. I am sure if you live in those countries long enough, you adapt.

From Kyoto, we took the 'bullet train' back to Tokyo. On the last night, which happened to be my birthday, we were invited to the Anglo-Japanese Society where a choir sang carols exquisitely. The big hall was crowded and everyone was given dinner boxes, with European or Japanese food. We left Japan the next day ('Have a good fright!' said the ground hostess) and set off for London via the North Pole.

I had enjoyed travelling with Tom, a civilised Etonian, who could be very entertaining, took an interest in national differences, and seemed to care for what we were trying to do with new schools. He was energetic with his money, worked hard on his farm near Oxford, and looked for 'causes'. He could have lived the life of a rich playboy, become paternalistic and adulterous, and finally retire into complacent somnolence.

After Christmas, we advertised for directors for Bangkok and Osaka. For Bangkok we got Robert Swan, a colourful character who had worked at the British embassy in Bangkok. He was engaging and knew Thailand. The candidate for Osaka was very different: a tall, serious Englishman in his thirties, ginger-haired, with an intent look. He had spent a year at a Buddhist monastery in Japan with his wife, also English, where they were only admitted after the ritual sitting outside in the snow for three days. 'The Japanese appreciate someone who has spent a year in a monastery,' he told me. 'Some firms send their employees there, or will only take those who are "graduates". It's a kind of test – like a public school,' he added with unconscious humour. Graham had also spent time in San Francisco, and was imbued with a combination of American management ideas and Japanese attitudes to life and society. He spoke fluent Japanese and was confident about building up schools, seeing the operation as a business enterprise adapted to Japanese needs, which he seemed to know so well.

I had doubts about his rigid attitudes. But the great thing in his favour was his confidence, his knowledge of Japan and the fact that he spoke the language. He knew little about the intricacies of teaching English, but would have a director of studies. Looking back, I am sorry we did not follow Brita's suggestion that all school directors should do a teachers' course to shake them out, to help them understand what we were all about. Of all our affiliated schools, those started by our former teachers tended to be the most successful and expand the furthest. Perhaps we needed a specific director's course? In any case, we chose simplicity, and in a few cases paid the price for it. Graham and Robert flew off to Tokyo and Bangkok respectively, to follow up the preparations we had made.

A few months later, I returned to see how they were getting on. In Bangkok, Robert had rallied his old friends and rented a building similar to the one we had looked at, with a palm tree in the garden.

Classes were going well although he found, as we had anticipated, that only the richer students, mainly from firms booming from the Vietnam war, could pay the fees – a pity because our aim was to reach the needy as well. Robert also found Thai students too shy and retiring for our teaching methods, bewildered by the 'dynamic' approach of the first teachers we sent out, though some of the Chinese seemed to welcome lively teaching. But we could not run separate streams. There were already Thai-Chinese tensions and this would have established a competitive situation, the last thing the Thais wanted. The Thai authorities limited immigration to strict national quotas, and places on the British list were scant. They understandingly agreed to put our teachers on a 'waiting list'. Our teaching was moderated by the climate. Air-conditioning was rare, and the pace somewhat lethargic, producing a compromise between Thai and Chinese preferences. The 7 a.m. classes I observed, avoiding the heat of noon, were more gently paced but still encouraged conversational participation, even from the more diffident Thais.

Thai girls must be among the most beautiful in the world, and there were complications on this account. Cindy, a blonde English teacher we had sent out, complained that a British company director used her as hostess at his dinners and cocktail parties, almost as if she were his wife – but there was nothing else. The old complaint, 'He just wants to go to bed with me!' was reversed to 'He just wants me to be his hostess at parties!' The director had a Thai girl-friend who knew no English, but with whom he would retire at the end of the evening. Cindy told me that she and a lot of European women felt clumsy and big-boned beside the exquisite Thai girls, although she had never been short of boy-friends in England. 'This is like Shangri-la,' she said. 'Suddenly it's as if you're old, and find that men no longer want you. This makes many relationships between Europeans break up!' Vowing to try to send only male teachers to Thailand in future, I flew to Osaka to see how the school was doing.

Graham had been successful, although classes were generally more subdued than in Europe. Conversation was 'bad manners' for Japanese girls. Graham had, however, taken the risk of getting teachers to call students by their first names, which helped because normally this only happened at home. It made some students almost as spontaneous as Italians. A few students seemed intrigued by our *gaijin* (foreign) ways, though they sometimes did not know the limits of a very different culture. Cathy Connolly, one of our trainers who spent two years in Japan, related an instance of this. After a free discussion about boy-girl relations in Japan and Britain, a student came up and asked if she was a virgin.

Knowledge of written and spoken English was also quite different. Some Japanese teachers of English who came to us for 'training' could speak no English. All we could do was to put them into a beginners' class, where they progressed rapidly, often taking the Cambridge Lower Certificate in six months. Like icebergs, they had an enormous mass beneath the surface; our job was to bring it up. The teacher's role was in some ways easier than elsewhere because the *sensei*, the teacher, is revered in Japan – though this could work negatively. Graham sacked a teacher, who took a waitressing job and served one of her students. 'You can't do that in Japan,' explained Graham seriously, 'The school loses respect and therefore students, however good classes are.'

Graham had devised the Business English Test, sold to firms and supposed to measure their employees' language ability. He said firms trusted the results; an employee who did badly might be refused promotion or be sacked. I was sceptical. Surely it was almost impossible to assess talent for languages through a kind of questionnaire-cum-psychological test. Someone who might appear to have no talent could suddenly discover motivation and confidence and become a brilliant student. But Graham said the test was Japanese-oriented, as if they were just differently-powered motor engines.

Back in London, I felt it was time to broaden International House's base. With Osaka and Bangkok and the schools already affiliated in Rome, Algiers, Tripoli, Lisbon, Beirut and Cordoba, with the teacher training, the English teaching theatre, the teachers' centre and the various magazines, it was all getting too intricate. It was all being run by one man, me, not even full-time at that, even if ably seconded by Brita, torn between her profession and three small children. So I founded a limited company with Tom and a new friend, Michael Delmear Morgan, a director of the Brown Shipley bank. He was descended from an English nurse made pregnant by Alexander II of Russia, whose children she was supposed to be looking after.

I was so untutored in the ways of the world that I became chairman of the company without realising it. This gave me little executive power officially, although I had a majority holding. It was all arranged by Donald Biddle, who hoped we would ultimately be quoted on the stock exchange.

PART 6

Strengths and Weaknesses

32 · Home

Our children were growing up. Katinka was sensitive with artistic tendencies and a lovely singing voice. She composed pieces on the piano and sang to her guitar, while Richard was wild and clever. Jimmy, the youngest, was pampered by all and had determined crazes: *Magnet* magazine, skate-boards, composing and playing music which he called 'pop-jazz'. He turned his room at the top of the house into a bizarre cave with carpets on the walls, angled lights, and joss sticks and bowls of pot pourri.

We still lived in Blackheath, but had sold our Span house for £6,000 and bought another for £5,000 with a crumpled roof which we had seen from the road and fallen in love with. It was built, we discovered from an ancient newspaper left in a partition, in 1827. There had recently been a fire in the attic, caused by a tenant chasing a mouse by candlelight. The whole room had been blackened like burnt toast, but was habitable once we had scraped off the cinders and soot and redecorated. A water pipe burst before we moved in, flooding down for a whole day from a tank in the roof. We loved that house: the unexpected corners, the wooden floors, the small study looking out onto the garden, the sense it had of a cottage in the country. My old friend from India, Peter Atkins, whom I had bumped into in Blackheath, thought the house looked frail. He bounced up and down on the wooden bedroom floor experimentally, so that it seemed about to crack. But it has survived to this day.

The garden, too, was wonderful, first with crocuses which seemed to form a blue pool reflecting a cloudless sky at the end of the lawn, then daffodils and tulips, camellias and forget-me-nots, laburnum and forsythia, fruit blossoms and a Japanese cherry-tree, like a fireworks display in March and April, and roses and clematis for the rest of the summer. Beyond our garden was a great woodland, inhabited by owls and foxes. When we moved in, there was still a pond fed by the narrow Kidbrooke with a rowing boat, under the green filigree of a weeping willow. But now most of it has silted up. The descendants of pears, plums, redcurrants and raspberries remained from the original estate's orchard, and a gnarled apple tree, which an old lady could remember being decorated with Chinese lanterns to celebrate Mafeking night!

From Sweden, Brita's mother Suzanne, now a widow, had bought a little cottage in Walberswick, a village in Suffolk near the sea. Suzanne used Walberswick as a staging post between Stockholm and London every summer, to see us and the children and to go to the Aldeburgh music festival.

Olive continued in Torquay, still playing tennis at least once a week at seventy. She did a bit of gardening, listened to her wireless, and filled innumerable scrapbooks with stories, mostly funny, from the newspapers.

My brother Colin had left the *Observer* and joined the publishers Bodley Head. He had married a girl who worked at the local grocer's to finance her art studies, and later became well-known as the novelist Alice Thomas Ellis. They produced seven children, five of them boys, and lived in Gloucester Crescent in north London, for which Camden Council gave them an interest-free £4,000 mortgage. He then moved to the publishing firm of Duckworth's, which counted DH Lawrence among its better-known authors, though it now published mostly religious books. Colin was offered 50% of the firm if he rejuvenated it. The owner then died of pneumonia in New York, and Colin was offered the remaining shares by his widow, with the exception of the few held by a minority director.

Colin was thus, suddenly, a publisher in his own right. He acquired development capital by selling Duckworth's premises in Henrietta Street. As with us at International House, it was a period of price stability and low rents. He moved the company into an old piano factory near his house in Gloucester Crescent, with a large, open floor where books could be displayed, stored and packed. The rent was one pound a square foot. He published anything that caught his fancy – novels, Horace, knitting patterns. I never tried to publish with him. It would have seemed incestuous, nepotistic. Anyway we tended to get tetchy and irritable with each other over business.

The Walberswick cottage gradually expanded, acquiring a sauna going cheaply in a sale, rooms being joined together, an extra bedroom created from the garage, and another with a separate work desk in the roof, with great windows looking out over the sea. There was also a skylight through which we could see the stars and moon from our bed. In thunderstorms it was a mobile panorama, with flashes racing through the night before our very noses.

Blackheath and Walberswick became a contrast to the extrovert bustle of International House. This fulfilled my dual elements of monk and actor. We had no great social life in either place, except with the children's friends, as we already had quite enough conviviality at work. We both spent time on our books: Brita on pronunciation, me on any teaching idea I felt needed expressing, or on novels which seemed too extreme, often too fantastic, ever to get published. Anyway I didn't hawk my novels around enough. If I got two rejections, I wouldn't try again – unlike some, for example John Braine, whose *Room At the Top* was accepted by the seventeenth publisher he sent it to. I was too easily discouraged, supposing my novel not good enough – as though there were some objective criterion – and would get on with the next one instead. By this time I had finished five novels, all unpublished.

In the end, I went back to my first success, *Babel In Spain*, with commissioned books on Latin countries: *The Italian Labyrinth* and *In Search of the French Revolution*.

33 · Snakes and Ladders

We earned enough to do what we wanted, including foreign travel to visit schools. Our salaries seemed derisory beside those of our contemporaries (Brita worked and taught unpaid until 1972, when a nominal figure was stipulated; for the whole of 1978 my salary came to £7,000). We had royalties, though, particularly from my BBC books, and by limiting our salaries we were putting money back into our own school for the future. Under the Labour government, higher income could be taxed at 60%. I saw no point in contributing money produced by our students to what I considered excessive government spending. I preferred to invest it in a profession which needed subsidies desperately. The less we took out, the greater the ploughed-in investment and the more valuable the company, should we ever decide to sell.

About now I had a letter published in *The Times* accusing the government of having a vested interest in inflation because salaries rose continually, and taxes with them. During an ensuing BBC interview I discussed the demotivating effects of large-scale direct taxation, and the benefits of VAT in contrast. I was also reluctant to earn much more than our staff and made no secret of it, displaying monthly accounts in the staff room. To me the organisation was a cooperative venture with everyone knowing everything, even if it was my ultimate responsibility to make decisions. Bureaucracy and hierarchy could only make thing less effective. The general atmosphere was very relaxed. Everyone was on first-name terms. Brita and I never behaved like bosses. We were all teachers. Brita still is, and I taught a class for a month every year until I retired in 1990. We were stimulators rather than lecturers. This approach rubbed off on our organisation, although it sometimes alarmed new teachers.

Our teachers were mostly lively and loyal, although they occasionally challenged our right to present our own creations. As they had all done the teachers' course, they shared our attitudes to foreigners and teaching, and knew International House before they started teaching. We did not insist on a degree but most had one. One exception was a man who had been a house-painter and became an excellent teacher. I sent him to Bangkok where he ended up marrying a Thai princess!

In the sixties, teachers often came for a year or two after university, perhaps wanting to go abroad before settling down to something 'more serious'. Because they were not yet committed, they were often more adventurous – Pat Smith, for example, who went to Tripoli and then Beirut, where she married a Lebanese. She felt the idealism in teaching English and helping poorer nationalities. There was Lin Hutton, daughter of a well-known Oxford economist with whom I had once debated world government. She became our first head of teacher training, Brita being too encumbered to take it on herself. Lin had taught in Libya and in Paris, took a break to rear her two children, and came back ten years later as teacher and then teacher trainer. From early on, our teacher trainers kept their increments when teaching regular classes. This encouraged them to go on teaching students, thus keeping up to date with classroom issues. By putting into practice what they had discussed with their trainees, they avoided one of the pitfalls of teacher trainers who easily drone on about things they have not tried out in the classroom for years. Similarly, directors and directors of studies kept their increments if they returned to teaching.

Thus evolved a team with experience of teaching, of teacher training, and of administration, both in London and abroad – Ben Warren, Helen Morwood, Tony Duff; Georgie Raman had a Swiss mother and a bank manager father in Ascot, and was rebelliously left-wing. In my experience such people often made the best executives. They cared, had integrity, and spoke their mind. Georgie became head of teacher training and then of the school. She champed at anything Brita did because she had the fixed idea that a boss's wife must be there through influence not ability. She insisted that promotion should be by selection board and not some whim of mine. She married a Hindu from Madras who taught in the British state system.

Georgie was very tender with her two buoyant half-Indian children and her innumerable dogs. She had a great following among the female staff, to whom she was very sympathetic in her feminist way. She was a firm director. She finally left for a job as director of studies at the Inner London Education Authority school in Peter Street, which had longer holidays and was not private enterprise but state-run. She felt, too, that the students would be poorer than ours and therefore more worthy of her care!

From 1968 unrest swept Europe, particularly in Italy. Ausonio, a Christian Democrat driving a Mercedes, was a natural target. He had started another school, in the Viale Manzoni. He was not averse to Italian subterfuge and reminded me of Louis XVI. I told him to be careful not to end up the same way. No tactician, he would tell a crowd of protesting teachers that he couldn't afford salary rises, then concede when they got angry. This was a time when employees in Italy were in a strong position. They could not be sacked, and the *scala mobile*, or sliding scale, compensated them for inflation. Italian workers had been exploited mercilessly in the fifties and sixties and were now exacting revenge. Much as I liked Ausonio, I felt he exploited his teachers, of whom the non-Italians protested the most. Some of his British staff treated Brita and me like unscrupulous lepers. Their union was led by a small man, formerly an accountant in Britain and now a firebrand manipulator. I remember an American couple who were very amiable, almost obsequious when we first met in Rome. But the next time, they snarled at us because we belonged to the 'employer class'.

But despite everything, the teachers wanted the best, regarding both salaries and teaching effectiveness. We resented being called exploitative capitalists and deplored the new self-righteousness and lack of humour, but we had what we wanted. Standards were high, the school flourished, and higher salaries brought stability. Some of the Rome firebrands came to London to teach on a summer course and tried to spread their doctrine. Our London staff were not really interested.

In Rome, the real loser was Ausonio, in terms of both his pocket and his feelings. He believed in a paternalistic, amiable approach, and here were these bloody British treating him with scorn. But he had great design and artistic flair. He already had an art college in Viterbo. Now he drifted away from his language schools, still intervening tempestuously but only occasionally, leaving administration increasingly in the competent hands of a sensible English teacher, Susan Conte, married to an Italian, author of an excellent book on pasta, who had been with Ausonio from the beginning. Ausonio started ploughing money from the school into his artistic projects, running up debts by postponing payment of his taxes. It was amazing how he survived without having to sell his classy villa with swimming-pool outside Viterbo. I remember going with him to a vast monastery near Viterbo which he had rented from the bishop for his art college, the monks' cells becoming studios for painting, sculpture and lithography. But Ausonio quarrelled with the bishop – over a communist teacher who was brilliant, but whom the bishop wanted dismissed on political grounds. Artistic sensitivity won over political persuasion. Ausonio transferred the college to Milan, where it became the first private art university to be recognised by the education ministry. Ausonio continued his Rome school listlessly, then sold it to the teachers, headed by Susan Conte. Thus even the accountant firebrand became a capitalist owner!

There was an English school explosion in Italy. Schools started and multiplied like amœbas, splitting into two and then four. There were eventually four 'Ausonio' schools in Rome, later directed by poet and linguist Jimmy Campbell, succeeded by Tony and Sheena Thompson from our London school. Our old building in the Via Marghera concentrated on Italian and was manned largely by our Italian teachers, with a director evocatively named Tiziana di Dedda.

Ausonio and Guy Wilson, joined by Nick Dobree from Beirut, started a school in Turin in a house which turned out to be near the red light district, its upper floors occupied by an elderly relative of the landlord's. Its first director was Marton Lemon from London. Martin married one of his teachers and was to play a considerable directorial role in first Paris and then Tokyo, as IH expanded. He stayed in Turin for three years until the school was sold to Tim Priesack, who had taught for Colin McMillan in Portugal. This was becoming typical of International House: new directors were chosen in London, or from affiliated schools where they had taught and shown administrative talent.

Bill Edwards started his own school in Arezzo. He was one of the bravest, most equable and cooperative people I have ever known. He had had a terrible car crash in the Australian army, leaving him with not only a wig but also a wooden leg, though to judge by his cheerfulness one would have thought there was nothing wrong with him at all. Once the school in Arezzo was going well, Bill and his partner John expanded to Perugia, where they set up a small school set in the famous Etruscan city wall with a view right over the surrounding *campagna*. Then they opened another in Prato near Florence, in a surprisingly charmless suburban house contrasting strongly with Perugia.

What worked so well with the affiliation system was not only the quality of the teachers we sent to schools, but also the pooling of so much energy. Instead of one central, overcharged generator, we had a whole series of interlinked dynamos, inspected and polished where necessary. In what had, up to then, been something of a ragbag profession, our system provided a career – as with Martin Lemon, at first director in Turin, then teaching in Tokyo and Paris, and finally starting his own school in Torquay; or Edward Woods, who transferred to the public sector, taught at Berlin University, and then moved to Lancaster University where he wrote an English grammar textbook. In the end, our teachers' course graduates peopled BBC English, the British Council, and the EFL departments of innumerable universities.

The central department was non-profit-making, covering the salaries of the five people running it from London and the rent of their offices. Everything was cheaper because salary costs could be shared: half of my salary, of the accountant's, and of my secretary's was paid by the London school, the other half by the central department. One crucial full-time post was head of teacher selection, who chose everyone sent from London. The first was Robert Swan, who had caught polio in Bangkok. We brought him home and gave him this job, which he performed with panache and humour, successful candidates becoming known as 'Swan's Selection'. The directors inspected the accounts at the annual conferences, and could balance their payments by commission on students they sent on courses to affiliated schools in Britain. The convenient dove-tailing made it all very economic. Our foreign students helped our image abroad, often meeting teachers in London who had taught in their home town, perhaps using the same text-books. Students often felt they were going from home to home, from one International House to another within one world organisation. This was coupled with a high degree of delegation, to take into account the differences between one country and another.

Most of our teachers were women, perhaps because EFL still did not offer a lucrative career for an ambitious man expecting to support a family. Many schools in England, Spain and the Middle East were directed by men, or by married couples, although in Italy Ausonio's sister Gui directed the Seregno school, with her able director of studies, Marcella Banchetti.

In La Spezia, a school already established by Lyndy Cronin was affiliated, and Lyndy was to do much to get all the Italian teachers to work closely together. She was married to a genial Italian who worked for the Italian Navy, his job consisting of hooking up a water ship on its monthly visit to the island of Palmaria, where they lived by the water's edge. He knew everything about water-life and was capable of putting a hand into a rock crevice and pulling out a lobster. He did the cooking and looked after the children, while Lyndy went to her school every morning by naval launch. Lyndy was vastly enterprising. She had summer distractions for children which were really 'Play in English' courses. They had all the *divertimenti* such as egg-and-spoon and sack races, new to Italians. The children loved them, learning English through play. Lyndy also embarked on special business courses with the EEC in Sardinia. Like other Italian school owners she was burdened by taxes but, unlike many others, she declared everything and paid 51% social security dues on all salaries.

Another school that affiliated, the English School in Palermo, belonged to Pat Durden, married to an Italian lawyer. She was happy in Sicily, although a little afraid of the possible effects of the Mafia and drugs on her children. She was particularly helpful for my book *Italian Labyrinth*, and through her I got to know the novelist Leonardo Sciascia and met Cardinal Papalardo, the first great clerical enemy of the Mafia in Sicily. Pat took us to a fascinating farm owned by the church and run by former drug addicts. It was amazing how much help school directors could give me for the book. Their students seemed to include every profession imaginable.

'Could you get me a judge?' I asked Tim Priesack in Turin.

'No problem!'

Ausonio seemed to know the entire Italian church. At our two Rome conferences, he had arranged audiences with the Pope. In Viterbo, knowing the Pope was due there, he took Brita and me to a small square where John-Paul II was addressing children. Suddenly the local saint appeared over the roofs raised on gigantic poles.

'Ah, Santa Rita!' the Pope delightedly greeted.

'*Santa Rosa! Non è Santa Rita,*' protested all the children.

A grinning Pope apologised profusely.

Ausonio once took us on an expedition to Tuscany, to the long-buried town of Ferretro. The day ended in disaster when he mis-judged a manoeuvre with his car and brought down his entire stock of wine which was in great racks at the end of his garage. A red flood surged along the concrete, interspersed with broken glass.

Bill Edwards introduced us to the goldsmiths of Arezzo and the Duke of Aosta. I had never appreciated the scale of contacts English language teaching could provide. A foreign journalist wanting to get to understand a country would do well to contact resident English teachers.

Meanwhile, expansion continued elsewhere. In Portugal, Colin McMillan's school in Lisbon was thriving and a second one had opened in Coimbra. When the revolution started, the Coimbra building was almost stormed, being next door to the headquarters of the hated secret police. Our family, including Olive who had never been to Portugal, went on holiday with him and his wife, Tere. They had met at International House in London and had three children: Mark, Simon, and tiny Carla who switched effortlessly from Portuguese to English, Spanish and even Catalan, the language of Tere's mother. We stayed at San Martinho, on the sea between Lisbon and Oporto, and swam and played tennis. We went out with a fisherman and caught mackerel every time we put a line into the water. '*Otra puta!*' we would exclaim as the line grew heavy again. We eventually had so many fish that we gave them away to anyone on the beach who felt like a decent supper. A few miles away was an inviting sandy beach stretching round in a crescent, with great white waves breaking on the shore. But there was no one on the sand or in the water, and we learned that even paddling could be a death sentence: dragged down instantly by the crashing waves and mighty currents, a corpse would surface far out at sea. The Atlantic could be treacherous: it drowned one of our teachers off the Moroccan coast, and claimed Colin's young son Simon in a surfing accident.

Colin's thinking matched our own. He spoke excellent Portuguese and Spanish, and had spent a sabbatical year from London University teaching in Seville, just when we were leaving Cordoba. Like us, he loved almost all things Iberian. He was so well read that I would ask his advice on good new novels. He was very enterprising, starting new schools in Coimbra, Viseu, Braga and Barreiro, over the river from Lisbon. Some places already had schools – the one owned by Carlos Rodriguez at Oporto, and the Aveiro school belonging to an American, Tony Laurel. They both became affiliated.

Colin was also a wonderful raconteur. He was very funny about his attempts to get permission for his original school in Lisbon when Salazar was still in power. The education ministry was largely peopled by girls in black dresses with alpaca sleeves to protect the dresses from the dusty tables. Whenever he produced a document required – his degree, a certification of the signature of the university vice-chancellor, an attestation that he had never been to prison – he was asked for something else, to the great amusement of the girls. This went on for a whole year. When he had finally got everything together, he was told that all that now remained was to take an exam on Portuguese and Brazilian literature and history. This exam would only take place when enough foreigners had enrolled, perhaps this year but maybe next, failing which the year after. Colin almost wept. It was out of Kafka, the ministry girls like mocking harpies. He gloomily saw himself giving classes at the Berlitz School, or in his small pension room.

Then he met a guardian angel in the shape of Mr Muir, the British Council representative, who said all these requirements were unnecessary. He promised to intervene personally with the director of private schools. Colin went from the depths of depression to the heights of exuberance. He got permission within a few days, and presented the director of private schools with three bottles of whisky, an extravagance he could only just afford.

Then he rented a school building and started his long climb to pre-eminence.

34 · Monsieur La Brèche and Colonel Gaddafi

Our biggest headache now was Algiers, although students were flooding in and seemed really to want to learn English. The problem was government interference. Algiers had generated a second school, in Oran, run by Peter North. Guy and Angela Wilson apart, it was always difficult finding good directors for Algiers. The initial glow of idealism I had felt was burning low. Boumedienne had ousted President Ben Bella and confined him to a secret prison in the desert. People I knew – Margaret Pope for example – were being expelled for intrigue. There was dogmatic nationalisation by a government with no experience of running anything. There were sunlight and beautiful beaches but hardly any tourist facilities. Teachers were still drawn to the north African coast. The better ones included Ben Warren, who would later be director in Tripoli and start a group of affiliated schools in Catalonia. Gordon Bentley, who still teaches at IH London, was another. The brilliant illustrator Doug Case, who later taught in London, performed in the English teaching theatre and moved on to the BBC, was our only teacher to marry an Algerian.

In 1967 there was strong anti-British feeling in Arab countries because of Harold Wilson's threat to intervene in the Middle East war on Israel's side. Derek Risley wrote from Tripoli about anti-British marches. In Algiers, a mob came by one evening on their way to storm the British Council. Our teachers put out the lights until they passed. The Wilsons having moved to Rome, we transferred Peter North from Oran to Algiers, where a problem cropped up with the forms the education ministry required. They referred to state schools for children, but the ministry seemed unaware of this. The police arrived one morning, to close our school because we did not have the right permit. They wanted to seal the doors with blood red wax. Peter persuaded them to postpone matters and rang me. I flew out next day. We turned the teachers' room into a bedroom, thus foiling the police who were reluctant to seal off *une domicile*.

I went to see a Monsieur la Brèche, in charge of the recognition of schools. In a bleak room with heavy wooden furniture, smelling of French ink like my old classroom at school in Menton, I stressed that we had had education ministry permission right from the start. Monsieur la Brèche dismissed this as 'early days'.

'But it's still legal!' I insisted. He still looked doubtful. So I asked him which legal system Algeria observed. Pointing to some large leather-bound volumes of French law, he said, 'This – for the moment.'

The British embassy was closed because of the Six-Day War. I didn't know what to do. We went back to La Brèche, now openly hostile, his lips thin and his eyes cold. I pleaded but he remained indifferent. I emphasised that we had come because we wanted to help this new country. A disbelieving smile appeared. I threatened to close the school, depriving hundreds of Algerians of their English classes. La Brèche shrugged his shoulders: *les Anglais*, hypocritical capitalists, intent on exploiting whatever they could get their hands on. We had brought the famous forms all filled in, despite their not applying to adult pupils. He softened a little as he handed us another dossier. 'If you fill this in, your dossier will be complete,' he said as if doing us a favour. How I came to detest this word *dossier* which just means file! No sooner was one task completed than the evil magician produced another!

'Does that mean the school can reopen?'

'When the dossier is complete.'

Next day we gave him the form and, the school reopened, I flew back to England. But the next year the whole process was repeated.

'It's the same in every country,' said La Brèche. 'In England too there must be regulations.'

'Yes, but anyone can open a school of English for adults!'

'And in France too!' added Peter North, who had worked for some years in Lyons.

'We are now under Algerian law!' said La Brèche, apparently contradicting his former assertion about observing French law.

I went to see Monsieur Taleb, the minister of education, a cheerful young man who said he would do his best to keep the school from being closed every year. Peter returned to England. I got fed up with the school opening and closing like a swing door. And there were the taxes – 90% of what we took a year, unless we had 'friends'. I discussed things with Mike Donnelly. Wouldn't it be better to have an Algerian director, able to deal with the bureaucracy? I knew someone who seemed suitable: Mohammed Sadoun, who had worked for the BBC and spoke good English. We appointed him, but he did not know how to treat English teachers. London was bombarded with complaints, even walkouts. So we refused to send any more teachers. After much thought, we decided to give Mohammed his independence.

Meanwhile the Oran school was flourishing, run by Elisabeth Henningham, an Englishwoman with an Algerian husband called Sherif, a perfect combination. Sherif ensured that the school was never closed. Elisabeth ran a school magazine, held a Christmas show, and taught and supervised as director of studies.

The school in Tripoli was also going well. Ben Warren was now director, despite difficulty getting a visa because the Libyans assumed Ben was a Jewish name! The school was full, with separate groups for women who took off their veils once inside the classroom and were taught only by women. We also had 120 army lieutenants on a special course.

Colonel Shelhi, virtually in charge of the country as old King Idris was ill, wanted us to start in Benghazi. Ben got me to come out to make a decision. In Benghazi we were shown premises in the barracks. I could not imagine a school dependent on the Libyan army being successful. We had a meeting with Shelhi and General King, in charge of British troops in Libya. We found it difficult to tell Shelhi, who was amiable and persuasive but touchy, that we didn't want to share premises with his army. I remembered the row over the lukewarm reports for our Libyan students in London. An offence to Shelhi's pride might lose our whole Libyan operation. I tentatively suggested starting in independent premises, but Shelhi said it wasn't necessary. His soldiers would feel honoured to welcome us to their barracks, and we would have complete charge of our school. What about timetables? What about noisy bugle calls, or parade-ground shouting? Shelhi replied that if there was anything that displeased, we had only to tell the commander who would deal with it immediately.

I was convinced – what else could I be? Ben was a reliable person, enterprising, tactful, persuasive when necessary, even though it was his successor, John Shackleton, who would actually be in charge. And there was always General King if anything dire happened. Benghazi was a relaxed, pleasant town, with Roman temples under the sea which you could swim down to, and the great empty uplands of Cyrenaica within easy reach.

We got a team of excellent teachers together in London. But two days before they were due to leave, there was a report of a coup in Libya. King Idris had gone to Turkey for medical treatment, and a Lieutenant Gaddafi had taken over after a brief struggle between the army and the police. Shells had gone over John Shackleton's house, while he sensibly cowered inside. Apparently Colonel Shelhi had planned a coup of his own, but was beaten to it. He was arrested, tried and imprisoned – for how long, we never found out.

The Tripoli school was unaffected, although the lieutenants' classes stopped. Their teachers went regretfully back to England. The streets were suddenly full of troops, greeting our teachers with waving rifles and enthusiastic cries of 'Teacher! Teacher!' The Benghazi school never started. Some teachers originally going there volunteered for the Gulf instead, where we had two newly affiliated schools. Their directors were amazed by the rapid response to requests for new staff. In Libya oil production increased, the professions were taken over by people of other nationalities, and the Libyans sat back, bemused and idle with their new wealth. Doctors tended to be Bulgarian, sewage inspectors Yugoslav, and hotel staff Tunisian. Remaining positions were filled by Egyptians, in favour for a time because of Gaddafi's admiration for Nasser: many were teachers. Our English classes reflected all this, and became almost as varied as in London. The reign of Gaddafi had begun. As one teacher commented, it was good to live under his dictatorship because it made you realise how wonderful Britain was when you returned.

35 · French Liaisons

In London, I now shared both office and secretary, Silvana Orlando, with Tom Hall. He came in twice a week to see what was happening. This was fine by me. At one stage I even gave up my office, only using it to dictate and sign letters, receive messages and make telephone calls. I spent the rest of my time talking to teachers or students, teaching, observing classes, seeing how delegated projects were evolving, visiting schools abroad, writing the textbook *Action* with Brita at home, and going to see people. I felt, anyway, that a director should avoid all the concerns which can so easily fill his day, in Bourbon-style management with the king in his palace and commoners approaching on bended knee. I favoured the Bonaparte syndrome with the leader out most of the time, winning battles. Part of it was my intoxication with foreign places, the colour and variety of people from different countries, new challenges and prospects, the feeling that we were luckier than most and had better take advantage of it.

Now that we were a company, shareholders and contributors presented themselves: Michael Delmear Morgan of the Brown Shipley Bank more or less donated £3,000. My old friend Charles Hodgson, the actor, lent me £1,000. A new partner, Michael Sokolov Grant, invested £6,000, becoming very active and occupying a third desk in my office.

Of Russian parentage, Michael was cheerful, interesting, and trilingual in French, English and Russian. He had style and a great sense of humour with an actor's panache. Sometimes I felt that in arguments he chose the side that gave him the more dramatic role. His father had been in the imperial Russian navy and survived the battle of Tsushima, where the Japanese delivered the final blow to the Russian fleet. After the revolution, Michael's parents had wandered from Turkey to Spain, to France, his mother giving birth to a son in each country. At 11 in France, Michael was noticed by a British refugee worker, Francesca Wilson, who became a good friend of ours. She had a soft spot for Russians as a Russian had been the love of her life, and she adopted Michael because he gave her one of his ravishing smiles. Michael was educated at King Edward School in Birmingham. In the war he was attached to a French battleship which had joined the Allies. He married Sheila Grant Duff, granddaughter of Lord Avebury. She had been an adviser to Winston Churchill and had gone to Czechoslovakia to write articles for the *Observer* revealing Nazi designs on that country.

Brita and I explored the possibility of a school in Paris. In the summer of 1967 we had met Odette Sabaton who taught English at a lycée in Paris. Odette felt a good school would be in great demand. Everything seemed favourable. There was little competition. She hoped to start an Anglo-French centre within the school. The only things we lacked were the most urgent: premises, and cash. Odette rang from Paris. She had found a wonderful place in the centre of St Germain, just beyond the Pont Neuf, down the picturesque Passage Dauphine, between Rue Dauphine and Rue Mazarine. The buildings, all vacant, were owned by a single landlord – perfect for a 'village anglais' with a school, a pub, a bookshop, an international club, a theatre, even fashionable English shops. As with other enterprises, we would concentrate on starting the school and get reliable specialists to take on the rest. We might even invite the British Council, whose Paris classes were run by London University, to come in with their advanced and literature classes, while we taught beginners and intermediate students.

We were very excited. Michael and I went over to look. It seemed just as good as Odette had said: ample space for International House in this former dental college, empty now except for a few ancient chairs. The pub could go in the building opposite, the theatre in the broad first floor above the Rue Dauphine entrance. The Passage itself had sloping, cobbled paving, right out of a thirties photograph, mules and straw hats just round the corner. It had once been part of the Augustine monastery abutting the old walls of Paris and built by Philippe-Auguste in the thirteenth century.

Back in London Tim Rix at Longman, the leading publisher of EFL books, had already proposed collaborating in Paris, Longman putting up the money, us contributing the know-how. I rang Tim and described our find. Tim was excited and went over with Michael to have a look at the 'village'. It captured his imagination too. We produced a budget which turned out over-optimistic, and signed an agreement.

Things were going well in Shaftesbury Avenue. The number of students grew. We rented more space opposite, classrooms totalling over 90. Meanwhile along Piccadilly, various schemes had come and gone. Our premises had expanded continually for ten years now, and it looked as if we might well be here for another ten, at low rent. We hung the flags of most nationalities at the main door and from first-floor windows. Every morning a flood of students streamed into classrooms, right up to the fifth floor and overflowing, through a labyrinth, to rooms overlooking Rupert Street. Fortunately neither Tom, Michael or I were interested in taking profits. They would have been minimal anyway, as we tried to keep fees as low as possible. Any surpluses went into expansion or improvements. Abroad, a second IH school had opened in Tokyo, above and below the British Council which, thus sandwiched between us, provided a library and offices while we gave English lessons. Both our schools and the Council were crowded. Together, we helped to form Tokyo's British cultural centre.

In London we had rented a theatre space next door, as a base for the English Teaching Theatre and a new sister-version, the French Teaching Theatre, organised along similar lines by one of our French teachers, Anne Grunberg. The first floor had once been a famous Victorian restaurant. The dark wooden floors were bare and dusty now, and art nouveau glass panes leaned against walls whose paint was peeling. Downstairs was a broad space which we now used for our club. An American impresario, Ed Berman, became interested in helping set up a theatre in half the space, leaving the remainder for our club. I agreed, provided we could use the theatre from early June to the end of October, when most of our students came. To begin with, Ed was heavily amiable. But once he had equipped the theatre and called it 'The Almost Free' – because you paid what you liked for tickets, he became tactically aggressive. He would come and see me, self-importantly. With his big, black beard, he looked like Moses descending from the mount with his tablets, while I became a deluded worshipper of the Golden Calf! At least he stuck to the agreed dates. But what he really wanted was the whole area of our club as well when it was his turn to use the theatre.

'If you refuse, I'll serve you an injunction!' his American accent would rasp. 'I'll give you till I've smoked this cigar to come to your senses – or else . . .' he added ominously.

'Oh go away!' I would reply, 'You're in the wrong country!'

At this he would fume over his cigar, like a forest concealing a volcano. Then, thundering about dire legal penalties, he would tramp heavily away down my narrow staircase.

We now had a place to welcome groups of new teacher trainees, to tell them about the course and what facilities International House could offer them. There was room for Saturday conferences on topics like the Silent Way, a new method teaching vocabulary through different-sized coloured rods. I had watched an American teacher use this technique in Yugoslavia, and invited her to International House on her way home to demonstrate it. This led us to invite the inventor of the method, another arrogant Moses-figure called Doctor Cattegno, with whom I had the pleasure of disagreeing publicly without him realising I was his host.

'I'm surprised you have any students at all, except masochists, if you treat them as brutally as you do us!' I told him after a particularly vitriolic outburst, directed at some of his audience. This obviously unaccustomed resistance made him almost civilised!

As well as looking after the teacher training on our joint summer course with the English Speaking Union and the BBC English by Radio, we began to train young teachers for Voluntary Service Overseas and others from the International Volunteer Services. About 250 of them had a one-week course in small groups before going to Ethiopia, India, New Britain or South America. We excluded discussion on electronic or technical aids – even tape recorders – because they probably would not have any. We concentrated more on making and using visual aids, on objects brought into the classroom, and on playing on their students' powers of deduction. It was remarkable how school leavers seemed to do better than university graduates, who might analyse and demand 'intellectual challenge'. The school-leavers accepted that teaching was essentially a simple, dramatic affair.

These courses ran successfully for five years. Then a former British Council representative in Greece called Barron inspected our course. He vowed he could do better, despite having no EFL experience. The next thing was that he replaced us and gave a lecture on 'Training VSO Teachers' at a conference I attended. It turned out that, as he hadn't actually started the training, all he wanted was advice. So I gave him fourteen points I hoped were of use, and in the summer filled our classes with students and other trainees instead of the volunteers. It was a pity. His course only lasted one summer.

Another new development was the international association of teachers of English as a foreign language, IATEFL, founded by Bill Lee, an enterprising freelance teacher and EFL writer. He wanted to organise annual conferences where teachers could talk about their own fields. He ran courses for teachers in Czechoslovakia and felt strongly for eastern Europeans and their currency problems. Through scholarships to his conferences, he helped bring east and west closer. I was a founder IATEFL member and stayed on the organising committee for twelve years – although everything was done by Bill, the rest of us mainly listening. Today, about 1,500 people attend IATEFL every year, speakers having to apply six months in advance.

This was when I was also on the committee of ARELS, the Association of Recognised private English Language Schools inspected and recognised as efficient, originally by the Department of Education and Science. I later suggested that the British Council would be a more appropriate inspector for EFL organisations, a suggestion they adopted.

ARELS was founded in 1957 by Frank Bell and Malcolm Campbell, two prominent EFL school directors assisted by Roy Barnes, of the Studio School in Cambridge, Peter O'Connell, school director in Folkestone, and Paul Lindsay, of the St Giles School. On the fringe was Peter Fabian of the London School of English.

To me, ARELS was an interesting talking shop with potentially great educational influence. I was interested in raising standards, and pressed for a ruling that all teachers should have an EFL qualification. Some saw this as International House trying to impose its own rules; others felt teachers were just as good without special training. I was suspected of recruiting for our teacher training courses. ARELS' valiant general secretary, General Egerton, spent much time manoeuvring between lobbies and seeking not to offend members who might then express resentment at crucial meetings. I suppose this was inevitable in an assembly of rivals; but it was disappointing. IH started a school in Brussels with ARELS. After a glorious start, the school flopped – partly because a very cold winter kept students away and partly because of over-anxious interference by the board and the expensive appointment of a gentleman whose job was 'statistics'. This did little to help the new school; it needed advertising rather than having its short life measured.

After several years on the committee and standing for the chair in vain, I resigned. An uneasy trade association was not my scene.

Meanwhile, building was progressing in Paris. The former dentistry school was looking very different, a ramp and staircase sweeping past reception and up to a dozen classrooms with different-coloured doors and plush chairs, with mini desks attached. The teachers' room was in the large loft, lit by skylights; the language laboratory was on the first floor in the centre of everything. We had a party for anyone who had been a student in London. Hordes came to drink wine in front of the white, linoleum-covered ramp. The best part was the club, in what had been a factory next door. One of the walls, now hung with hessian, had been part of the fortified wall of Paris. Looking down on the sunken stage, backless wooden tiers rose to the rear of the hall, scattered with large multicoloured plastic poufs.

I had left the planning of the Passage Dauphine to Odette and Michael, and the finance to Michael – a mistake. I visited occasionally to see how things were going and to take part in discussions with the architect – how big should the classrooms be? where to hang blackboards? was the reception area satisfactory? should the classroom walls have corkboards? In London, we had an office for the supplementary books, visual aids and cassettes, called the 'horse-box' because the person serving leaned out through the top half of a stable door. Where to locate this in IH Paris became a grave question. The air resounded with opinions about *le orse-box*, our latest Franglais word!

We were all impossibly tense as the Passage took shape – including Brita who felt, perhaps rightly, that it would have been better to start small as in Cordoba. Tim Rix and I consoled Michael, who had overspent and said he felt suicidal. The publicity man had used exaggerated remarks about me for our advertising and brochures, calling me the symbol of *l'amitié* of International House combining it with lengthy disquisitions full of abstract ideas.

At last the school was ready. I had persuaded ARELS to hold a conference a few days before, its first in a school abroad – but then where else did students come from? The club was only just ready, the hessian going up the night before, to the anxiety of some who felt it would never be ready for the next morning. It was. '*Vive le chaos!*'

Guy and Angela Wilson were our first directors. Ben Warren was also in Paris, having left Tripoli just when Gaddafi's coup had brought him to power. I put him in charge of our intensive English courses for ESSEC, a *grande école*, every morning from 8 a.m.

Everything looked promising, when to our alarm Odette heard that a municipal law forbade opening a pub within fifty metres of a school. If only the pub had been opened first! – there was no objection to opening a school within fifty metres of a pub. Local pub owners were determined to stop us. Meanwhile we were paying rent for the pub building, the empty theatre, and the buildings further down the Passage which we were reserving for the 'village'. But things still looked good. We had enrolled 150 students in the first week and the new school began to function. Under Ben Warren's leadership, the ESSEC courses had gone well: the students appreciated our conversational methods and the presence of English native speakers. They liked the image of *le gentleman*, which had long fascinated many French people, and the contrasting one of youthful England as represented by the Beatles.

I was at our first teachers' meeting, and the club seemed colourful and full of light. Odette, I knew, had plans for some interesting *évènements*. We returned to England with a light heart, little anticipating the complications in store.

36 · Paris, Queen of Cities

Odette Sabaton was in her mid-forties, a slim, fashionable Pari-
sienne. She knew Britain, spoke English well and taught at a well-
known lycée, but had higher ambitions. She had been enchanted
with swinging London, but now complained about our hippy English teachers and their habit of sitting on the floor eating sandwiches
in her elegant club. Being shortsighted, she would sweep past them
in the street, and even indoors, ignoring them. She thought they
should speak better French and be more enthusiastic about the
vernissages and other cultural events she arranged. She also found
Guy and Angela lacked enthusiasm for her plans. For them, of
course, it was the school that really mattered. They felt her activities
did not bring in many new students. And they were two to her one.

They fell out openly over a minor lighting matter in the club.
Odette resigned with dramatic furore. Michael and I took the night
ferry to Paris to talk everything over. As a result, Brita and I decided
to go over for a few months to help find a solution. Fortunately a
large top flat was available in the Passage. We enrolled Richard,
aged twelve, at an international school, where he learned little
except how to flick cherry stones so that they stuck to blackboards.
Katinka, who was thirteen, went to the justly reputed Ecole Alsa-
cienne, and seven-year-old Jimmy to a local primary school, where
the teacher said he was unruly because he got up and walked around
when he felt like it, instead of staying in the neat ordered rows of
desks.

With our arrival, the Wilsons and Odette made an uneasy truce
and got on with their jobs, on the understanding that a decision
would be made before we left in June. It was all very fraught. I had
a greater reason for loyalty to the Wilsons, old friends who had
stepped in as directors for us more than once at short notice.
However, Odette was a key figure in our grand scheme.

In Paris we did everything we could to recruit new students. Brita and I canvassed companies with brochures. Odette got articles in *L'Express* and *Le Nouvel Observateur* on our use of drama in teaching and our plans for the 'village anglais'. We also had a series of English Teachng Theatre performances by our teachers, directed by Fiona Morel. Tony Duff, an acclaimed London teacher, became head of Paris teacher training. He managed to include our Richard and Katinka as Rosencrantz and Guildenstern in his excellent production of *Hamlet*, which drew praise from the French critics. We developed French classes with Daniel Salem, who had worked at the BBC French service in London. Fiona produced Pinter plays, then all the rage in Paris, in English on our sunken stage, and we had a British week with lectures and debates on the UK. International House had recovered a role which was not just language teaching, although that was at the heart of it. Brita staged pronunciation workshops in the club, enthusing our French students to bend their intonation in English ways. Andy Caswell, Diana Gibbs and I experimented with getting students to rehearse and perform sketches. We were surprised how willingly French students did this, throwing themselves about with far less inhibition than in class.

On June 21st, *Saint Jean*'s day, we had an exuberant celebration bringing together the French, British and Swedes, Brita having contacted a group of Swedish folk dancers led by a French musician she had met at a concert. The swirling dances and colourful dresses made a wonderful impression. We lit a small bonfire in the street so that, in proper *Saint Jean* fashion, we could leap over the flames. Some old ladies living above were frightened and called the fire brigade, who sped up the narrow Rue Mazarine, hosepipes poised. We protested that there was no danger, just a traditional celebration. The students plied the firemen with wine and borrowed their helmets. The firemen joined in and jumped over the fire themselves. A concertina struck up and dancing began, interrupted by a second fire engine whose firemen said they must do something as traffic was backed up as far as the Place de la Concorde. They dallied a little too and had some wine, but eventually switched on their hose, and the last few plumes of smoke rose into the pink sunset.

The time came to decide between Guy and Odette. I had to side with Odette. We had a stiff farewell party. Brita and I agreed to stay on for a while to help smooth things over. In London Peter North, who had been in Algiers, would be acting principal in the Shaftesbury Avenue school.

The new autumn term in Paris went well and, now used to IH Paris, we had more time. Living not far from the Seine was a delight. We had weekend excursions in the soft autumn to show the children Versailles, Malmaison, Fontainebleau – as my brother and I had done with Olive thirty-three years earlier. The 1968 disturbances were still fresh. Not that it affected us much, but it perhaps made the police more officious, whistling even more often if you trod on a patch of grass. Richard was getting negative school reports and seemed to spend much time at Le Drugstore, in the Boulevard St Germain, of course picking up French the whole time and now almost bilingual (although to my fury, once back at his school in London he came 23rd in French). It was ironic that, after all our efforts to improve our students' spoken English, our son's French should be measured in the traditional writing-and-grammar way.

Things were going only reasonably in London where Michael, now in charge, was proving arbitrary, obsessed with everyone paying their bills punctually. He got rid of his compatriot, poor Vera Traill, over a six months' rent bill. He sacked the director of the Rabat school for 'financial reasons', and disaffiliated the Gulf schools for paying their fees late. I was not consulted, and only discovered all this when I got back. Given the low Shaftesbury Avenue rent, it made little difference whether Vera paid us hers anyway. What was important was that she give good service, as her au-pairs often enrolled as students. The Gulf schools just needed a visit. Michael gave the Rabat school to a Morroccan, exactly the type of director we existed to prevent; we soon disaffiliated him for taking shortcuts at the expense of educational quality. Michael wanted a 'tight ship', and was inevitably backed up by Tom Hall, the ex-army man. But I knew this couldn't work with schools spread all over the world. The standards had to be definite, but they had to be enforced with endless elasticity and tact.

Our Paris school was officially opened by Sir Christopher Soames, the British ambassador, and Lady Soames, Winston Churchill's daughter. Monsieur Larquetout, the landlord, was sufficiently over-come by the occasion to tidy up the Passage, removing all traces of the car park he was digging underneath – into which I once said International House would eventually slip. We gave our guests a demonstration of English Through Acting to show what we could do (while our son Richard proudly showed a white mouse to Norman Reddaway, representing the cultural department of the Foreign Office, who fortunately made approving noises). Michael greeted the Soames, whom he already knew, with Brita, me, Tom and various people from Longman. Sir Christopher and I went into the crowded club to give short speeches. But the crowds were too much for him. 'So many people!' he whispered. 'Do we have to give a speech? Can't we give it later?'

I was dumbfounded. Surely he was used to crowds and giving speeches? 'No, we must!' I insisted, and guided him firmly through to the platform, where he recovered and gave everyone a witty, warm welcome. I can't remember what I said, except for explaining what we were doing in Paris, *la reine des villes*, as I called it – which of course went down a treat.

Everyone went back to London, leaving me with a knotty accounting problem. I am not an accountant. So we advertised for one and got a very well qualified lady. Longman's financial advisor, Philippe Jacob, warned against employing her as she was an executive – which seemed to me exactly what we needed. But Philippe said she would be difficult to get rid of if she proved unsatisfactory. I deferred and continued doing the accounts myself, like a garage mechanic struggling with Einstein. We needed both British and French style accounts, and they were bafflingly different. One thing was obvious, though: financially, Paris was a black hole.

In London, at a board meeting which I couldn't attend, Michael proposed that Tom Hall replace me as chairman. I still can't quite understand why. I felt Tom had experience of running farms and battalions, but knew less about schools of English. Perhaps it was the beginning of the schism which later developed between those who had never taught and those who had. Or perhaps it was just a dramatic gesture, or Michael siding with Tom whose wealth was reassuring. Or perhaps he was determined to put any blame for what happened in Paris squarely on my shoulders, after his initial overspending. Or perhaps he just thought I was hopeless. Michael's proposal was ignored. But to me it seemed a backhander at a time when I was toiling away for everyone. I did not really know what was going on in London, or what plans Michael was hatching with my two backers, Tom Hall and Tim Rix.

Paris buzzed with activity – something not really appreciated either by Longman, recently toughened by its merger with the journalistic conglomerate Pearson, or by International Language Centres Limited, the company which now controlled International House, London. Both were inevitably more concerned with their investments. Odette continued to organise *spectacles* to make us better-known. The American playwright Robert Wilson came to be interviewed at our club. His play *Le Regard des Sourds* had been acclaimed by the poet Louis Aragon as one of the few surrealist works in France. Wilson arrived in a black car, dressed in black and masked, an incense burner round his neck, and looked like a Satanist priest. I sat him down in the semi-darkness and interviewed him in English, with an interpreter for the huge audience. It was eerie, a real surrealist evening. For one thing, I couldn't be sure it was really Robert Wilson. There could be anyone behind the mask. He was acerbic, ridiculing my questions about his play. Had he tried to get it performed in London? 'London!' he repeated scornfully. The British didn't understand surrealism! The incense burner clanked, and dark eyes stared out indignantly through the black mask.

After about half an hour, the audience interrupted with questions in French – whereupon Robert Wilson, or whoever it was, got up, bowed superciliously and, with no word to the interpreter or me, walked out as if to say he was not going to be interrogated by the hoi polloi, and in French! Frenzied discussion broke out. Why had he been so rude? Was it really him? Most people had seen his play but had never seen him.

As French people love a fashionable phrase, I was trying to come up with an abstract word to describe what we did. (French speakers at this time thought there was magic in the word *audiovisuel*, and would ask if we practised it before enrolling. If you asked what they meant, most had no idea. They just wanted you to say *oui* to be sure your methods were *respectables* and *modernes*.) I suggested the word *linguidrame*, which turned up in the *Nouvel Observateur* two weeks later, in an article that mentioned us: '*à International House on pratique le linguidrame*'. I imagined the word getting into the French dictionary in permanent tribute to our work, though I don't know if it ever happened.

I started 'English walks' on Saturday afternoons, walking through St Germain with a dozen students and describing some of the things we saw in English – the words for bicycle parts, for example, of course using the real thing. They then had to describe a bicycle with all its vocabulary – or a car, the façade of a building, a square. We talked English the whole time, pointing at things without translating. People could get quite agitated when we pointed at their cars or bicycles. One cyclist got off in alarm thinking something was wrong, as we happily recited 'Mudguard, mudguard!' This was typical of our 'dramatic' English teaching. But it was very much the icing on the cake, designed to stimulate students to speak. I got them to write down vocabulary as we went along. Afterwards they wrote an account of what had happened, and showed it to me.

Part of the Passage premises was empty, and one day we got a chance to recoup some of the rent we paid. I was visited by Eeri Vespi, the chairman of Eurocentres, an international trust devoted to teaching the local language, rather than a foreign one – French in Paris, Spanish in Madrid, English in London and so on. Most of its students were Swiss. Eeri was a cheerful person. After several beers, which I paid for because we were on my territory – a habit that has stayed with me ever since Spain and perhaps earlier – he said he was interested in renting premises from International House, if he could have the monopoly on teaching French. I was reluctant. Our French courses were going well with little competition, and we had started French teacher training courses. They were also a way of advertising other things. Someone from the Saudi Arabian embassy learning French, for example, was likely to recommend our club or our English classes to his friends. What would happen to Daniel and our French teachers? Could Vespi's school absorb them? I felt we were being forced to restrict ourselves to what we were in essence: a school of English marooned in its little 'village anglais' – which of course had a lot going for it, Britain having just been admitted to the EEC. I put Eeri in touch with Longman and IH London. Both were in favour. I stipulated that he absorb all our French teachers on the same terms or better.

Michael began to change his attitude towards me, displaying a strange air of importance. He actually threatened me, saying I should be more careful in what I said about the agreement with Eeri, or there would be trouble in London. He could not have shown a redder rag to a bull. I wrote saying it would be better if he stopped working for International House when we returned (though we have remained friends ever since). Looking back, it is sad how many 'executions' there were in Paris. Much was due to the rocky finances.

It was almost Christmas. Brita was overcome by her mother's impending death. Our whole autumn had been darkened by her advancing cancer. We went to Stockholm over the holidays with the children, to find Suzanne just conscious in a large, ordered hospital. Then, as if she had kept herself alive only until she saw us again, she departed this life on Boxing Day. Outside the window, a white plastic swan was caught in a frozen pond.

37 · Untimely Deaths

Our year in Paris was up. Brita went to Stockholm to sort out Suzanne's affairs, Katinka to stay with friends in Cordoba until her school started. Richard had an entrance exam for a school in Sevenoaks recommended by friends. He and I stayed in a flat in Basil Street while he attended a 'swotters' college, where he learned very little except how to puff a secret cigarette in a sophisticated manner. But I missed the trees and grassy slopes of Blackheath. Working in the West End was different from actually living there.

International House, too, seemed alien. Before, it had been 'mine', in the best sense. Before going to Paris, I knew the students and all the teachers. This made even a large community seem small. I felt a little like Yunus, our excellent bilingual Malay teacher, away at college during the year and with us in the summer. He said International House had lost its friendly atmosphere. I told him it was only because he didn't know so many people now, that it would soon change for the better. Although I hadn't fully realised it, the school now no longer belonged completely to us. We were majority shareholders, but I had no money. I was beholden to Tom for investment in the Japanese schools and in Paris. He and Michael had both invested in London.

There was, too, a sense of failure. Last year, in that great surge of optimism, we had talked of inviting all the London teachers over to Paris for the inauguration of the 'village anglais'. But it no longer existed, having become more of a 'village franco-anglais-suisse' – perhaps even more international! I had a feeling of missed opportunities. Surely I should have talked to Norman Reddaway about official financial backing. Brita or I could have contacted Randolph Quirk, professor of English at London University. From a distance, he helped run the British Council teaching operation in Paris and had been a good friend of Brita and her father in Stockholm.

Brita and I were soon absorbed in the world organisation. There was a new director in Tripoli, Jeff Mohamed and his wife Sue. I decided to pay them a visit. Both had taught with Nick Dobree in Beirut, where I had observed their classes and found them excellent.

Jeff and Sue had met at Durham University. They were strongly left-wing. Sue believed that International House students should pay less and teachers earn more. Their Tripoli earnings went on taking friends to restaurants back home. Jeff refused to get a mortgage, which he regarded as immoral.

Tripoli airport made me realise how lost a foreigner can be in an airport without English, unless he speaks the national language. I thought of all those Libyans who had blundered through London, Paris and Rome, missing their flights or ending up at the wrong destinations.

Jeff and Sue were running a first-rate school under difficult bureaucratic circumstances: twenty-two stages in applying for permission to get a teacher from London. Although both got on well with most Libyans, they had to work hard not to offend anyone, Gaddafi being so ostentatiously anti-British. It was interesting how many of our teachers approved of Gaddafi, forgetting that before Gaddafi there had not been the vast oil revenues to clear away the shantytowns, to build new supermarkets and modern buildings. Libya's oil income was now the equivalent of ten thousand pounds a head annually.

I went on to Cairo, where we eventually had two schools. I had been visited in London by an enthusiastic man called Colin Rogers, who had already worked as a teacher trainer for the Egyptian education ministry and claimed to know everyone there. Colin was convinced that under the more pro-western Sadat there was now a great opportunity, and that the demand for English was enormous. I gave him a free teacher's course on which he got grade B, and suggested that on his way to Cairo he call in on Nick Dobree to see what a really good school of English was like. He was short of cash, so I lent him £250.

Before I knew where I was, Colin had married an Egyptian girl, Soumaya. Her father was a pasha who, under Nasser, was taken round Egypt to see what had happened to his confiscated estates until he had a heart attack and died. He had had a personal railway built to his country home. Within a month, Colin had got Nick Dobree to back him from Beirut, and obtained permission to start the first English school in Egpyt since the Suez invasion in 1956 – largely with the help of Norman Daniels of the British Council, well-known for his research into Egyptian antiquities. Daniels took a paternal liking to Colin who, once he had the permit, rented a large building in Medinet el-Sahafeyeen, a suburb of Cairo.

He held an inauguration in the garden one balmy evening, with the British ambassador and the Egyptian minister of higher education, Dr Hafey Ghenein. Food was from the fashionable caterer Groppi's. I reflected happily on how different everything was the last time I had been in Cairo, in an occupying army. The city was choked with traffic, but otherwise much the same. The building, where Colin was already enthusiastically pulling down and erecting walls, as he was to do for the next five years, was bursting with 2,000 students. On the first evening of enrolment there were so many applicants that the steel entrance doors had to be closed, and even then they bent under the pressure. In the end the police had to be called, though not for the sort of riot they were used to. Colin told me that the schoolroom furniture ordered had not turned up in time. So the night before the first classes, he desperately imagined hundreds of students all sitting on the floor. A friend said the only places to get enough chairs at short notice was at funeral parlours. So Colin went round and hired them as if for a vast multiple funeral. The chairs arrived a few hours before class, borne by a long procession of mules.

Another affiliated school soon opened in Heliopolis, the other end of town, also financed by Nick Dobree and directed by another Colin, Colin Davies. They too had to call the police at enrolment time. Rodney Blakeston, director of studies, remembers Colin going out to meet the mob with scores of blue tickets which allowed people to enrol. He disappeared in a turmoil of legs and arms and flying blue tickets. Both schools were to have more than 4,000 students and develop their own teacher training courses. They also gave Arabic lessons.

Colin Davies was extraordinary, having spent much of his time at Cambridge playing in different bands. His great passion was the American guitarist Buddy Holly – he was founder-president and sole member of the Middle East Buddy Holly Society. The Heliopolis school was custom-built with a roof terrace, the opposite of Medinet el-Sahafeyeen, a sprawling affair though about the same size. I once went to dinner with Colin Davies in his flat which, like a lot of Heliopolis houses, was full of long corridors and bathrooms and balconies to accommodate enormous families. I met his wife, Liz, and a Scottish teacher, Christine. (She later died, falling from the top of the Great Pyramid at night in a strong wind.) Discussion touched on education in England and the inequality created by public schools. Everyone except Liz, who was Canadian, had been to one. I interrupted Colin's tirades to point out that we were discussing a purely provincial, British problem, while Colin's caretaker and wife were sleeping on the bare floor downstairs under a ragged blanket.

The schools survive, but the overwhelming enrolment crowds have dwindled. Students once believed English lessons would get them jobs, perhaps even in Britain or the USA. But immigration restrictions stopped all that. Colin Rogers had difficulty obtaining British visas, partly because an entire group of thirty-two students had taken illegal jobs in England the previous summer. Now Colin Davies has gone to Washington, where he works for a student organisation with offices all over eastern Europe. He broadcasts on Buddy Holly for a radio station. The school in Heliopolis is in the capable hands of Paul Mason. Colin Rogers is still at Medinet el-Sahafeyeen, and has built a school for 1,700 Egyptian children, as well as his International House.

*

Ben Warren, who had lived in the flat next to ours in Paris, also decided to start a school in Spain, with his Spanish wife Carmen. They chose Sabadell, a small industrial town north of Barcelona where there was plenty of demand but no school. He had a Catalan partner but needed us to invest initially. Michael and Tom were not keen, in view of the continuing risks in Paris. I had always believed in encouraging teachers to start their own schools, and greatly admired what Ben had done in Algiers, Tripoli and, recently, in Paris with the ESSEC students.

I had a spare £1,000 from *Getting On In English* royalties, and invested it on a personal basis as long as I had no liability. Ben accepted, in return for a reduced 14% of equity. I went to Sabadell for the inauguration. I shall never forget looking up from the street at Ben and Carmen and their baby son as they gazed out of a window. This was not in itself remarkable, but it caught me at an emotional juxtaposition: there was something isolated about the little family looking out together, unaware they were being watched. Perhaps it reminded me of our own start in Cordoba. Ben and Carmen were then at the beginning of their real achievement. In the next five years, Ben started no less than nine schools in Catalonia, and helped found three others in Madrid and another in Zaragoza – the first of the Madrid schools under Jeff Mohammed, recently back from Tripoli. Investment was shared with already established and new IH directors: Eulogio Cremades from Cordoba, Javier Lacunza from San Sebastian, Cedric Scheybeler from Santander. Together, they built up one of the most successful groups of International House schools in the very country where the organisation had its first roots.

Ben was still young. After a geology degree at Cambridge and an IH teacher's course, he went to Algiers, then to Tripoli as director. He was in his late twenties when he started in Sabadell, just like us in Cordoba. Carmen was a Cambridge Proficiency student at IH London. Together they went to Tripoli and got married on their return to England.

He was meticulous and exacting without being pompous or patronising, and unfailingly fair to his staff. He had an openness to him that was immediately appealing and made people trust him. When put in charge of the ESSEC programme in Paris, he gave up teaching for administration. He soon felt out of touch with the classroom, forever presuming newly trained teachers would be better than he was. I tried to persuade him it was, at least partly, a matter of fashionable staffroom jargon and 'new' methods suddenly in vogue. Ben got satisfaction from seeing his schools grow. He went round regularly, checking on administration, finance, enrolment, and advertising. Like other 'visitors', I would help as much as I could with observation of classes, critiques of what I saw, interviews with teachers. I also gave talks and seminars, talking, listening, congratulating, criticising gently where necessary, planting new ideas.

On that first visit to Sabadell, I almost killed Ben after the ceremony. I was carrying a stack of chairs upstairs, when one tipped off and crashed down the well onto his head. He was rushed to casualty, where fortunately it turned out to be only a superficial wound.

Ben always felt he ought to make money. He had partners who lived on their school profits. He built a comfortable house at San Cugat near Barcelona, where he lived with Carmen and his boys. To build it, he had to raze the house he had lived in for years – a pity, because the old house was picturesque with wistaria climbing over it. But there were damp stains on the paintwork and the rooms were full of moisture in winter. So, one day the demolition men arrived with pickaxes and lorries. A few days later there was just a broad scar in the ground.

The new house, like the old, stood on a broad terrace looking onto an open space with a winding road fringing a chestnut forest. It had three floors, all the doors fitted exactly, the showers worked with rare efficiency. It has been a source of wonder to me, the way Spain and Britain seem to have changed places in the forty years since we first arrived in Cordoba. Spanish roads today are impeccable, while in England pot-holes are now the rule. Trains are generally punctual in Spain but not in Britain. Showers are often primitive affairs in Britain, no doubt because of the traditional preference for baths.

Now, though, it is a sad house. I can still see him hurrying along the corridors, or out to the garage with his briefcase, an attentive smile on his lips. But Ben is no longer there. One morning, at the first conference after I had left International House, Ben did not turn up. No one thought anything of it; he had been long enough in the organisation to be absent when he felt like it.

That evening, we were invited to Anne and Donald Biddle's for dinner. The phone rang. It was Tony Duff, my successor. He told me Ben had been murdered.

He had been for a walk in Mayfair late the previous night, and was on his way back to his hotel. An unknown man had come up and stabbed him. It turned out he had just left someone else half-dead on the pavement not far away. A passing taxi driver had witnessed the attack on Ben and called the police, who acted quickly and arrested the murderer. Hearing this on the phone, I felt as though my father's senseless murder had come full circle. I was quite overcome, and hardly spoke all evening, dazed and imagining it all. I told no one, not even Brita, because I did not want to turn the Biddles' dinner-party into a wake.

It is a decision that has tormented me ever since.

When the evening was almost over, I blurted out what had happened. A school director from Brazil hysterically accused me of trying to censor her right to know, of being cold and excessively self-controlled.

38 · Farewell to ILC

In London, we were affected by the three-day week and the miners' strike. The French were especially touching, with their belief that we were shivering and hungry in the dark. French students even got sent food parcels. Inevitably we had smaller classes, and had to raise the fees slightly. I explained we would be charging the equivalent of a packet of cigarettes more per week, which raised no objections. Given the crisis, Tom pointed out that my projects, such as the new video – the first ever used in a private language school in Britain – the teachers' club, and even the teacher training courses were costing a lot of money. I argued that they were essential to the provision of good teaching; they were also excellent publicity.

Tom would guarantee the overdraft, but only if he had a bigger share in the company. I couldn't blame him. He had never received a salary, which in any case would only have been a minute, highly taxable contribution to the wealth which he, his wife and their parents had accumulated. He had generously backed many projects – the schools in Bangkok, Paris and Japan, and smoothed over our various financial crises. Tom now felt he knew enough about running language schools, unaware perhaps that it was fatal to treat them like military units. He wanted more power. As far as I was concerned he could have it, provided I did not have to serve under him, and provided he had reliable subordinates to create and carry out sound educational policies. So I sold him all my International Language Centre shares for £14,000.

Looking back, I feel that my accepting this with such tranquillity was bizarre. For one thing, it seems such a small sum, considering everything Brita and I had done. I think I was anxious to do nothing to jeopardise an already precarious International House. I remember going with Tom to a dark solicitor's office and signing our agreement without sentimentality or regret. I have never really cared about actually owning something. What is important is seeing ideas take shape, not possessing them. This was one reason why the system of affiliation worked so well. Ownership was vested in the schools themselves, yet everyone was bound by definite regulations which ensured educational quality.

I think too that I wanted to be free of the manoeuvring and arguments about money in which I had found myself since Paris. It seemed to have little to do with teaching and writing and the enjoyment of a fascinating profession. Of course I was always prepared to manoeuvre to fulfil a straightforward teaching aim. I didn't mind our organisation being big, as long as it was split up into small units which remained close and familiar. Perhaps I was trying to consolidate my own kind of creativity, familiar and personal. People have often been surprised at how freely International House gave away ideas. But it was part of the same concept of having no secrets, no carefully nursed monopolies. I was, anyway, arrogant enough to feel we had most of the new ideas in English language teaching.

I sold my shares in the Paris and Tokyo schools. Michael and Tom cut Paris right back, even getting rid of the club and poor Odette. I also sold what I owned of the magazines *Modern English* and *Modern English Teacher*, partly because I wanted simplicity. But I remained educational head of the organisation, which was what interested me the most. All IH schools, including Paris and Tokyo, were affiliated through the central department; and that still belonged to me. Teacher training was already under a registered charity, the Haycraft Trust. Over the years we had ploughed back earnings into the organisation, which had thus almost been an educational trust from the start. This now became reality, with Lady Eccles as chair and such EFL eminences as Louis Alexander, the well-known textbook writer, and David Wilkins as trustees, balanced by Donald Biddle, Sidney Heaven who used to work for the prison service, and the writer Anthony Sampson. I wanted regular advice from people I respected. So Brita and I settled down to a new, more peaceable existence. I still had my office; Tom and his underlings were over the road at 33 Shaftesbury Avenue. I had an excellent new secretary, Jean Peto, who did the accounting and arranged the timetable for teacher training. We were self-sufficient.

My second BBC course, *Choosing Your English*, had come out in 1973, practising the language of feelings. At home, Brita and I worked on finishing our beginners' book, *Action*. A simple play unfolded in each lesson. Anwi Buckingham, who now ran the language laboratories, produced exercises, and Ken Wilson wrote appropriate teaching songs. The originality was that the book was operated almost entirely through the teacher's book. Lessons were practised in spoken form, the reading and writing following in the student's book, all consolidated in the homework book. *Action*, though, involved more work for teachers, which they turned out reluctant to do. Some students too had difficulties hearing new vocabulary without seeing it written. I remember a young man from Cartagena perpetually weepy from homesickness, and a stolid nun from Orvieto, neither of whom seemed to retain a word. It worked well for open-minded students and was a much used in-house publication. When ultimately published by Macmillan, it had little success and sank slowly into the limbo of unwanted books. More successful was *Think, Then Speak*, experimenting with teaching language through conversation skills such as deduction, logic, summarising, fluency, imagination, association, empathy and so on. Anyone ignoring these skills inevitably expressed themselves poorly in English, or in any other language.

Il faut reculer pour mieux sauter, as the French say: 'take a step back to get a better jump'. After about a year, in which the number of trainees on teachers' courses increased, and we apportioned classrooms harmoniously within the school, Tom told me he had lost £25,000 over the summer. This seemed incredible, July and August usually being the most crowded months. But he said running a school was not as easy as he had imagined, and he wanted to sell it back to me. I agreed, for £10,000, the sum our educational trust had made in the last year. Tom also asked me to go to Tokyo with him, where teachers and directors of studies were rebelling against Graham. So we flew over the pole, peering out at the freezing white landscapes thousands of feet below.

The trouble at the Tokyo school was Graham's reluctance to hold weekly teachers' meetings. Staff did not know what was going on and complaints and problems were not discussed. Graham was very remote, and few staff had even met him. One director of studies had left after causing major disruption. Another had been disloyal, whispering agreement with discontented teachers, without informing Graham of what was going wrong. Behind everything was Graham's feeling that it didn't really matter what British teachers thought, so long as he had behind him the superior Japanese, whose values he so admired. I felt he resisted staff meetings because they smacked of democracy, a disorderly procedure at odds with the Japanese habit of precise, more formal consultations. We ended up having to ask Graham to go. We had tried to get to know him better, going to Kobe where we once had a school, and to the Buddhist temple at Nara. But he was frozen into a role where his Japanese and American experience both played a part. Perhaps he imagined he was the revered abbot of a Japanese monastery or the young up-to-date president of a powerful American firm. He never really accepted that he just directed a language school full of skilled young teachers, exuberant and enterprising, intrigued by Japan but wanting ultimately to go back home, a place with which on the whole they were well satisfied.

Graham was very hurt. What upset him most was that none of his Japanese staff resigned in sympathy except one, his personal assistant. Tom made a commanding officer speech to everyone and left Peter North, director in Algeria and then London, in charge. On the flight back, the night sky was very clear as we flew over England at 2 a.m. From thirty thousand feet, all the way down from Scotland the cities were like diadems scattered over the dark floor by their careless owners.

After Japan I went to Portugal, still growing with a new school in Oporto and another in Torres Vedras, which reminded me of the fortifications built by Wellington in 1809. There was a third in Braga, and Tony Laurel's school in Aveiro. I visited Gay Adamson, director of the Coimbra school, in her wonderful flat overlooking the Douro valley. I remembered the novel I had written about the Peninsular War at the age of eleven; the names came flooding back, recalling those creative Sunday evenings as I read my passionate flow aloud to the boys in the dormitory.

Colin McMillan secured a triumph by getting a series of English lessons onto Portuguese television. He used filmed sketches from the English teaching theatre, each illustrating a particular structure, followed by a live lesson taught by himself, with students, to reinforce it. It was a brilliant idea and became the most popular programme in Portugal: viewers were entertained by the sketches, and identified with the the students' stumbling efforts and final success. I saw the new school in Madeira, a partnership between Colin and two Portugese businessmen who thought a school was simply a way of making money – which is why it soon foundered. I shall never forget tiny, precarious Madeira airport, like a bright handkerchief stretched over a ledge in the distant cliff. A previous flight had overrun and tumbled into the sea, but we got down safely. I was exhausted. As always when visiting Colin, we talked over drinks into the small hours. On very little sleep, I was expected to observe classes without nodding off. I also gave a talk to Portugese teachers on various English teaching approaches.

I re-visited Beirut that summer after three years. In Athens, Nick Dobree had started up a most wonderful school. It had a language laboratory, a teacher training programme, and a superb team of teachers. The director was Simon Cole whose impulsive German wife, Oda, wore boots and kicked cars that got in her way. The staff included Sue Lake, who had taught in Greece for several years and later produced an excellent Greek textbook using International House techniques. It was in Omonia Square and initially had a lot of students. But something was wrong. Numbers gradually diminished until Nick had to close. According to the officially-required Greek director, Nicos Vacas, this was partly because the school was not allowed to advertise any connection with International House or Britain. There were hundreds of *frontisteri*, as language schools were called, in Athens. They were terrified of an International House school. It was the time of the colonels' dictatorship and, according to Nicos, there was a rumour that anyone who went to International House was a communist. So students were afraid to come.

In Beirut, though, Nick's schools were flourishing. There were now two: the original one with Mary Zeine in the western, Muslim quarter which occupied a whole building, and another in Tabariz, the eastern, Christian quarter, which was modern with a balcony looking down over a square. I flippantly said it would make an ideal machine-gun post. The Tabariz school was directed in turn by two highly responsible young women: Pat Smith who had taught in

London and Libya, then Felicity Henderson who had been in Beirut from the beginning, aided by Philip Padfield.

I tried what I thought was an interesting experiment. I had lost my voice, which someone said was a pity because I could not give a teaching demonstration. So I gave one in mime, with the help of the blackboard, teaching the present perfect tense, one of the trickiest for foreigners and which the class had not yet done.

I was introduced simply as 'another teacher'. I was fascinated by the rapt attention of the class as they deciphered my gestures and responded, instead of simply listening as usual. Of course I was a 'new' teacher and therefore interesting anyway, and they somehow knew this class was special.

After observing other classes and getting students to do some English Through Acting, Nick and I had a hoarse discussion about the chances of civil war in Lebanon. A bus crammed with Palestinians had recently been attacked by the Christian Falange. 'I'll give it till September,' seemed to be the general opinion. I couldn't believe it. Here we were playing squash, going to visit the solid stone houses in Mary Zeine's hillside village, discussing the delights of skiing up in the mountains and the dangers of strong currents in the sea. Despite the road blocks, everything seemed as normal as it had been since 1918, when Lebanon stopped being a mere enclave in the Turkish empire. Under French influence it grew to become the 'Switzerland of the Middle East', complete with corniche, banks, swimming-pools, skyscraper hotels and night-life.

The Dobrees gave a party on my last night. The drink arrived at the last minute and the waiters were recruited hurriedly and were unskilled, though jolly. A whisky-and-soda was a dash of soda and a lot of whisky; the same went for gin-and-tonic. After half an hour the élite of Beirut's European society were blotto, as glasses were dropped and smashed on the floor. An oil journalist became a satyr and chased the girls around. The Venezuelan ambassador told us loudly, in poor English, that everyone in his country spoke English perfectly. As the guest of honour I had only one whisky-and-soda, which finished me off anyway. I was stiff and controlled, behaving as well as I could. I spent the evening being wheeled about the room to smile amiably at person after person. As Chloë Dobree said afterwards, 'I've never known you so boring!'

It was all a bit like the Duchess of Richmond's ball before the cannon at Waterloo.

39 · Murder in Beirut

As predicted, fighting started in Beirut that September. Crossfire prevented students and teachers from getting to the west Beirut school. Eager snipers kept up continual fire. One afternoon, Nick Dobree returned to his flat and hesitated between making a phone call or going to the loo. He was lucky to choose the latter. A few minutes later a car bomb exploded in the street outside, showering his telephone table with shards of splintered glass.

'You were relatively safe from shells,' said Nick afterwards, 'as long as you had a wall between you and the explosion.'

To begin with, people did not know how to cope with war and there were many casualties. But they gradually learned what precautions to take. Nick once watched a savage bombardment from the safety of the hills, and was surprised at the news that there had been only two or three casualties. Chloë booked a flight and then cancelled it, which was just as well as the plane was blown up.

According to some counts, there were seventeen ceasefires in that first year, before the 'proper' war started. Both Beirut schools began a rhythm: open during them, closed when they were broken. When the war really got going, the Tabariz school was occupied by Syrian soldiers, thus confirming my earlier suspicion. They sold the language laboratory, although who could have wanted one just then remains a mystery. They amused themselves by chucking the reels of tape around the room, which was soon knee-deep in the stuff. They built bunk beds in the classrooms and used the place as lodgings and local military headquarters. Pat Smith had lovingly accumulated books and tapes, and was in despair. She had started the school in 1969 and run it for five years; suddenly, everything was shattered. Something similar happened in the west Beirut school, but much later, during the Israeli invasion. Beirut was flooded by refugees from the south, who broke into empty buildings and stole what they found. But Nick had the brains and the humanity to offer them the school premises, there then being no students. Families occupied the classrooms, and Nick went round ensuring they were all right. Where English dialogues had rung out with Levantine accents, shrouded figures now cooked meals and slept on colourful blankets on the floor, to the cries and chatter of their children. Nick said the refugees were clean, and respected his property. The fact that he had offered them this refuge earned their gratitude, and they complied with whatever he asked.

I visited Beirut in 1982 during a lull, flying from Ankara where we had affiliated a school belonging to a Kurdish businessman and army boxing champion called Nazif Bey. From a small southern village, he had secured a contract teaching English to members of parliament, even to some ministers. He had the boxer's crumpled face and upturned moustaches: in his pale winter coat and cap he looked like an imperial Turkish cavalry officer about to gallop forth with raised scimitar. He owed his good English to his persistence: he had won a scholarship to London for selling more copies of the Language Tuition Centre's magazine than anyone else in Turkey.

Nazif was very much a businessman, and couldn't really believe that all this 'charity trust' talk was anything but a front. When Brita and I had our twenty-fifth anniversary celebration in London he stood up and, instead of a congratulatory speech, announced he had brought over some splendid Turkish copper trays, and if anyone wanted to buy one very cheap they could do so at reception. Later, visiting a new affiliate in Oman, I was amazed to see Nazif surrounded by Turkish carpets in a hotel lobby, including one for £400,000 which he was trying to flog to the sultan.

He realised the importance of quality and the advantages of belonging to a prestigious international organisation. He kept on asking for 'experienced' teachers. But, I pointed out, he didn't offer conditions to attract anyone except those straight off the teachers' course. I once stood in for a teacher of his who was ill. I was reminded of our students in Cordoba – the same warmth and directness, the dignity of what had once been a great empire, now a developing country with a European veneer. Nazif started schools in Ankara, Istanbul and Izmir. The economic situation was difficult, with galloping inflation and insufficient government money to provide oil in winter. Morale sank when two of our teachers were asphyxiated by gases in a cave near Ankara.

Accused of making irregular export bonus claims, he was imprisoned. After sixteen months in a cell, during which he published two books on economics, he was declared innocent. In his absence the school was run by his wife, a gynæcologist, advised by former army officers. Nazif had always favoured them as the only Turkish profession with sound administrative experience. The result was an impossible bureaucracy in which a director in Izmir had to apply to Istanbul for permission to buy a pencil. Unfortunately the situation did our reputation in Turkey no good. It may not have been entirely Nazif's fault. But in the end we had to disaffiliate his schools. Although their educational standards were reasonable, we received too many complaints from teachers to recommend new ones to go there.

Nick met me at Beirut airport, which had just reopened. At his flat, I didn't like him going out onto the balcony to see what was happening whenever we heard machine-gun fire. At night, there was the hum of shells flying over the city. In the morning, I walked up to the school in the sunlight, past the precarious, dead buildings that littered a way I knew well from throbbing, crowded days. A woman was sweeping up her electric lamp shop where a bomb had exploded the night before. The floor was covered with scraps of china and glass, and shattered lamp holders dangled from the ceiling. The school looked much the same. I recognised some of the teachers from previous visits. Some were still there because their husbands had jobs which kept them in Beirut despite the war. Others, older ladies, had lived here for most of their lives and would stay on no matter what happened. International House had found jobs in other schools for many of those who had left. London was full of Lebanese. A few months earlier I had had a Muslim and a Christian in an intermediate class. After an embarrassed, frosty introduction, they got on well together, sharing unexpected nostalgia. Because some of the teachers now in Beirut had been hastily grabbed without training, classes were not brilliant. But student motivation had increased because English was essential for travelling abroad – yet another example of the need for English, making me once more lament the failure of so many British governments to take the teaching of their own language to foreigners more seriously.

Nick and I had lunch with the Zeines in their flat on the eighth floor of a tower block, fortunately undamaged. They had a horrifying view of devastated Beirut. The Zeines were despondent, he because the American University had been closed and he saw no end to the war, she because they felt lonely: some of their children had married foreigners, others had emigrated to the States.

The next day, I went to lunch at the house of Philip Padfield, the director of studies, on a slight hill with a terrace. Philip had stayed on partly because of friends, partly for his dog. I could understand this. It seemed so tranquil, sitting on his terrace in the sun, eating our lunch and discussing the difficulties of maintaining teaching standards. Despite day-to-day problems, Philip seemed happy. He loved Beirut. I remember him saying, 'There's no real danger, except the accident of a stray bullet, or a piece of shrapnel. It's bracing, too, protecting the school against all these challenges!'

That evening Nick and I went to the cinema, to see *Barry Lyndon*. We sat in cushioned armchairs, licking ice-cream, and it seemed incredible that we were in war-torn Beirut. We could have been anywhere. An irony of war is how peaceful the truces can be.

Back in London, it was not long before I heard that Philip had been kidnapped with a friend when leaving a bar at one in the morning. Colonel Gaddafi was being threatened by the Americans, and had sent word to Beirut suggesting a few hostages. The full Britain-based American raid happened the following week, and

Philip and his friend were shot, their bodies left by the side of the road.

I remembered his words about 'no real danger'.

40 · Severing Bonds

When she was sixteen, Katinka went to Oakham, a mixed school in Rutland where she was very happy. Then she got into Saint Andrew's University, but found it too much like school and transferred to Sussex to read philosophy and English, also singing in madrigal choirs and an opera. She then spent sixteen months in India studying Indian singing and yoga. All our children were independent and, like their parents, seldom in the employ of other people. Richard and Katinka did a teachers' course and took up EFL for a while.

Back home, Katinka had twelve Indians come over from Orissa to perform at the ICA and Womad festivals around Britain and Europe. Qualifying in shiatsu, yoga and voice therapy, she combined her interest in healing with her other skills, putting on shadow puppet plays in schools and doing voice workshops for the English National Opera schemes for Down's syndrome children and old-age pensioners.

Jimmy took three 'A' levels and, like Richard, declined to go to university. Feeling there were better ways of spending three years, he launched into drumming. He auditioned and rejected 87 prospective singers for his group, and ran a recording studio in a crumbling warehouse in Rotherhithe, on the banks of the Thames with a dent in one wall where a boat had crashed. He then invented a new form of equipment for laser games which he sold as far afield as Spain and Saudi Arabia.

We now had six grandchildren. Katinka, with fellow performing artist and clown Francis Agnew, spent another six months with their little son Merlyn in India doing street theatre for children. We visited them there. It was strange going back to India as a visitor, rather than a member of the ruling class. I was relieved not to be called 'sahib', though many things were much the same, with traces of the Raj still everywhere – especially on the railways, with stations girders reminding us of country halts in Devon, menus still offering Ovaltine and Horlicks, or fried eggs for breakfast, or places I knew: Fatehpur Sikri, Mysore, Hyderabad.

Jimmy met an attractive girl at a party, but failed to get her address and knew only her name, Melissa, and that she came from Yorkshire. He was in despair when, driving his car one day a week later, he saw her on the pavement and swept her up. Five years later they had two girls, and he says they plan to have four more.

Richard married a French girl, an IH Proficiency student he met while running our bar. It was the first time the bar made a profit, and it also made Richard. Perhaps because he was also learning to fly, or because of his girl-friend Claudine, he suddenly became responsible, changing from the wild adolescent who 'borrowed' our car to go to Wales one summer and crashed it. He got his commercial pilot's licence, though his teachers' course proved more useful when he left for Paris and tried to find work. He was given a warm welcome by Claudine's family who were so taken with him they asked if we had any more Richards at home! In Paris, he abandoned his ambition to fly, it being an expensive business. It was hard to get a pilot's job with so many redundant after the Vietnam war. He started teaching English, and he and some other teachers founded their own business English school at La Défense. He then started another company, this time teaching the use of computers, from offices below where he and Claudine lived with their three little sons – who soon started coming over to learn English with us in the summer.

Olive continued to live alone in the same house in Torquay until the mid-seventies. She came to visit two or three times a year, or we went down to her. She was much the same, her hair a little greyer, her body a little bulkier. She still played tennis in her seventies, still bubbled with jokes she had heard on the wireless, still stuck paper butterflies to the wallpaper, still rearranged the garden with new gravel paths and stone borders, still as exuberant and independent as ever.

Then she rang to say she had been robbed. Early one morning she thought she heard birds in the attic. She went up to investigate and found two men hiding. Coolly, she said, 'I thought you were birds.' They handed over the few possessions they had taken, including my father's sword and a silver fruit-bowl. She told them to go, and they tramped down the stairs. She called the police, who thought she had dreamed it all because there was no sign of entry. She came up to Blackheath, with a constant tick in her cheek and she began to talk nonsense, repeating 'What do you think I should do, now, John?' There was something forlorn about her, as if she were a little girl insisting, insisting, not hearing the answers. My brother Colin came down and wept in front of her. We didn't see much of him and his family as they lived in north London. But this seemed somehow the dissolution of a family, of links we had always taken for granted, of all the memories of sunlight and tennis, of Italy and hibiscus, of laughter, of the warm sea. Olive seemed almost to have a fragrance of these things.

I called a doctor friend of ours. On his recommendation, Olive went to a private nursing home and had elecric-shock treatment. This was miraculous, and seemed to return her to her old self. We decided it would be better if she lived with us. But that seemed like caging a wild bird, so she bought a flat next door. I went down with her to Torquay and she packed up the books she loved, the diaries and scrap-books, the untidy bed linen, the rugs from Burma and Naini-tal that my father had trodden on, the stacked photographs of her past. She didn't think I knew enough to be of any real help, but attacked the task with incredible energy, bundling up her life – and in a sense mine – and getting the house empty and cleaned up, ready for sale.

She settled into the flat next door to us in Blackheath, coming over for meals, suddenly taking buses round southern London. 'She's fine!' said her psychiatrist. 'She must take her medicine, though. She fibulates, and the medicine will cure this as long as she takes it regularly.' Perhaps because of her old illness after my father's death,

Olive had always shunned doctors, feeling they intruded on her privacy. She had always been healthy, apart from that one time, and had never needed attention. Medicine was alien to her.

It was Richard's birthday. The family were sitting down to dinner. Brita had cooked a feast. The presents were colourfully wrapped. But there was no Olive. I went to fetch her from her flat, but there was no answer to the bell. I wondered where she had gone. Had she forgotten? I used my spare key. I found her slumped over a chair like a paper doll, still breathing but apparently not conscious. I called the ambulance and phoned home to break the news. Greenwich hospital took her into a geriatric ward. She would have loathed it if she had realised. We clustered round her bed from where she looked out listlessly, but at least conscious.

A doctor took me aside. 'I can't do much for her,' she said. 'You must realise she's just a vegetable!' Olive a vegetable! I remembered watching her hands as she played the piano under the lamplight in Alassio, thinking in agony that one day those hands would be stilled.

'She can't be a vegetable!' protested Jimmy. 'It's just that she can't talk. But I bet she can write.' So we wrote, asking how she was. Did she feel any pain? To our delight she responded, taking the pen and the back of an envelope, writing in her normal hand. Apart from the difficulty of talking, she felt all right.

As the days passed she began to talk, but confusedly. Quotations from Shelley and Keats began to appear during our written conversations. She wrote down stories we had not heard before about people long dead, from her childhood. Her days were now an unclear fog, enlivened by imagination. 'I hear the Russians have landed,' she remarked one evening. It didn't seem to worry her. It was as if everything came to her from an unemotional dream world. She lived in that hospital for eleven months and eight days. The nurses called her 'love' and 'dearie'. One evening, an Irish voice rang to tell me that they were sorry but Mrs Haycraft had just died of pneumonia.

Olive had joked that RIP stood for 'Return If Possible'. I was tempted to put it on her gravestone, with something to show the love and sorrow and memories we all felt.

PART 7

Palazzo in Piccadilly

41 · Harold Macmillan Inaugurates

After eighteen years, our Shaftesbury Avenue lease was about to end. I went to see Joe Levy, our landlord, who talked about light at the end of the tunnel. To us it looked more like eternal darkness. An American advertising man suggested renting our frontage for advertisements: 'We'll make it worth your while! I'm sure your students won't mind working by electric light!'

I read in the *Guardian* that the St James's Club at 106 Piccadilly had gone bankrupt. They had asked members to lunch more at the club, but too late. The remaining twenty-year lease was going for £100,000. There was an annual rent dating from 1922, the year the lease began: £3,500 a year, or 23p a square foot! I was shown round by the gloomy footman left in charge to discourage squatters. The palace, which in effect it was, resembled the Petit Trianon at Versailles: the same black-and-white-chequered stone floor at the entrance, and about the same size. The Royal Academy, Palmerston's mansion at number 94 and the St James' were the only 18th-century buildings in Piccadilly to survive the Edwardians and the blitz.

Built by the earl of Coventry in 1762, it contained a first-floor suite whose magnificence was revealed once the huge shutters were folded back. At night it was magical. One great drawing-room had an Adam ceiling painted by Zucchi, only slightly smeared having been the club dining-room. A balcony stretched the whole length of the building, looking over Piccadilly and the trees of Green Park. Connected to this large room was what had once been the bedroom of the countess, with another Adam ceiling. It had been the club bar. Both rooms had beautifully carved-marble Adam fireplaces.

According to drawings in the London Museum, the adjoining boudoir was the only octagonal boudoir in London, painted in blue, pink and rose. But the club had used it as an upstairs pantry, with a hot plate defacing the ceiling with greasy splodges, and a wall had been torn down for the electric lift. Small yellow cupboards had been cut into the other walls. Something so unique and delicate, turned into an ugly little room that smelled of fat!

A magnificent staircase, built by Cundy in 1832, led down to a waiting area with massive porphyry pillars, like an inclined rowlock with a landing where it separated and a large, clear window above. A narrow side staircase led to the gentlemen's bedrooms on the third floor, and the servants' quarters on the fourth. I could easily imagine Club members stumbling up, after billiards and brandy, trying to find their rooms and wandering into the maids' instead. On the ground floor was the large glass-roofed billiard-room. Next door was a splendid bar, decorated by Osbert Lancaster. The basement held a vast kitchen, almost big enough to be a separate house, with an enormous black stove in the middle. The mansion had been a private, aristocratic home, the Coventrys' town house, within easy reach of Buckingham Palace. Then it became the residence of Napoleon III's ambassador to Queen Victoria, the Comte de Flahut, Talleyrand's illegitimate son. It became the St James's Club just before the Prussian army beat Napoleon in 1870.

The thing about 106 Piccadilly was that it *looked* expensive, and seemed in need of massive redecoration. I was glad to see that the building was too rambling, too old-fashioned, to be easily marketable. It was grade-one listed, meaning much of it could not be touched or divided into smaller rooms for a hotel or offices.

I set my heart on it. It would be a worthy headquarters for our world organisation, with a personality of its own. I calculated that it would hold two dozen classrooms, with the billiard-room as a teachers' rooms and teacher training, lectures and parties on the main, first floor. The wine cellar would make an excellent language laboratory, cool in summer and warm in winter. The only real barrier seemed an objection to 'students'. To the firm which owned 106 Piccadilly, this meant rowdy, undisciplined youths. They almost died imagining 'students' beneath the chandeliers in the St James' Club – and foreigners to boot! But the alternative to us in 106 was probably an oil sheikh, and this spurred them in our favour. The lease specified that neither a school nor a hospital could occupy the building – 'school' no doubt meaning children; but we were in the same sort of category. I argued, truthfully, that we were essentially a teacher training college for British teachers to teach English to adults. Of course we needed adult students for our trainees to observe and practise teaching.

We were, so far, the only people really interested in the building. The club wanted £100,000 for the lease. They laughed when our agent Peter Banks offered £20,000, but finally compromised at £65,000. Westminster Council agreed to a change of use. We now had to convince them we were respectable. They wanted to visit 40 Shaftesbury Avenue to see how we ran the training there. I told all our teachers to wear something tidy. Ann Samson got everything polished, from wooden floors to door handles. Punctually at ten, four directors arrived in dark suits, like undertakers. After they had observed a few classes, we went to my office. On the stairs they were pushed rudely aside by a long-haired individual carrying a rucksack. I have never known who this was or what he was doing there – probably a trainee late for class. The startled directors asked with pursed lips if this was the type of person we would introduce to the former St James' Club. I said he was a temporary canteen worker. They were mollified. We next had to confront the whole board of directors, thirty-two including a peer of the realm, ranged solemnly round a room with portraits of ladies in diaphonous dresses and gentlemen with powdered hair. It was like the last task in a fairy tale before the princess's hand is won or lost. I had prepared answers to twenty-eight likely questions: the proportion of trainees to foreign students, where our foreign students came from, how advanced most were, how many British trainees passed the course annually, why the course lasted only four weeks, whether we had had teacher training at the beginning in Cordoba. All the questions came up. The phone call came a few days later. 'Once you have paid what you owe the St James's Club, the building is yours!' They also said we must add £100 for the coal left in the cellar, surely the work of a small-minded administrator, or the club's revenge for our beating them down by 35%.

We paid, and celebrated with a staff tour. Many seemed hesitant, reluctant to leave the cheerful familiarity of 40 Shaftesbury Avenue for such bleak grandiloquence. I realised how insensitive we can be to the potential of a new development, particularly if the developing is being done by someone else. 'John's fantasy!' said some, making flippant comments about students freezing in the vast refrigerator downstairs, or being crushed by a falling chandelier.

A flattering article in the *Evening News*, comparing my EFL work favourably with the British Council's, generated indignation not from the Council but from private school owners and staff. The *EFL Gazette*, mouthpiece of the British language-teaching profession, attacked 'the growing power of International House' and said no one should use its teachers' courses to lay down how EFL should be taught. People from other schools made our staff feel guilty to work for this megalomaniac organisation. The guilt filtered back into the general atmosphere of the school. We were still using 40 Shaftesbury Avenue while 106 Piccadilly was being redecorated. Our designer Peter Graville hired workmen from Devon, who kipped down in the enormous kitchen like a hidden army.

We invited Randolph Quirk to our first teachers' club meeting, to speak on English language structure. To ensure security, we told everyone to ring the doorbell. Quirk was not informed, and I caught him just as he went steaming off indignantly into the night. We had a small party afterwards. The unconsumed wine was later discovered by the workmen, rising from their depths like thirsty mice. We found them asleep under the Adam ceiling next morning, still drunk.

The work still unfinished, we held the annual directors' conference there. Most affiliated school directors attended, eager to see the new premises. These conferences, held ever since we had schools abroad, lasted three or four days. We tried to make attendance obligatory – as at the annual directors of studies' conference.

One objective was to share ideas which might transform a school overnight. It also gave a sense of unity and a chance to find out how everyone else was doing. The brief, usually fascinating account of each school by its director could bring advantages – an unexpected contract, for example, with a businessman who had enjoyed his own classes at an IH school somewhere else. The agenda was drawn up in London absorbing suggestions from affiliates. All schools, including London, paid the IH central department an annual 1%–2.5% of their income, for finding teachers, organising annual inspections and conferences, and handling emergencies. Surpluses or losses were carried forward, the fee rising or falling accordingly. The 'grapevine' effect was amazing. London knew almost immediately about any significant event in a school abroad. The schools produced new ideas and trained staff. It was a cooperative, rather than a large London-centred bureaucracy, a family with common roots, objectives and standards. Enthusiasm and teaching ability were amazingly high.

At conferences I did not allow voting. IH was not a political organisation. Schools were affiliated to our educational trust, whose trustees decided what should or should not be done – though they usually followed joint recommendations from the schools. During my time, six schools were disaffiliated for not maintaining educational standards. There were only five resignations, mostly temporary from Tom Hall's group.

Aspiring affiliates could attend conferences, learning more about IH than I or anyone else could tell them. Javier Lacunza, a Spanish Basque, was a good example. In 1936 his republican parents had sent him to a monastery in Devon, which he had recently revisited, evoking happy days in a green country at peace. Now in his fifties, he had three English schools in San Sebastian, the first opening the same year as ours in Cordoba. Brita and I got to know him better when visiting San Sebastian, then in crisis with ETA, the Basque independence movement. During one teachers' meeting we had to close the shutters because of stone-throwing outside. As few of his staff were specifically trained, we sent out a teacher trainer. He employed Spanish teachers for beginners, while our rule was to

employ only native British, American or Commonwealth teachers –
though I now thought this excessive. It was really the students, with
their faith in *el profesor nativo*, the native-speaker teacher, who
demanded this. But foreign teachers, who had analysed English from
the outside, could appreciate their compatriots' learning difficulties.
The crucial questions were their command of English, and how well
they had done on a teachers' course. Javier galvanised us into setting
wider criteria, no longer limiting ourselves to native speakers of
English.

For this first conference at 106 Piccadilly, we held a grand
inauguration inviting Harold Macmillan, also an EFL publisher, and
the guitarist Paco Peña, one of Brita's first pupils in Cordoba, to
open our new building officially. They made a harmonious team.
Paco made us, personally, feel we had come full circle since our
beginnings in Andalusia. Macmillan was as witty as ever. He
contrasted the St James's Club, where he had played many a game
of cards, with its new tenants, a 'respectable seat of learning'. His
one stumble was when he said, 'I think we should thank Mr, er,
hm,' sifting frantically through his few papers, 'Mr, er – yes,
Haycraft!, for this venture.'

The conference was a success, but we soon had accountancy
problems. Our new accountant, Max, was not only fully qualified,
he had just completed a postgraduate course in philosophy, and
seemed pleasant. The first ominous note sounded when he failed to
produce the accounts on time. 'John,' he said with his charming
smile, 'I'm finding it difficult to adapt to things around here.' I
suggested he catch up the following weekend; I would pay extra.
Accurate, punctual accounts were vital. The Devonian hordes in the
basement were running up vast bills. Our two accounting clerks,
Saswathi and Sandra, could keep routine business going. But where
Max should have been, there was a black hole. So we looked for
someone else. Max was publicly talking of unfair dismissal and
saying teachers' salaries were suffering because of the 'extravagant'
redecoration. There was a wave of sympathy for him.

After frantic interviewing, we found someone more suitable. Peter
Lawson had worked for a bank from age sixteen, then for Berlitz

schools on the same kind of work as ours. He soon discovered we were short of £90,000. Apart from the expenses of moving, our fees were barely adequate and could not be raised before January. When I explained things to our banker, he grew increasingly remote. 'We don't give further advances to firms going bankrupt!' he said abruptly.

As I burbled, 'But we had a lot of students this summer – ' he withdrew to an office where I couldn't get at him.

Back at IH, Donald Biddle and I sat in my fourth-floor office, once the butler's bedroom. The sunset glowed, pink and peaceful, on buildings and roofs outside.

'The worst thing is, the trustees will have to close the school.'

'Close it! Why?'

'Because they are personally liable if they knowingly keep the trust going in a state of bankruptcy.'

Close us down? Impossible! It would mean abandoning 106 Piccadilly in a cloud of debt, our employees jobless. The affiliations would crumble. A quarter of a century's work would end in humiliation.

Downstairs, it was break time for the evening students and they were milling about exuberantly, scarlet traces of sunset gleaming through the great windows by the porphyry pillars, casting sunspots on the carpet.

'I can't let it go!' I said. 'Look at all this! It's successful. It works. All that's missing is sordid cash! We can't let it die, leave these rooms empty again, with nothing but an echo of International House!'

'But you can't encumber the trustees, either. You invited them in.'

'I wouldn't dream of making them liable. There must be some other way.' We talked in low voices, by the roll of honour for those who had died in the first world war.

'There are other banks. But they would need security . . .'

'We've got a house, and Brita inherited some shares from her mother.'

*

Brita had always supported even my most doubtful IH ventures.

'Of course there's nothing in it for us,' I told her at home that evening. 'We're an educational trust. We could lose everything, including our house. But I'm sure we can make 106 Piccadilly work.'

'If you're sure . . .'

So next day I went to our old bank in Shaftesbury Avenue and saw the manager, Peter Hoyle, who agreed to lend us £90,000 provided we produced up-to-date accounts, and security in the shape of our house and shares.

Thus were provided the strong flower pots needed to protect our fragile plants from the bleak winter winds.

42 · Through the Iron Curtain

In 1982, a Hungarian on a teachers' course called Laszlo Simonfalvi asked if I was interested in starting an English school in Budapest. I said I was, but thought no more about it. I felt a communist government was unlikely to favour our type of free enterprise. To my surprise, Laszlo rang ten months later. He had started an English school inspired by International House ideas, and it was crowded with students. He asked if I would come and visit the school. A month later, I did.

It was my second visit to a communist country. Brita and I had taught on a British Council summer course in Slovakia in 1974, bringing the children as conversation practice for the Slovak teachers at meals. The Slovaks were fascinated. We tried learning Slovak with a new technique, saying what we wanted to learn and how. Before going shopping, we asked for dialogues to rehearse and put into practice in the little morning market.

On our last night, ten-year-old Jimmy fell seriously ill. We could not move from our hostel whose new arrivals were Russian wrestlers now hanging up red banners and emblems. We found a German-speaking doctor. To our horror, she said Jimmy had meningitis. He

was rushed to hospital, where the head pathologist, Kamila Getli-
kova, was delighted to meet westerners with whom she could speak
both French and English. She clasped Jimmy to her large bosom and
comforted us by saying, with great rolling 'r's, '*Je vais cur-r-rer votr-
r-re fils!*' It was not meningitis. We now had nowhere to stay, so she
took us along to her tiny flat. There were gherkins soaking in the
sink.

'*Vous*,' she said, pointing at the sitting-room floor, '*vous pouvez*
sleep there. I shall sleep *avec les* gherkins.' Generous, but we
couldn't accept. She helped us find the one hotel room available.
Jimmy was in a ward with a little Slovak boy called Miroslav. After
a week, he was allowed to travel, although limping slightly. We
drove down the broad plain past ripening plum trees, defaced Jewish
cemeteries, and ruined castles with legends about ageing countesses
who had slaughtered young maidens in order to drink their blood
and remain young.

But I went to Budapest alone, to a splendid hotel by the Danube,
and observed classes in a variety of premises. On Sunday we drove
to Kecskemet, a sprawling town with three churches and the Kodaly
music institute. We drank cherry brandy in the back room of a bar
and discussed plans.

I was impressed by the Hungarian facility with languages; many
spoke almost perfect English. Laszlo said we would need something
big, and the Kodaly institute might provide premises. What about
teachers? Laszlo had been passing on ideas from our teachers'
course, but found it a poor subsitute for the real thing. Visas were
still hard to get. Couldn't we provide teacher trainers to instruct
Hungarians? We did, and things improved. But Laszlo found it
difficult to cope with a staff of over twenty, a number reached
rapidly in Budapest, as ours was the only adult English school.

Laszlo's staff started leaving to found a second school, and then
another. Soon there were three – International House, International
Language Centre and International School – all flourishing in colourful premises: Laszlo on an upper floor with the smell of fresh

bread suffusing the staircase, George in the centre of town with a large lecture-room, and Anna sharing with a youth club in a street called Bimbo. The building had been a brothel, then a prison; the cells made convenient classrooms. Although he was the first person to start an IH school in Hungary, there was no love lost between Laszlo and his teachers. Standards slipped because he did not communicate with London. He asked for teachers too late, and gave no employment or accommodation details. At one of the new schools, I praised his initiative in starting the whole enterprise. My audience protested. Perhaps they thought, quite unjustifiably, that I was prejudiced in his favour because he was getting my book on the French Revolution translated into Hungarian. Laszlo disaffiliated later. I often wonder what happened to him, with his extraordinary mixture of initiative, stubborn independence and creativity. Anna Siko's Bimbo school alone survived, still full despite increasing competition, running teachers' courses and producing new ideas.

About now we started schools in Poland and extended our contacts in Russia. At an IATEFL conference in Athens and again in London the following year, I had met Natasha Gvishiani, English professor at Moscow University, who, I discovered, was like a Red princess, married to Kosygin's grandson and related to Stalin's wife. Late in 1989, on the eve of the communist collapse, Natasha and her former tutor, Svetlana Ter Minosova, head of all Soviet foreign language institutes, invited Brita and me to lecture in Moscow and Leningrad.

Walking us round the golden domed churches, Natasha pointed to the slopes by the Kremlin wall, saying 'I used to toboggan there.'

Terry Sandell, the British Council representative, put us up and we met a whole new world of Russian English teachers. We were also delighted to see Bruce Monk, a teacher from our London executive school who had been at Moscow University for nine years. He much preferred Russians discussing the purpose of life or the nature of love to Americanised Europeans complaining about their dishwashers. He had recently co-written *Happy English* for Soviet secondary schools, with a print run of three million but hardly any royalties.

We were asked to run a course at the Foreign Language Institute in Tibilisi, and flew with a group of IH trainers who all had luggage mishaps. At Moscow they assumed it would automatically be loaded for Tibilisi. Rodney Blakeston lost everything, so I lent him sweaters and underwear. He bought some boots for twenty roubles; made of cardboard, they only lasted a week. Martin Parrott heard over the intercom, on the plane back to Moscow at the end of the course, that his luggage was on board! Kate Leigh alone retrieved hers only one day late. We stayed at the Tibilisi Hotel, built in 1912, where the waiters mooned lugubriously. The only cure for the bitter cold in our room was to sit on the lavatory and flush it; the water mysteriously ran hot. Despite the shortages, though, the hospitality was wonderful, with constant invitations from new people. Tibilisi reminded me of Izmir, with similar wooden ornamentation, balconies and tree-lined streets. Snowy mountains shone behind great chunks of ice in the sunlight.

Before the course we visited Gori, Stalin's birthplace – not for that reason but to see the sister of Mr Bestavachvili, our Georgian builder in Blackheath. She offered us an enormous lunch. She remembered Stalin's mother doing laundry for people. We tried the Stalin museum, but it was closed, though the house where the Little Father was brought up was open. Gori was one of the few places in Russia not to tear down his statue; the vast black menace still stood in front of the government buildings. Demonstrating students eager to destroy it after Khruschev's 1956 revelations were pushed to the river by the local militia and shot.

The Tibilisi course was extraordinarily lively. There was a new freedom of expression, impossible a few years earlier. People said Marx was nonsense and boasted they had always been secret Christians. As in Hungary, the standard of English was remarkable – perhaps because learning it had been a kind of protest. Our teachers were more 'intellectual' than most westerners and loved poetry and plays. Most were part of the 'intelligentsia', a concept which for good or ill hardly exists in Britain.

Intellectual expectations became apparent when we were invited to a performance of *King Lear* in Georgian, directed by Robert Sturua, familiar to London theatre-goers. Because we had not seen or read the play for years, we had trouble unscrambling the plot. 'Who gets blinded? What for? What's the nice daughter's name? Which one is she?' Yet in spite of the gaps in our culture we were appreciated by our trainees because we were that rare thing – foreign!

The only other foreigner I met was a Frenchman who hailed me on the university steps and told me he had fought in the resistance and, after the war, travelled to Moscow bursting with zeal. The KGB finally got him stuffed away in Tibilisi where they could keep an eye on him. He had lived here ever since, had a Georgian wife and children, and taught secondary school French, wondering what he had been doing in this alien town all his life.

We also explored Poland. Our chairman, Norman Reddaway, had been ambassador there until he retired in 1978. In 1939, as an undergraduate, Norman had been to Wilna, now Vilnius, then part of Poland. He speaks excellent Polish. Travelling with him reminded me of the fascinating introduction to Swedish history and politics given me by Brita's father.

In Warsaw, we stayed at an overheated hotel full of smiling prostitutes, opposite the sooty façade of an ugly skyscraper, communist party headquarters, a present from Stalin. We went to Poznan by train, the carriages mostly dark because there were no light-bulbs. I knew the English professor at Poznan University, Jan Fisiak, and had heard there might be a nascent English school. Jan arranged for me to lecture on methodology, not part of east European teachers' courses.

The school existed, run by Anna Zabrocka and her husband Tadeus, a university linguistician. It reminded me of Budapest, with rented rooms, bilingual staff and Englishwomen married to Poles. We discussed ways of helping, and the chances of renting former communist buildings. Politically, things were still up in the air. We went to a party which Fisiak couldn't attend because he was being sworn in as education minister in one of the last, shaky communist governments. I remember asking a university lecturer if his youthful idealism hadn't ended in disillusionment. He roared with laughter. 'Idealism!' he scoffed, 'I don't know a single Pole who ever felt idealistic about communism, at any age! The church, perhaps, but communism, never!'

We flew to Krakow, one of Europe's most beautiful cities but close to the Nowa Huta steelworks, the pollution affecting the drinking water and vegetables. And the steelworks ran at a loss! Maciej Wojciechowski was a former state school teacher who had found a new sense of purpose. He loved his new enterprise and was endlessly resourceful. His wife had waitressed in London, and both spoke excellent English. We met his bright director of studies in the school he had just started, in one big church-owned room. It was strange to see, in what was still communist Poland, crucifixes and religious pictures next to a BTA poster of Queen Elizabeth in full monarchical fig.

'This is temporary,' muttered Maciej. 'The Church haven't told the educational authorities, and they're worried they might get into trouble.' Our next time in Krakow, Maciej was redecorating a secondary school the church had leased him, a splendid building with a dozen classrooms and a large hall. We would hold a directors' conference there only two years later.

In Poznan, Anna and Tadeus had also got hold of a building that was big enough. Four years later, there were twelve IH schools in Poland.

43 · The British Council: Cooperation and Conflict

In our earlier years we always had good relations with the British Council. In London, we had a trustee from the British Council on the board, to involve them in what we were doing: Matt MacMillan, Roger Bowers, Peter Roe, Mike Potter, Ian Seaton, each one very constructive.

John Mallon, British Council representative in Madrid in the seventies, knew I had been forbidden in Franco's Spain. Yet we had a bond of entrepreneurial kinship. Despite the ban, he invited me to lecture at the Madrid institute; and I was part of a British Council EFL lecture tour to Oviedo University.

I remember an Anglo-American conference in Ditchley Park in the 70s. I had a great argument with Arthur King, the Council director of education, about English teaching. I knew Arthur; he had been a friend of Brita's father in Stockholm.

'We give training seminars for teachers, we don't deal with students!' Arthur said, firmly.

'But how can you train teachers unless you also teach students?' I insisted.

'It's perfectly possible to do without all that,' scoffed Arthur.

'Oh, so by training you mean lectures on literature and British life and institutions?'

'Well, that's what foreign teachers need . . .'

'I don't agree. What most need is to speak and understand English – which most of them, like us with French, can't do when they leave school!'

And so it went on. Arthur finally declared, with a shrug:

'The British Council will increase EFL teaching over my dead body!'

I appreciated Arthur, but felt he probably knew little about the reality of English language teaching in his academic tower. The

British Council had sold the family silver for a song. The institutes in Valencia and Bilbao had gone. The beautiful building in Seville with its library and patios had been sold for £5,000 on the never-never to Ned Thomas. Only the Madrid institute remained. They had even disposed of the one in Rome. Time gradually caught up with the Council. France spent money on the Alliance Française, Germany on its Goethe Institutes. The Council sputtered on with a few old institutes, unveiled a new building in Spring Gardens, and talked of 'educational and cultural activities' at embassies abroad. It had not one teaching institute in Tokyo or Paris, and had transferred its South American *culturas* to 'worthy' local committees. British newspapers were saying all it did was teach morris dancing to foreigners. MPs inspected, and official audits made the Council increasingly hesitant. A commission suggested I submit an account of what International House had done. But I felt the Council and we were allies, among the few British organisations with an international outlook. I didn't want to encourage parochial quarrelling.

Only very late did the Council realise it could only meet real needs and earn money by developing English teaching. In Madrid, John Mallon increased EFL and brought in an extra £100,000 a year. After some pondering, the Council took the plunge and started new schools, though they often failed because the lofty planners knew nothing about running lowly language schools. They moved John Mallon, by now their EFL whizz-kid, to Venezuela where they had two new institutes – one near a massively productive oil well at Maracaibo, the other in the sprawling jungle town of Ciudad Guyana, near a mountain of iron ore by the Orinoco. But almost at once they decided to close them, fearful they would lose money.

Although we had nothing in Venezuela, there were two successful IH affiliates in Buenos Aires, one in the *barrio* of Belgrano, both started valiantly by the Scottish teacher trainer David Thompson who had also taught in Bangkok. I was due in San Francisco for a TESOL conference, the American equivalent of IATEFL, and to visit Buenos Aires. John Mallon was pleased when I suggested stopping at Caracas on my way home.

Buenos Aires was flat and elegant, with broad avenues and a

French flavour. I found Argentinians consumed immense beef steaks and gallons of red wine. Some suburbs seemed almost English – the heritage of pre-1914 British railway engineers. I particularly remember the suburb of Temperley, with little villas and front gardens full of flowers, and a gothic church from which rang the familiar tones of Hymns Ancient and Modern. I opened the door a crack to peep in at a large congregation wearing hats who could have been in Blackheath.

Our friendly Buenos Aires students had a comfortable, old-fashioned view of England. I was to select two for scholarships. This involved interviewing twelve, and reading their essays on what they expected to find in London. They had clearly not wanted to offend: there were views of Buckingham Palace from bedroom windows, visits to Harrods before lunch at Fortnum and Mason, green parks full of flowers, a sense of warm Edwardian middle-class peace and prosperity.

I addressed the Pickwick Club, where anglophiles met for lunch. I talked about International House and how it had grown from nothing in thirty years.

'Is it British?' asked one. I said it was.

'How unusual!' scoffed another. 'I thought nothing progressive came out of Britain these days.'

I was there when the new IH building was opened by the British ambassador. The staff had prepared a sketch about the 'Malvinas', the Spanish name for the Falkland Islands. With curtain rings in their ears, spotted kerchiefs and beards, a British pirate and a Spanish one fought with cardboard cutlasses. Enter a British police-man, who declared the British pirate the winner but then arrested him for piracy – all to a lively bilingual commentary. The place was full of Argentinian students.

'Isn't this a bit risky?' I asked.

'Oh no!' I was told, 'Nobody minds. They've got a sense of humour, and anyway it's all ancient history now!'

The Falklands war was less than two years away.

*

I thought Caracas a halfway sort of city: rows of colonial houses being replaced by self-declamatory high-rises, brown hills topped by illegal squats, untidy villages which, I heard, would slide downhill in heavy rain.

The Maracaibo institute was competently run by Bill Hanlon, married to a Venezuelan and fond of motorbikes. He showed us the shallow lake which the oil came from. Ciudad Guyana was different. The institute was on land presented to the Council by the iron ore authority. Monkeys screeched from the trees which spread for miles. The British staff had a sense of exile, of teaching in the jungle in improvised, though well-equipped buildings. John and I discussed how to make the institutes viable. It seemed obvious what needed doing. Administrative staff duplicated each other. Thinning-out could save over £40,000 a year and improve efficiency. A director could teach ten hours a week and save a teacher's salary. Discount air travel would save thousands more. By recruiting our trained teachers we would improve quality. We had to make clear to everyone that the central objective was an efficient teaching organisation. This meant cutting the perks of 'official' comfort and status.

I submitted a report to our chairman, Norman Reddaway, and the British Council, which replied irritably and evasively, suggesting we raise a £120,000 loan to compensate for past losses and cushion against future risk. A British mining firm hoping to exploit Ciudad Guyana did not want the institute to close because they would need employees who spoke English. They had offered the Council a seven-year interest-free £100,000 loan to stay open. But the Council could not accept loans. So Norman Reddaway told the company we were trying to keep the institutes going and could use the loan. They agreed. We invested it at 15%. The institutes started turning a profit, and we only had to commit £33,000. Over the seven years, the interest repaid the loan.

The agreement with the Council lasted only two years. I suggested we continue elsewhere, and still think the combination would have been ideal. Council finance and diplomatic prestige, allied with our training skills, could have created quality English schools worldwide. Our rivals in ARELS might have been upset. But none was then an educational trust, or had teacher training or schools abroad.

It was a pity it did not happen; it could have done a lot of good for Britain. Instead, the Council and IH tussled in, of all places, Spain. There were now three IH schools in Madrid – such was the demand, there was room for everyone. But the real clash came in Bilbao, where we had been since 1983. The Council signed with the university, and offered Jeremy Taylor, our director, a better salary to direct their new school. He accepted. The Council started eyeing the Catalan towns where Ben Warren already had schools, and Santander where IH's Cedric Scheybeler was also in place – although nothing came of these threats.

Perhaps it was a demonstration of the Thatcherite demand that official organisations bring in more money, in open competition. But things were different abroad. It was ludicrous for British organisations to lure each other's customers and employees away, especially when one of them was financed by the British taxpayer – which included me! In the past, the Council had always encouraged British organisations that disseminated our culture and language. I remembered my conversation with Arthur King. I suggested what I thought a civilised compromise: neither organisation should start in a town where the other was already established if the population was under 300,000; otherwise, we would probably both fail. The Council ignored this. But when Eulogio Cremades announced he was opening in Granada, where the Council already had an ailing institute, they protested that Granada was too small!

To increase income, the Council were now admitting twenty-five students per class, which I felt was too many. Their fees were also usually higher than ours. The affiliates got worried, and managed to sue the Council for going beyond its agreement with the Spanish government. They lost, but the Council got bad publicity. The British ambassador told me he would henceforth do nothing to support any International House school – not that it made much difference!

During all this ridiculous brouhaha in Spain, we and the Council made £25,000 each on the Venezuelan institutes. We spent some of ours in South America, getting the Portuguese-speaking Colin McMillan to tour Brazil giving talks on International House. This brought a valuable new affiliate, the Britannia School, owned by a vibrant Anglo-Brazilian, Susan Mace. Her husband Roberto was one of Brazil's leading *cachaça* exporters, *cachaça* being very strong rum. The view from their house overlooking Rio made one giddy. Susan was very interested in cooperating over teacher-training. We sent an administrator, Hugh Davis, and several trainers including Martin Parrott and Jane Glover. In the best IH world exchange style, London got some people who proved excellent trainers themselves – Jenny Parsons and Olivia Date; both had worked a long time for Susan.

44 · 'Las Malvinas'

There were blustery demonstrations in Buenos Aires, speeches from Galtieri. Our ambassador withdrew unaccredited, the British Council evacuated their few people, British concerns closed – but not International House. As so often during crises, IH teachers had so many friends among their students that the main school stayed open, though the smaller Belgrano branch did close. Some students stopped coming, but David Thompson continued classes much as usual. Some teachers wanted to leave, and students helped David get them across the River Plate and home via Uruguay. He found that their Anglo-Argentinian replacements, although less well trained, spoke English almost as well as those who had gone.

During the crisis, most Argentinians remained friendly, rather like what we had felt in Spain over Gibraltar: you were not blamed for your government's actions – any more than, in a country with no democracy, they blamed themselves for those of their own leaders. Some thought our teachers might be staying because they were spies, while others confided to these 'friendly enemies' their detestation of Galtieri and the generals. Mothers with sons in the Malvinas garrison could, understandably, be hostile. On the whole, though, classes stayed pleasant, the students wanting the teachers to feel at ease. There was always the question of what might happen afterwards; whoever won, Britons might be mobbed in the excitement. The endless propaganda added to the insecurity, and it was often difficult to know what was actually happening.

It was an anxious time for David Thompson. The Belgrano school was shut, student numbers were down, the emergency airfares had cost much of his reserves. Would he have to close? He thought not – but one never knew what a victorious, or a defeated, government might do. From London, we could do little. We kept in touch by telephone, relayed messages from parents of our teachers still in Buenos Aires, and looked after our own Argentinian students as tactfully as possible.

I went to Buenos Aires after the war and congratulated everyone. IH had been the only British organisation to stay open virtually throughout. Perhaps being 'unofficial' helped. But the basic reason was that, whatever the political wind, people still needed English.

I spent much of my pre-retirement years visiting schools abroad. I returned to Venezuela to visit the two institutes, which were going well. John Mallon and I lectured at Merida University, with a perilous flight almost shaving Andean peaks and flying low up endless valleys. We lectured only in the morning, spending the afternoon signing and distributing pompously decorative attendance certificates. It was all taken very seriously, so in London I started a certificate ceremony at the end of each four-week course. This went down very well, appealing especially to the sense of ceremony of our 'Latin' students. What simple lessons still remained to be learned, even after thirty years!

I finally got to Rio de Janeiro, surely one of the world's most beautiful cities with the bays and narrow, towering mountains, the valleys filled with white houses, the hang-gliders dropping like dragonflies from the sky. On my second trip I inspected the excellent school and its new executive premises. Here too, as in San Sebastian, there were non-native teachers who were fine but – such is the myth of the native teacher – sadly lacking in confidence. On that same visit, my trousers were stolen while I was swimming off Copacabana. But thanks to the wild abuse of a Brazilian girl sitting nearby, they were actually returned, and with apologies.

I came a third time with Brita for a conference of all English-teaching schools for adults in Brazil. After dinner one evening, she and I strolled down to the sea, where the full moon shone with an unearthly silver light. We were dazzled, and wandered out along the empty beach.

A small man came walking towards us purposefully, perhaps to ask us the time, a dark shape under his arm. We slowed down and suddenly, a few inches from my mouth, was the jagged end of a broken bottle.

'Money!' shouted the man hoarsely, 'Money!'

I had nothing, apart from Brita's purse which I had put in my pocket, for safety.

'I have nothing,' I said. Brita started throwing sand at the man.

'Don't!' I cried, afraid he would turn on her.

Keeping his weapon under my nose with one hand, the man searched my pockets. I was tempted to overpower him with my two free hands – surely not difficult, but was it worth it? Before I could decide, he found the purse and clicked it open to reveal sixty pounds.

He lowered the bottle.

'Thank you!' he said, reaching out to shake my hand – which, bewildered by this sudden courtesy, I gave him. Suddenly realising the deplorable poverty around us, I was almost glad for him to take the money.

45 · Tying Things Up

Other ventures were less dramatic. In Hamburg, I affiliated what became a flourishing executive school started by Patrick Woulfe, a former teacher of ours, and another in Munich, which could have done well but had the wrong director. There was a new affiliate in Lyon. Across the Atlantic, Jonathan Dykes, an IH teacher trainer from Barcelona, dropped in to a school in Manhattan which wanted to affiliate. Under enterprising director Elisabeth Stark, two more schools later opened in San Francisco and Fort Lauderdale. A teacher from Scotland, David Will, started an IH school in Cairns, in Australia, with crocodiles in the mangrove swamps nearby.

In London, we launched a new scheme for teachers abroad who had no advanced diploma course close to hand, called 'distance training through correspondence'. It started with a week in London in summer. Back at their schools, candidates did about three hours a week reading, and writing essays which they sent us, using their teaching as a sounding-board. The course ran at a loss, but I was determined to persevere, to prevent those teaching abroad being disadvantaged. Designed and developed by Charles Lowe, and for the last ten years run by Graham Workman, the course produced consistently excellent results with many 'distinctions'. The formula of extended course plus real teaching programme proved highly effective.

Having a suite of big rooms at 106 Piccadilly for use as lecture halls helped expansion. The teachers' club grew until we had events almost weekly. We became a central EFL forum at which leading teachers and text-book writers spoke, and with ARELS we arranged weekends on specialised subjects. Our social programme included talks, debates, English Through Acting and the 'conversation exchange', where a foreign student talked in his own language for half an hour with an English person, who then 'repaid' with his.

The writers' club would invite well-known authors to talk about one of their books, which the students had already used in class. Our list was impressive: Roald Dahl, who embarrassed the Japanese students by asking if there were any women in Japan as he hadn't noticed any on his visits; PD James, particularly well known in France; John Le Carré, who told me that although many people invited him to talk in Europe and America, no Englishman ever had, presumably because they were shy. Our Adam ceiling hosted many famous names: Beryl Bainbridge, Brigid Brophy, Nina Bawden, Paul Bailey, Sue Chitty, Margaret Drabble, Francis King, Thomas Hinde and Bernice Rubens, among others.

Our staff continued to produce textbooks, at all levels and involving most publishers. Many had an accompanying teacher's book showing how to use each lesson – an excellent adjunct to teacher-training. Some were to enjoy worldwide success, earning fortunes for their previously skint authors. I have never asked for a commission for IH. The knowledge was perhaps garnered on International House time, but the books were written in the authors' own time. And anyway it made us proud and all added to our reputation.

Practical training was now essential for anyone wanting to make EFL a career. The British Council came to prefer it to postgraduate linguistics diplomas. International House provided the initial training for entry into EFL. The new teacher had a couple of years' experience, preferably abroad, then took the diploma and could be considered a 'real' teacher, ready perhaps to go into teacher training or become a director of studies. An excellent trainer named Beverley Dobbs moved to Cambridge in 1975, and wanted a job. I persuaded Frank Bell, of the Bell School of Languages, to take her on under our ægis. It worked well, and the Bell School soon took over teacher training itself.

Three years later, the Royal Society of Arts suggested creating a new certificate for our teacher training, the course itself remaining unchanged. Despite the obvious need for training, few language schools had followed our model as they considered us rivals. Finding it absurd to maintain a barrier to the expansion I had set my heart on for over twenty years, I agreed to the RSA suggestion. Several affiliated schools criticised me for ending our prestigious monopoly, mostly those that ran training themselves – Rome, Paris, Lisbon, Barcelona, Tokyo and Cairo.

Some years earlier, we had been approached by various schools in Dublin, wanting short training courses for their summer teachers. I suggested one central location, but each school wanted its own course on its own premises. I went to Dublin to try and sort things out. At a really positive joint meeting, everyone was cheerful and welcoming. But within a fortnight it all collapsed and was not resurrected. This decided us to try affiliating schools in different parts of Britain, if not in Ireland. They would be in direct competition with us in London, but they might absorb the growing demand for English courses outside London, and would give IH extra publicity. Everyone would benefit from students wanting to explore somewhere different each time they came to Britain.

We had already affiliated a school in Hastings, owned by Maurice Conlin, another in Newcastle started by Gillian Mitchell, an old hand from Tripoli, and in Torquay, under Martin Lemon, now back in England with his wife Mikael and their three bonny children. Maurice Conlin had inherited the Hastings school from a retired colonel after a whole succession of directors of studies, all incompetent or fraudulent, had kept numbers ridiculously low or taken students away to start their own schools. Only Maurice had been loyal, and the colonel bequeathed him the school in his will. He offered us 25% of his holding. So we trained his teachers and sent him students – I remember a Libyan contingent who decided they didn't like London. With other students sent by affiliated schools abroad, he expanded into a large building on the seafront, where we set up teacher training.

While Hastings grew, Tom Hall was getting into difficulties, surrounded by aggressive, uncaring incompetents who, apart from Jeff Mohamed and John Naunton, both fine directors in Tripoli, seemed to regard Tom as a captive treasure ship for plundering.

One morning the phone rang. It was Maurice. Tom had offered to sell cheap, finally fed up with losing sums even he found large. He had already closed down Libya, as the increasingly dominating Gaddafi was making things ever more perilous. The upshot was that Maurice bought Tom out. He sold the schools in Tokyo and Osaka to a Japanese firm and they ceased to be part of the IH world organisation, which I thought a pity. There were complications about the name. One minute Maurice would insist we all call ourselves International House, and the next start a new school and call it International Language Centre. He saw himself as director of an independent ILC organisation, not just of IH Hastings. It was not long before his advertising put forward the pre-Copernican idea that all IH schools, including London, gravitated around Hastings!

In London, we had recovered from the problems of taking 106 Piccadilly. Peter Lawson brought in the competent Alan Legge, also from Berlitz, to expand the accounts department to cope with new developments. Fees rose by twenty percent, salaries by ten. We were no longer one of the cheapest schools in London, but the economic situation was now very different from our distant beginnings in Endell Street. Then, Britain had been the richest country in Europe, and we had good reason to help our more impoverished students. Now, Britain came eighteenth on the world prosperity list, many of our students displaying wealth few of our teachers could match. Living had been cheap in the sixties and seventies; teachers had tended to come from comfortably-off backgrounds; EFL had been a temporary job, even if potentially fascinating. Now, however, EFL was becoming more of a career.

To continue offering affordable classes to those who needed them, we kept fees low for the 'guinea-pig' classes, and students who came to us through the recognised refugee organisations were charged nothing at all. These volunteer classes may have been less formally structured than the regular classes, and were of course taught by trainee teachers; but they had the unique advantage of featuring as many as six different English voices in a single one-hour lesson.

Guinea-pig students could also meet the trainees after class – not always possible with regular teachers, who usually had another class to run off to.

International House was still as cheerful as ever. There were fewer au-pair girls or waiters in the increasingly expensive classes. But with a lot of young people from all over the world, it was difficult to be anything but humorous and exuberant. Teachers who took things too seriously would soon get it knocked out of them in the relaxed, but highly professional and productive atmosphere that still prevailed.

There was a teachers' union, which I thought could only do more harm than good. In an educational trust, any available money went on expansion and salaries, almost nothing on my or Brita's miserable earnings. There was also a short-lived monthly 'parliament', chaired by an elected staff member. The only tangible result was that accounts were displayed in the teachers' room, for anyone who could understand them! We quietly started an executive school – over Maurice Conlin's objections: he feared it might drain custom from his own executive school in Hastings. My most successful schools have always been the ones created without undue fuss – Cordoba, Shaftesbury Avenue, Rome. I circulated all our London students, asking if they were interested in commercial English. Thirty answered positively. We provided trained teachers with commercial experience, and gradually expanded. The executive school grew, and we bought a building in nearby Yarmouth Place, later expanded by Tony Duff into bright modern premises.

46 · Letter from a Younger Man

I recently discovered a letter I wrote at the age of seventeen in a moment of whimsical boredom. I was in the library at Hawarden, Gladstone's old home, for a week's study for my Oxford exhibition.

I found the letter the year before retiring from International House. Addressed to me forty-five years later, it runs:

Dear Ancient,

How do you feel being so old?

Don't you wish you were only 17 as I am, with the whole world in front of me, and the war almost over?

What have you done with your precious life and your potential? Have you published any good novels? Or have you been distracted by some tedious, lucrative job, or some affair with a girl who has taken you over and made you marry her and have endless children?

Or have you gone into politics, or become a journalist, or an army officer, like our father?

At least I hope you have done something you are happy with to compensate for the creaking and pains of old age.

Or perhaps you have died and this will have no effect on you.

I wish I could send you some of my youth and energy. It's sad that in return you can't give me advice on my bewilderment and uncertainties. Perhaps, though, you can't remember these because they belong to your distant youth!

Love, John.

P.S. It seems strange to think we are actually the same person!

I had been lucky to have a 'toff' education for only £10 a year because of my father's early death, and then educational grants and scholarships.

I had taken up EFL when its enormous potential was unknown. We trained ourselves over six years teaching in Cordoba and Sweden, followed by the development of our own ideas in London, when there were few other EFL teachers or ideas around.

Then came President Kekkonen and my first BBC textbook, while Brita was pulling off the tour de force of 40 Shaftesbury Avenue. I have always had a relevant resource: my writing, which has kept me alert and continually interested, and tolerant of possible 'characters'. I have learned, from my writing and International House, how an initial aim can fail while a secondary one knows nothing but success.

I have had two really effective ideas. First, the teachers' course. It now has a sonorous name and is the main way into what is a 'respectable' profession. It has established what I have worked for ever since we started in London.

Second, and related, was the idea of affiliating rather than owning schools, quality being the main condition. This has enabled teachers who have succeeded on our courses to travel to most parts of the world and work in good schools, starting careers as teachers, directors of studies, teacher trainers, textbook writers. Or as school owners.

Administrative experience at Wellington and in the army gave me confidence. I have been surprised how, as an Englishman, I have usually been welomed and respected everywhere. The Americans have inherited our imperial mantle, and now at last we British can be liked.

'Once a nomad, always a nomad!' comments a friend who has just published a book on Freud (*Why Freud Was Wrong* by Richard Webster, published by HarperCollins). For me, languages have always been linked to 'nomadic' reality – French at school in Menton, which laid the foundations of my education; German with my grandmother and at school during the war, followed by practice with German POWs; Italian in Alassio, and later researching a book on contemporary Italy. I brushed them all up during those fourteen tours through Europe for the travel company. Swedish came with marriage, Spanish through endless dalliance. To anyone who marvels, I tell them Brita speaks all the same languages as me, only better. Anyway such were my opportunities, I would have been a blockhead indeed not to learn them.

Brita recently told me about a girl she met some years ago who taught in Salerno, small, blond and twenty-four, redolent of Surrey and a mother with sensible skirts, of tea on the lawn and barking dogs. She told Brita she had spent the previous year in Sicily, living in a chaotic flat and teaching a lot of students who belonged to the Mafia.

'I can't imagine a Swedish girl doing that!' said Brita, ' – or any other nationality – just mad dogs and Englishwomen!'

With few exceptions, International House has been wonderfully well served by its staff. Treat them as well as you can, be strictly honest, give them a sense of career possibilities, really get to know them, care, and protect them – and they will give you back a hundredfold. International House has been an adventure with young people, from Algeria and Hungary to Japan, to mention only three of the half-hundred countries where you can feel in your veins that you are helping. As Indhira Gandhi said, the best thing the British left behind in India was their language.

Thank you all, you teachers in Beirut, in Argentina, now and during the wars. Thank you in more peaceable climes. International House has only been able to achieve what it has through your help, your flexibility, your cheerfulness, your encouraged talent!

A year after I left International House, Norman Reddaway met the financier George Soros. He gave him an article of mine in *The Times* on English teaching in Romania, where I had met Sandra Pralong, the Soros representative. She too recommended me to Soros.

I took Soros round International House and we had lunch. He offered me the job of looking after English teaching for his organisation in eastern Europe. He asked, 'Do you want part-time or full-time?'

'Part-time,' I said. The carousel was in motion again.

It went on for three years, with 'flying' teachers, teachers' courses, and new English language schools in Kiev, Lviv and Timisoara, in Minsk, Kaunas, Vilnius and Tallinn . . .

But that is another story.

Epilogue: Under the Adam Ceiling

It was well after midnight at 106 Piccadilly. Our grown children, Jimmy, Richard and Katinka, were still there. They too were 'improvisors': Katinka giving puppet shows and arranging tours for Indian dancers; Jimmy a drummer and composer; Richard owned his own computer firm in Paris.

Brita gently reminded me it was late. The caretakers began edging into the almost empty rooms. I clinked glasses with Ann Samson, who had run reception and then much of the administration since 1964.

'We'll miss you,' she said. 'It won't be the same.'

'Of course it will . . .'

Slowly, we went down the stairs.

I looked at the roll of honour, lit up in golden letters near the main entrance. From the first world war, it had belonged to the old St James' Club, with aristocratic names: Lord Kitchener, Lord Longford, baronets and honorables from the best regiments. All killed in action. That world-scale massacre had affected all of us, had generated Hitler and Stalin and many of the bitter ills of this terrible century. Many of the three thousand students who passed this roll every year had also had fathers and grandfathers killed. I imagined them all, my own father too, as pale, distorted shadows emerging from a mist. The worst of the horror seemed over. It was extraordinary how many of the ideals of my youth had come nearer fruition.

I went cheerfully through the main door for the last time as director-general, and down the steps to the dim street. The trees of Green Park were tall and motionless in the summer night.